On Being Female, Black, and Free

On Being Female, Black, and Free

Essays by Margaret Walker, 1932-1992

Edited by
Maryemma Graham

The University of Tennessee Press • Knoxville

The quotation from "Speak the Truth to the People" by Mari Evans, published by Wm. Morrow & Co., 1970, is reprinted by permission of the author.

The quotations from "Note on Commercial Theatre" and "The Negro Speaks of Rivers" from *Selected Poems* by Langston Hughes, copyright 1926 by Alfred A. Knopf, Inc., renewed 1954 by Langston Hughes, are reprinted by permission of the publisher.

"Chief Worshippers at All World Altars" originally appeared in *Encore* 1, no. 12 (June 23–July 4, 1975).

"Natchez and Richard Wright in Southern American Literature" originally appeared in *Southern Quarterly* 29, no. 4 (Summer 1991).

"On Being Female, Black, and Free" is reprinted from *The Writer on Her Work*, vol. 1, edited by Janet Sternburg, by permission of W. W. Norton & Company, Inc. © 1980, by Janet Sternburg.

"Race, Gender, and the Law" originally appeared as "Discovering Our Connections: Race, Gender, and the Law" in *The American University Journal of Gender and the Law* 1, no. 1 (Spring 1993).

"The Writer and Her Craft" originally appeared in *Teaching Creative Writing: Proceedings of the Conference on Teaching Creative Writing*, Library of Congress, 1973 (Washington, D.C., 1974).

"Their Place on the Stage" is reprinted from *Their Place on the Stage: Black Women Playwrights in America*, edited by Elizabeth Brown-Guillory, with permission of Greenwood Publishing Group, Inc., Westport, Conn. © 1988 by Elizabeth Brown-Guillory.

"Whose 'Boy' Is This?" is reprinted from *African American Women Speak Out*, edited by Geneva Smitherman. © 1995 Wayne State University Press. Used by permission of the Wayne State University Press.

The paper in this book meets the minimum requirements of the American National Standard for Permanence of Paper for Printed Library Materials. ⊚ The binding materials have been chosen for strength and durability. Printed on recycled paper. ☉

Library of Congress Cataloging-in-Publication Data

Walker, Margaret, 1915–
    On being female, black, and free : essays by Margaret Walker,
    1932–1992 / edited by Maryemma Graham.—1st ed.
        p. cm.
    Includes bibliographical references and index.
    ISBN 0-87049-980-7 (cl.: alk. paper).—ISBN 0-87049-981-5 (pbk.: alk. paper)
    1. Afro-Americans—Southern States—Social life and customs. 2. Afro-Americans—Civil
rights—Southern States. 3. Afro-Americans—Southern States—Politics and government. 4. Afro-
Americans—Education—Southern States. 5. Southern States—Race relations. 6. Afro-American
women authors—20th century. 7. American literature—Afro-American authors.
I. Graham, Maryemma.
II. Title.
E185.92.W35 1997
975'.00496073—dc21   96-51235   CIP

To our children and grandchildren:

Barry, Joy, Khari, Sigismund, and Jamian Alexander;
Karen and Katherine Coleman;
Jarrett and Gwendolyn Gail (G.G.) Williams;
Malika, Robeson, Marona, and Rance Graham-Bailey

Contents

Part III.
On Black People, Mississippi, and U.S. Politics

Part IV.
What Is to Become of Us? Notes on Education
and Revolution

Acknowledgments

THESE THIRTY ESSAYS have been compiled from speeches and assorted writings by Margaret Walker which form an incredible archive that she has maintained since her first poems were written in the late 1920s. From the very beginning, Walker gave me full access to her papers and responded fully to all my questions, no matter how trivial. For her constant collegial, intellectual, and personal companionship, and for her unfailing memory, I owe a special debt of gratitude. I also wish to thank Walker publicly for trusting me with her words and believing that my revisions, at times substantial, would not violate the integrity of her work. More importantly, our dialogues over the years—beginning with that first class I took from her at Northwestern University in 1969—have made me heir to a unique tradition of African American intellectual history which no book or classroom could have ever provided.

A community of scholars, especially undergraduate and graduate students, have participated in the preparation of this manuscript—typing and transcribing speeches, tracking down references, persuading unusually busy publishers to grant us permissions at less than the usual rates. Susanne B. Dietzel and Sheri Divers, my former graduate students who are now both scholars in their own right, did more than what graduate students typically do; they persisted with perceptive comments which helped to shape and re-shape the direction of this volume. Gina Rosetti carefully tracked citations and pursued publication copyrights with a vengeance. To Meredith Fritz must go a very special thanks for commitment and thoroughness to a project, without any promise or hope of compensation. Certainly this book has benefited enormously from her superior technical and research skills. Finally, I acknowledge with grateful appreciation the support provided by my own academic institution, Northeastern University (especially the English and African American Studies departments), the Smithsonian Institution's National Museum of American History, the Association for the Study of Afro-American Life and History in Washington, D.C., and Ron Bailey, who more than anyone else understands why this book had to be.

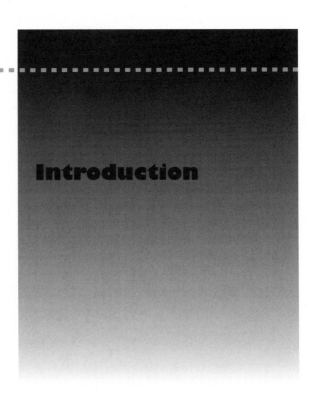

Introduction

NOW AND AGAIN, there comes along a writer who is also a visionary. Such a visionary is Margaret Walker, a writer for whom literature is all-encompassing, passionately individual, and yet critical. For Walker, to write is to invoke tradition and the past, to celebrate plurality and difference, to translate complexity into human understanding, and to construct a model of human society as it is, but more importantly to transform that model as it can be. The wisdom of her many years has not only enriched that vision, but it has also made her enormously productive and unusually active—in the last decade several books have appeared (*The Daemonic Genius of Richard Wright, This is My Century: New and Collected Poems, How I Wrote* Jubilee *and Other Essays on Life and Literature*).

Margaret Walker and I began our collaboration with these very books, one of which she was well on her way to finishing when Ron Bailey and I joined the faculty at the University of Mississippi—at her urging—in 1983. In my mind, there has been no one more crucial to the development of contemporary African American poetry and fiction than Walker, and yet, as Trudier Harris so

aptly comments, Walker is often viewed as someone "whose achievements were in the past, someone who had earned respect but to
whom no undue attention need be given. . . . Although her younger
contemporaries might have been reluctant to praise [her] . . . she is
spiritual if not designated godmother to them."[1] Although Walker
had given some thought to publishing her essays, she viewed herself primarily as a poet and a writer of fiction for whom teaching
was a difficult though thoroughly rewarding means to earn a
living.

   As a literary scholar—and Walker's former student—I entered
this collaboration with the hope of presenting Walker in her own
right, and as much as possible to reveal the artist as well as the
woman behind the poetic voice. This effort, of course, is the job of
biography. But no one need speak for Margaret Walker, as anyone
who has ever known her understands all too well.

   This second volume of essays emerging from our ongoing collaboration comes out of the "Mississippi connection," and it owes
much of its existence to the people and students in the state of Mississippi, for whom Walker has always been accessible; her frequent
public appearances make her a true poet of the people in the tradition of Langston Hughes, whom she knew well and greatly admired.

   Short of a full-scale autobiography, these thirty essays capture
Walker's uniqueness as a literary foremother and cultural icon and,
at the same time, they reveal her critical perspectives on American
and African American literature and her own poetics.

   Our first published volume, *How I Wrote* Jubilee *and Other Essays on Life and Literature,* presented a record of Walker's literary
journey. In placing her among her contemporaries—Richard Wright,
Langston Hughes, Robert Hayden, Melvin Tolson, Margaret Danner,
Owen Dodson, and Gwendolyn Brooks—that volume also resonates
remarkably well within the tradition of black women's writing that
runs from Phillis Wheatley through Frances Ellen Watkins Harper to
Walker's immediate forebears in the era of the Harlem Renaissance—
Georgia Douglas Johnson, Anne Spencer, Angelina Weld Grimke, Zora
Neale Hurston, and a host of other women. These are women whom
Walker had known—many personally—whom she had often spoken
to me about, but whom I, like many scholars, have only recently discovered.

   On Being Female, Black, and Free is a very different kind of book.

Although it shares *How I Wrote* Jubilee's keen political insights and witty perceptions and bears the strong influence of her classical training and moral preferences, this volume seeks to present the historical essay in a form that gives Walker yet another voice with which to speak to and for her people. Here, Walker not only speaks directly about her experiences, but reveals the nature of her art and her activism as they have evolved over time.

Unlike poetry, the essay is not constructed to create the image of conflict and resolution; traditionally, it confines itself to the exposition of an idea or a prophesy and may involve a religious or secular subject. In a country that takes freedom for granted, Walker uses the essay as a way to examine the world of art and education as central to the process of liberation.

Thus, in Walker's first known essay, published when she was only seventeen, she eagerly asserts her knowledge of the reality facing twentieth-century black America. In this remarkable piece, Walker adopts the familiar posture of the spokesperson for "her people," in this case, black youth, in a carefully constructed revision of the prevailing Booker T. Washington philosophy. In short, Walker signifies on Booker T.:

> The Negro has a bucket, the tool is in his hand, he has used it and given it to others all over the world, his manual labor has brought enormous profits and stupendous results to nations who have used him as the tool to realize their dreams and ambitions, to materialize their ideas and plans. Now he must use what is his own for himself, he is putting his brain to school daily. It should be and it must supply him with the idea, the scheme and the plan. And now the two together— his brain and his brawn—must work out his own salvation.[2]

Nearly sixty years later, her message still haunts us:

> Too many of us are impractical dreamers and full of unchanneled emotion and imaginative fantasies. It is very important not only to know our heritage, but it is equally important to know how to make a practical application of our theoretical knowledge. We need to reexamine the uses of our education and strip ourselves of the unnecessary baggage clinging to our liberal arts

education. We need to know how to do certain things well and with skill, first in order to liberate our people, second in order to actually accomplish complete social and intellectual freedom, and third, in order to entertain and occupy ourselves in time of leisure.[3]

This state of perpetually becoming, of confronting different realities at the same time, might serve us as a general theme for this collection of essays, each one marking a particular moment in time, illuminating and affirming various aspects of the process of historical evolution of Black Americans. The process, however, is not without its ideological, political, and cultural boundaries, which have dominated American life and presented the most significant challenges to institutional reform: slavery and the Civil War; segregation and civil rights; persisting economic inequities and the continuing struggle for equal rights.

For Walker, reminiscent of the great abolitionists and social reformers Frances Harper and W. E. B. Du Bois, longevity is not simply a blessing, but an opportunity to continually voice her bitter opposition to all forms of racist discrimination and injustice and her insistence upon the right and responsibility of the artist/intellectual to create a vision of a better world. Fearing that this sentiment is going out of fashion, Walker reminds us in "Agenda for Action: Black Arts and Letters":

> If we are to meet the challenge of our crucial times, if we are in truth to define the paradigm for our children's tomorrow we cannot afford the pussyfooting, in-fighting, and petty jealousy that ape the white world and divide us between town and gown. If we are to take seriously the mandate of all black people for freedom in our time, we must solemnly go about our business of creativity, expressing the highest essence of black art and intellect, that which is most authentic and germane to the black experience, for in doing most what we do best, we serve with our greatest devotion our people's most glorious cause.[4]

The exhortation to action is echoed in a number of essays, but is nowhere more powerful than when it meets with the personal:

I have struggled against dirt and disease as much as I have against
sin, which, with my Protestant and Calvinistic background, was
always to be abhorred. Every day I have lived, however, I have discovered that the value system with which I was raised is of no
value in the society in which I must live. This clash of my ideal
with the real of my dream world with the practical, and the mystical inner life with the sordid and ugly world outside this
clash keeps me on a battlefield, at war, and struggling, even
tilting windmills. Always I am determined to overcome adversity, determined to be me, myself, at my best, always female, always black, and everlastingly free.[5]

Such freedom was not a guarantee when Margaret Walker was
growing up in the Jim Crow South, when, says Walker, "I knew
what it was to step off the sidewalk to let a white man pass before I
was ten." She credits much of her success with being born into a
deeply religious family that fostered excellence and placed spiritual
values and integrity above money.

This affirmation, in the highly personal essays, comprises the
first section of this volume. The essay "On Being Female, Black,
and Free" not only incorporates a strong sense of Walker's much
discussed humanistic vision together with an autobiographical
recall of the past, but outlines the cogent themes from the African American historical experience that mark her own existence:
the distinctiveness of black cultural life, which emphasizes tradition and change and continues the engaged battle for political
and social justice and equality for men and women. Reflecting
on the series of celebrations marking the fiftieth anniversary of
For My People (published in 1942), Walker told me:

From my early adolescence, I've been dealing with the
meaning of the turn of the century. I was born when it was
barely fifteen years old. And now we have less than ten years left
in this century. So, the body of my work springs from my interest in a historical point of view that is central to the development
of black people as we approach the twenty-first century. That is
my theme. And I have tried to express it, both in prose and poetry. I feel that if I've learned anything about this country and

century—I've expressed it already in the books I've been writing
and the few more I'd like to write. . . . Giving voice to all I have
come to know and understand is still the most important thing
for me as a writer—that has never changed for me, nor for the
people I've known and worked with through all these years.[6]

Whether it is the power of Walker's voice or the truth of her
vision that invites such rich, lyrical, and precise language that one
finds in her poetry, fiction, or criticism, she reaffirms the values
and the cultural distinctiveness of African American life through
oratory as perhaps its central and most visible feature. Writers
like Sonia Sanchez, Toni Morrison, Alice Walker, and Toni Cade
Bambara seem to echo this aesthetic in their own revising of the
black experience. And Walker has an entire following of other yet-
to-be-well-known writers[7] who have used her example, including
Arthenia Bates Millican, Julia Fields, the late Raymond Andrews,
Tom Dent, Tina McElroy Ansa, and Pinkie Gordon Lane.

In the first section, "On Being Female, Black, and Free," Walker
evokes the contemporary scholarship on race and gender. Walker's
own position is defined most articulately in the title essay, which
was written in 1980 for a volume entitled *The Writer on Her Work*,
edited by Janet Sternburg. Those familiar with such writers as Alain
Locke, J. Saunders Redding, and Sterling Brown have long since recognized the traditional role that the essay has played in African
American literary history. Virtually all these writers operated
within a discursive continuum where audience became a critical
determining factor. These and other critics alternated between jour-
nalistic prose and the literary essay and were equally skillful at
both. For women writers, the essay has often served as a means to
enter the public sphere, where issues of social and political importance could be debated forcefully without fear of immediate
reprisals. Thus, Harriet Martineau in England and Maria Stewart
in the United States made active use of a variety of prose venues
to argue their ideas. Like these writers, Walker's essays, many of
which were originally delivered as speeches or lectures, permitted Walker to explore the relationship between childbirth, illness, education, work and legal rights, all of which come together
in the creative process. Walker argues distinctively for a woman's
culture as a cultural and historical frame for understanding the in-

dividual and collective experiences of women through the ages. Freedom is defined as the ability to participate fully in the discourse of culture. Walker's awareness of this freedom to speak and to write came at an unusually young age. Her sense of herself as a writer and of other women artists is in itself an exercise of such freedom. The essays in this section not only configure race, gender, and freedom as necessary elements in one's personal achievement but as particularly important for the woman artist. Walker's intimacy with world religions contextualizes her wholehearted embrace of and self-interest in the role of woman not only in religion, but also in education, the economy, politics, and the arts.

In "Discovering Our Connections: African Heritage, Southern Culture, and the American Experience," Walker places an implicit value on regionalism. The South is home and her point of departure in any understanding of American culture. The unusual sharpness with which she describes the racial and political landscape, its "climate for genius," shows Walker to be a keen observer of the South's magnetism and contradictory impulses. In opposing the view of a somewhat homogeneous South, one that is unchanging and static, Walker launches a campaign against an apathetic citizenry and the elusive "southern" character. Walker's articulation of the region's complexities and contradictions, its divergent paths of modernization and tradition, her exposure of the forces of progress and destruction help us to envision a South as one that cannot be essentialized or romanticized. This exposition of southern culture is as much a composite of the African heritage as much as its myths and legends are peculiarly American. These essays interrogate certain notions of history and regional difference and project a view of the South as a place where narrative and metaphor meet. But it is Walker's critical activism, derived in part from her close connections to the 1930s radicalism as well as from the civil rights agenda that marks the South's remembered past—slavery and the Confederacy; segregation and civil rights—of national and shared importance. It is within this context that African American literature becomes the child of a marriage between the southern legacy and the national culture.

The section "On Black People, Mississippi, and U.S. Politics" provides an intellectual autobiography of Walker; at the same time it becomes a political biography of the nation as a whole. These are

perhaps the most "political" essays in this volume in the sense that
they view race, economics, and leadership as being connected to
empowerment, exploitation, and change at the local and national
level. The provocative "Whose 'Boy' Is This?" is a scathing indict-
ment of a political system that valorizes leadership without morality, and authority without accountability.

The challenge of educational reform in the 1960s and 1970s,
mainly through the rise of Black Studies, Women's Studies, and
Ethnic Studies in United States colleges and universities, is given
careful consideration in the final section, which is appropriately
titled "What Is to Become of Us: Notes on Education and Revolution." The main essay serves as a bridge between Walker's earliest
concepts and philosophies and her most recent speeches. A long–
time advocate of curriculum reform, Walker discusses many ideas
here that have now become implicated in the contemporary debate
over multiculturalism and demonized by the political right. Perhaps this is yet another reason for her importance and reliability as
an analytical guide to her own and indeed our changing times. Ultimately, what is "revolutionary" for Walker is that democratic
ideas must be at the center of educational reform. When we bring
the intellectual and moral virtues into harmony for the benefit of
the whole society, we are enacting our most important work as intellectuals and educators.

Given her self-prescribed role as a spiritual and intellectual leader—one her readers and reviewers gladly acknowledge—
Walker's penetrating analyses and carefully constructed images of
black life in America bespeak an uncompromising commitment
to the integrity of an African American world view, an aesthetic which she considers essential for "saving" America from its
own destruction. Perhaps no one speaks as forcefully, skillfully, or
as truthfully about a panorama of shared problems we collectively
face as Americans with a shared historical past, looking toward a
common future, with full realization of the responsibility for pre-
serving our common humanity. It is this simple truth pervading her
work, as this collection of essays will confirm, that has earned for
her a permanent place in the cultural discourse of America.

Notes

1. Blyden Jackson, Jr.; Rayburn S. Moore; Louis D. Rubin, Jr.; Lewis P. Simpson; and Thomas Daniel Young, *History of Southern Literature* (Baton Rouge, La.: Louisiana State University Press, 1985) 567–68.
2. From "What Is to Become of Us?" in this volume.
3. From "Humanities with a Black Focus," in this volume.
4. From "Agenda to Action: Black Arts and Letters," in this volume.
5. From "On Being Female, Black, and Free," in this volume.
6. Margaret Walker, interview by editor, tape recording, Jackson, Miss., 14 July 1991.
7. Arthenia Bates Millican, *The Deity Nodded* (1973), *Seeds Beneath the Snow* (1975). Julia Field, *The Green Lion of Zion Street* (1988). Raymond Andrews, *Appalachee Red* (1978), and *Baby Sweet's* (1983). Tom Dent, playwright, cofounder of Free Southern Theatre. Robert Deane Pharr, *Giveadamn Brown* (1978) and *The Book of Numbers* (1969). Tina McElroy Ansa, *Baby of the Family* (1989) and *Ugly Ways* (1993). Pinkie Gordon Lane, *Girl at the Window* (1990).

Biographical Note

MARGARET ABIGAIL WALKER was born July 7, 1915, in Birmingham, Alabama, received her early education in New Orleans, and had completed her undergraduate education at Northwestern University in Evanston, Illinois, by the time she was nineteen. Although Walker had written and published before moving to Chicago, it was in Chicago that her talent matured; it matured as she engaged in her roles as a college student, as a member of the Works Progress Administration, and as she shared intellectual, cultural, and professional interests with many black and white artists who were gathered there, the most famous of whom undoubtedly was Richard Wright. Wright and Walker shared a close friendship until Wright left for New York in the late 1930s. Walker herself left Chicago for graduate school at the University of Iowa in 1939, by which time she was well on her way to becoming a major American poet.

In 1942, Walker completed the full manuscript of a volume she entitled *For My People,* the title poem for which had been written and published in Chicago in 1937. The volume served as her M.A.

thesis in English from the University of Iowa, but, more important, it brought her immediate recognition as the first African American woman, and the second African American after Richard Wright, to achieve national literary prominence. *For My People* won the Yale Series of Younger Poets Award, was published in 1942, and is now an American classic.

Around the same time, Walker had begun work on a historical novel based on Margaret Duggans Ware Brown, as told to her by her maternal grandmother, Elvira Ware Dozier, a novel she would not finish until she came back to Iowa in the 1960s to complete her Ph.D. During the in-between years, Walker returned to her native Southland, joined the faculty at Jackson State University, in Jackson, Mississippi, where she and her husband, Firnist James Alexander, raised their four children. Still, Walker continued to write and to play an active role in the Mississippi phase of the civil rights movement. The novel she had woven from the stories told to her by her grandmother was published in 1966 as *Jubilee* and received the Houghton Mifflin Literary Award. *Jubilee,* which has never been out of print, has been translated into seven languages and has enjoyed tremendous popularity as the first modern novel of slavery and the Reconstruction South told from an African American perspective. Other poetry and prose volumes followed soon thereafter: *Prophets for a New Day* (1970), *How I Wrote* Jubilee (1972), *October Journey* (1973), and *A Poetic Equation: Conversations Between Nikki Giovanni and Margaret Walker* (1974).

Throughout her literary career, which extends well over fifty years, Walker has continued to earn awards and honors for extraordinary achievement and for her lifetime contribution to American letters as a creative artist. She holds six honorary degrees, numerous certificates and citations and in 1991, received a Senior Fellowship from the National Endowment for the Arts, and in 1992, the Lifetime Achievement Award from the College Language Association, as well as one from the governor of Mississippi.

Walker retired from her full-time teaching career in 1979, remained in Jackson, and began to intensify the work on several projects she had begun, especially a very controversial biography of Richard Wright, which was published in 1988 as *Richard Wright: Daemonic Genius*. In 1989, Walker brought her four poetry volumes together with a sizable collection of new poems which were published appropriately as *This Is My Century: New and Collected Poems*. This volume seemed to give Walker renewed energy for, although past seventy, she continued to appear in special engagements and give lectures at colleges and universities throughout the United States. A year later, we published the first volume of her essays, *How I Wrote* Jubilee *and Other Essays on Life and Literature*.

Currently, Walker is at work on her autobiography.

Part I

On Being Female, Black, and Free

(1980)

On Being Female, Black, and Free

MY BIRTH CERTIFICATE reads female, Negro, date of birth and place. Call it fate or circumstance, this is my human condition. I have no wish to change it from being female, black, and free. I like being a woman. I have a proud African American heritage, and I have learned from the difficult exigencies of life that freedom is a philosophical state of mind and existence. The mind is the only place where I can exist and feel free. In my mind, I am absolutely free.

My entire career of writing, teaching, lecturing, yes, and raising a family, is determined by these immutable facts of my human condition. As a daughter, a sister, a sweetheart, a wife, a mother, and now a grandmother, my sex or gender is preeminent, important, and almost entirely deterministic. Maybe my glands have something to do with my occupation as a creative person. About this, I am none too sure, but I think the cycle of life has much to do with the creative impulse, and the biorhythms of life must certainly affect everything we do.

Creativity cannot exist without the feminine principle, and I am sure God is not merely male or female but He-She—our Father-Mother God. All nature reflects this rhythmic and creative principle of feminism and femininity: the sea, the earth, the air, fire, and all life whether plant or animal. Even as they die, are born, grow, reproduce, and grow old in their cyclic time, so do we in lunar, solar, planetary cycles of meaning and change.

Ever since I was a little girl I have wanted to write, and I have been writing. My father told my mother it was only a puberty urge and would not last, but he encouraged my early attempts at rhyming verses just the same, and he gave me the notebook or daybook in which to keep my poems together. When I was eighteen and had ended my junior year in college, my father laughingly agreed it was probably more than a puberty urge. I had filled the 365 pages with poems.

Writing has always been a means of expression for me and for other African Americans who are just like me, who feel, too, the need for freedom in this "home of the brave, and land of the free." From the first, writing meant learning the craft and developing the art. Going to school had one major goal, to learn to be a writer. As early as my eighth year, I had the desire, at ten I was trying, at eleven and twelve I was learning, and at fourteen and fifteen I was seeing my first things printed in local school and community papers. I have a copy of a poem published in 1930 and an article with the caption, "What Is to Become of Us?" which appeared in 1931 or 1932. All of this happened before I went to Northwestern.

I spent fifteen years becoming a poet before my first book appeared in 1942. I was learning my craft, finding my voice, seeking discipline as life imposes and superimposes that discipline upon the artist. Perhaps my home environment was most important in the early stages—hearing my mother's music, my sister and brother playing the piano, reading my father's books, hearing his sermons, and trying every day to write a poem. Meanwhile, I found I would have to start all over again and learn how to write prose fiction in order to write the novel I was determined to create to the best of my ability, and thus fulfill my promise to my grandmother. A novel is not written exactly the same way as a poem, especially a long novel and a short poem. The creative process may be basically the same—that is, the thinking or conceptualization—but the techniques, elements, and form or craft are decidedly and distinctively different.

It has always been my feeling that writing must come out of living, and the writer is no more than his personality endures in the crucible of his times. As a woman, I have come through the fires of hell because I am a black woman, because I am poor, because I live in America, and because I am determined to be both a creative artist and maintain my inner integrity and my instinctive need to be free.

I don't think I noticed the extreme discrimination against women while I was growing up in the South. The economic struggle to exist and the racial dilemma occupied all my thinking until I was more than an adult woman. My mother had undergone all kinds of discrimination in academia because of her sex; so have my sisters. Only after I went back to school and earned a doctorate did I begin to notice discrimination against me as a woman. It seems the higher you try to climb, the more rarefied the air, the more obstacles appear. I realize I had been naive, that the issues had not been obvious and that as early as my first employment, I felt the sting of discrimination because I am female.

I think it took the women's movement to call my attention to cases of overt discrimination that hark back to my WPA days on the Writers' Project. It did not occur to me that Richard Wright as a supervisor on the project made $125 per month and that he claimed no formal education, but that I had just graduated from Northwestern University and I was a junior writer making $85 per month. I had no ambitions to be an administrator; I was too glad to have a job; I did not think about it. Now I remember the intense antagonism on the project toward the hiring of a black woman as a supervisor, none other than the famous Katherine Dunham, the dancer, but it never occurred to me then that she was undergoing double discrimination.

When I first went to Iowa and received my master's degree, there were at least five or six women teaching English in the university. When I returned to study for the doctorate, not a single woman was in the department. At Northwestern my only woman teacher had taught personal hygiene. I did not expect to find women at Yale, but it slowly dawned on me that black women in black colleges were more numerous than white women in coed white universities.

And then I began looking through the pages of books of American and English literature that I was teaching, trying in vain to find the works of many women writers. I have read so many of those great women writers of the world—poets, novelists, and playwrights: Sigrid Undset and Selma Lagerlof, Jane Austen, George Sand, George Eliot, and Colette. All through the ages, women have been writing and publishing, black and white women in America and all over the world. A few women stand out as geniuses of their times, but those are all too few. Even the women who survive and are printed, published, taught and studied in the classroom, fall victim to negative male literary criticism. Black women suffer damages at the hands of every male literary critic, whether he is black or white. Occasionally, a man grudgingly admits that some woman writes well, but only rarely.

Despite severe illness and painful poverty, and despite jobs that always discriminated against me as a woman—never paying me equal money for equal work, always threatening or replacing me with a man or men who were neither as well educated nor experienced but just men—despite all these examples of discrimination I have managed to work toward being a self-fulfilling, re-creating, re-producing woman, raising a family, writing poetry, cooking food, doing all the creative things I know how to do and enjoy. But my problems have not been simple; they have been manifold. Being female, black, and poor in America means I was born with three strikes against me. I am considered at the bottom of the social class-caste system in these United States, born low on the totem pole. If "a black man has no rights that a white man is bound to respect," what about a black woman?

Racism is so extreme and so pervasive in our American society that no black individual lives in an atmosphere of freedom. The world of physical phenomena is dominated by fear and greed. It consists of pitting the vicious and the avaricious against the naive, the hunted, the innocent, and the victimized. Power belongs to the strong, and the strong are BIG in more ways than one. No one is more victimized in this white male American society than the black female.

There are additional barriers for the black woman in publishing, in literary criticism, and in promotion of her literary wares. It is an insidious fact of racism that the most highly intellectualized, sensitized white person is not always perceptive about the average black mind and feeling, much less the creativity of any black genius. Racism forces white humanity to underestimate the intelligence, emotion, and creativity of black humanity. Very few white

Americans are conscious of the myth about race that includes the racial stigmas of inferiority and superiority. They do not understand its true economic and political meaning and therefore fail to understand its social purpose. A black, female person's life as a writer is fraught with conflict, competitive drives, professional rivalries, even danger, and deep frustrations. Only when she escapes to a spiritual world can she find peace, quiet, and hope of freedom. To choose the life of a writer, a black female must arm herself with a fool's courage, foolhardiness, and serious purpose and dedication to the art of writing, strength of will and integrity, because the odds are always against her. The cards are stacked. Once the die is cast, however, there is no turning back.

In the first place, the world of imagination in which the writer must live is constantly being invaded by the enemy, the mundane world. Even as the worker in the fires of imagination finds that the world around her is inimical to intellectual activity, to the creative impulse, and to the kind of world in which she must daily exist and also thrive and produce, so, too, she discovers that she must meet that mundane world head-on every day on its own terms. She must either conquer or be conquered.

A writer needs certain conditions in which to work and create art. She needs a piece of time; a peace of mind; a quiet place; and a private life.

Early in my life I discovered I had to earn my living and I would not be able to eke out the barest existence as a writer. Nobody writes while hungry, sick, tired, and worried. Maybe you can manage with one of these but not all four at one time. Keeping the wolf from the door has been my full-time job for more than forty years. Thirty-six of those years I have spent in the college classroom, and nobody writes to full capacity on a full-time teaching job. My life has been public, active, and busy to the point of constant turmoil, tumult, and trauma. Sometimes the only quiet and private place where I could write a sonnet was in the bathroom, because that was the only room where the door could be locked and no one would intrude. I have written mostly at night in my adult life and especially since I have been married, because I was determined not to neglect any members of my family; so I cooked every meal daily, washed dishes and dirty clothes, and nursed sick babies.

I have struggled against dirt and disease as much as I have

against sin, which, with my Protestant and Calvinistic background, was always to be abhorred. Every day I have lived, however, I have discovered that the value system with which I was raised is of no value in the society in which I must live. This clash of my ideal with the real, of my dream world with the practical, and the mystical inner life with the sordid and ugly world outside—this clash keeps me on a battlefield, at war, and struggling, even tilting at windmills. Always I am determined to overcome adversity, determined to win, determined to be me, myself at my best, always female, always black, and everlastingly free. I think this is always what the woman writer wants to be, herself, inviolate, and whole. Shirley Chisholm, who is also black and female, says she is unbossed and unbought. So am I, and I intend to remain that way. Nobody can tell me what to write because nobody owns me and nobody pulls my strings. I have not been writing to make money or earn my living. I have taught school as my vocation. Writing is my life, but it is an avocation nobody can buy. In this respect I believe I am a free agent, stupid perhaps, but *me* and still free.

When I was younger I considered myself an emancipated woman, freed from the shackles of mind and body that typified the Victorian woman, but never would I call myself the liberated woman in today's vernacular; never the bohemian; never the completely free spirit living in free love; never the lesbian sister; always believing in moderation and nothing to excess; never defying convention, never radical enough to defy tradition; not wanting to be called conservative but never moving beyond the bounds of what I consider the greatest liberty within law, the greatest means of freedom within control. I have lived out my female destiny within the bonds of married love. For me, it could not have been otherwise. In the same way I refuse to judge others, for if tolerance is worth anything, love is worth everything. Everyone should dare to love.

I am therefore fundamentally and contradictorily three things. I am religious almost to the point of orthodoxy—I go to church, I pray, I believe in the stern dogma and duty of Protestant Christianity; I am radical but I wish to see neither the extreme radical left nor the radical right in control. And I am like the astrological description of a crab, a Cancer—quick to retreat into my shell when hurt or attacked. I will wobble around circuitously to find another way out when the way I have chosen has been closed to me. I believe absolutely in the power of my black mind to create, to write, to speak, to witness truth, and to be heard.

Enough for a time about being female and black. What about freedom? The question of freedom is an essential subject for any writer. Without freedom, personal and social, to write as one pleases and to express the will of the people, the writer is in bondage. This bondage may seem to be to others outside oneself but closely related by blood or kinship in some human fashion; or this bondage may appear to be to the inimical forces of the society that so impress or repress that individual.

For the past twenty years or longer I have constantly come into contact with women writers of many different races, classes, nationalities, and degrees. I look back on more than forty years of such associations. Whether at a cocktail party for Muriel Rukeyser at *Poetry* magazine or at Yaddo where Carson McCullers, Jean Stafford, Karen Blixen, Caroline Slade, and Katherine Anne Porter were guests; or meeting Adrienne Rich and Erica Jong in Massachusetts at Amherst; or having some twenty-five of my black sister-poets at a Phillis Wheatley poetry festival in Mississippi, including many of the young and brilliant geniuses of this generation; or in Mississippi where I have come to know Eudora Welty and Ellen Douglass; or having women from foreign countries journey to Jackson to see me, women like Rosey Poole from Amsterdam and Essim Erdim, a young woman writer from Turkey, or Bessie Head from South Africa—all these experiences have made me know and understand the problems of women writers and our search for freedom.

For the nonwhite woman writer, whether in Africa, Asia, Latin America, the islands of the Caribbean, or the United States, her destiny as a writer has always seemed bleak. Women in Africa and Asia speak of hunger and famine and lack of clean water at the same time that their countries are riddled with warfare. Arab women and Jewish women think of their children in a world that has no hope or peace. Irish women, Protestant and Catholic, speak of the constant threat of bombs and being blown to bits. The women of southern Africa talk of their lives apart from their husbands and their lives in exile from their homelands because of the racial strife in their countries. A Turkish woman speaks of the daily terrorism in

her country, of combing the news each evening to see if there are
names known on the list of the murdered.

I have read the works of scores of these women. I saw Zora
Neale Hurston when I was a child and I know what a hard life she
had. I read the works of a dozen black women in the Harlem Renaissance, who despite their genius received only a small success.
Langston Hughes translated Gabriela Mistral, and I read her before
she won the Nobel Prize for Literature. Hualing Hieh Engle tells of
her native China, and my friends in Mexico speak of the unbelievable poverty of their people. Each of these internationally known
women writers is my sister in search of an island of freedom. Each
is part of me and I am part of her.

Writing is a singularly individual matter. At least it has historically been so. Only the creative, original individual working alone
has been considered the artist working with the fire of imagination.
Today, this appears no longer to be the case. In America, our affluent, electronic, and materialistic society does not respect the imaginative writer regardless of sex, race, color, or creed. It never thought
highly of the female worker, whether an Emily Dickinson or Amy
Lowell, Phillis Wheatley, or Ellen Glasgow. Our American society
has no respect for the literary values of intellectual honesty nor for
originality and creativity in the sensitive individual. Books today
are managed, being written by a committee and promoted by the
conglomerate, corporate structures. Best sellers are designed as
commodities to sell in the marketplace before a single word is
written. Plastic people who are phony writers pretending to take
us into a more humanistic century are quickly designated the paper heroes who are promoted with super-HYPE. Do I sound bitter? A
Black Woman Writer who is free? Free to do what? To publish? To
be promoted? Of what value is freedom in a money-mad society?
What does freedom mean to the racially biased and those bigots
who have deep religious prejudices? What is my hope as a woman
writer?

I am a black woman living in a male-oriented and male-domi-
nated white world. Moreover, I live in an American Empire where
the financial tentacles of the American Octopus in the business-
banking world extend around the globe, with the multinationals
and international conglomerates encircling everybody and imping-
ing on the lives of every single soul. What then are my problems?

They are the pressures of a sexist, racist, violent, and most materialistic society. In such a society, life is cheap and expendable; honor is a rag to be scorned; and justice is violated. Vice and money control business, the judicial system, government, sports, entertainment, publishing, education, and the church. Every other arm of this hydra-headed monster must render lip service and yeoman support to extend, uphold, and perpetuate the syndicated world-system. The entire world of the press, whether broadcast or print journalism, must acquiesce and render service or be eliminated. And what have I to do with this? How do I operate? How long can I live under fear before I too am blown to bits and must crumble into anonymous dust and nonentity?

Now I am sixty-three. I wish I could live the years all over. I am sure I would make the same mistakes and do all the things again exactly the same way. But perhaps I might succeed a little more; and wistfully I hope, too, I might have written more books.

What are the critical decisions I must make as a woman, as a writer? They are questions of compromise and of guilt. They are the answers to the meaning and purpose of all life; questions of the value of life lived half in fear and half in faith, cringing under the whip of tyranny or dying, too, for what one dares to believe, and dying with dignity and without fear. I must believe there is more wisdom in a righteous path that leads to death than an ignominious path of living shame; that the writer is still in the avant-garde for truth and justice, for freedom, peace, and human dignity. I must believe that women are still in that humanistic tradition, and I must cast my lot with them.

Across the world humanity seems in ferment, in war, fighting over land and the control of people's lives; people who are hungry, sick, and suffering, most of all fearful. The traditional and historic role of womankind is ever the role of the healing and annealing hand, whether the outworn modes of nurse, and mother, cook, and sweetheart. As a writer these are still her concerns. These are still the stuff about which she writes, the human condition, the human potential, the human destiny. Her place, let us be reminded, is anywhere she chooses to be, doing what she has to do, creating, healing, and always being herself. Female, Black, and Free, this is what I always want to be.

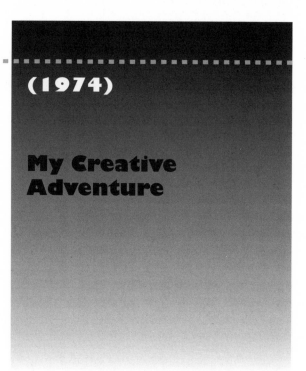

(1974)

My Creative Adventure

MY CREATIVE ADVENTURE is really my life as a writer. As such, my adventure began in New Orleans when I was a small child only ten years of age. I must have already felt even earlier that although I loved books and especially poetry, there was something mysterious about the process and only the elite were elected to be poets. So my first composition at age ten was prose. I wrote a Thanksgiving piece for my seventh-grade English class and I still remember how it began—"Picture to yourself a band of pilgrims."

In the next few years, however, I was busy trying to write poetry. We were living in the same house where my father moved us within two weeks after we came to New Orleans. Many mornings I would rise early and sit on the side steps writing. At school I scribbled poetry in my composition book and at home in the night when I was not reading to myself or my grandmother, I was trying to write. Home, school and New Orleans furnished a wonderful

This essay was prepared as a speech for the 1974 meeting of the National Council for Teachers of English in New Orleans. Walker became ill and was unable to deliver the speech.

environment that made me want to write. Music and books at home—my mother or my sister playing the piano continually, my father's books and the trees that I watched through the bedroom windows—all provided invaluable stimuli. I thought New Orleans must be the most beautiful city in the world and not having seen the world, I still think so.

My teachers were also encouraging and I especially remember my high school English teachers enlightening us as to the greatness of poetry, American and English Literature and memorizing pieces that I spoke at school, church, and special programs. When I showed my father my first efforts at writing poetry, he gave me a date book to keep them and said I should keep all my poems together.

He warned my mother not to get excited about having a poet in the family since it was probably just a puberty urge. However, when I came home from my first year away at Northwestern and I had nearly filled that book with three hundred poems, I asked my father if he still thought it was a puberty urge. He laughed and said that I would probably be writing poetry for the rest of my life.

Through the years, I have met many writers, professionals and amateurs, famous and obscure, but I am sure my desire and determination to be a serious writer received early nurturing from my parents and early teachers in New Orleans. What does an English teacher do for a young adolescent who not only expresses a desire, but seems compelled to write a few lines of doggerel every day? Well, first, she can encourage such a youngster. (I say "she" because my high school English teachers were all women and for two years in college I had women literature professors—once away at Northwestern and Iowa, my teachers were men.) Yet my composition teachers all urged me to write. I heard them read poetry aloud as I heard my mother read aloud at home first. Of course, I learned to revel in poetry in the same manner. Poetry should be savored orally in class. Students should also learn rhythms and images as they learn meanings.

I believe a poet thinks in figurative language and symbolic terms, at least one sees these initially. Ideas come later, but concepts are first and we conceive in pictures and feel the rhythms intuitively. Learning different kinds of rhythms, whether patterns of the line or emotional meanings of words, must be part of the English lesson. I mastered many things unconsciously and automatically before I became conscious and self-conscious. Once this happened I was more inhibited and I wrote less, whether better I cannot say.

Although I learned some scansion and versification at home in New Orleans, I really grasped English prosody and forms of poetry from my teacher, Professor E. B. Hungerford, at Northwestern. Yet, it was not necessary for me to reacquaint myself with the differences between iamb, trochee, anapest, and spondee as well as their sound, meaning, and effect upon a line of verse, particularly mine.

It was not until I graduated from Northwestern and was writing on the Federal Writers' Project that I found my voice as a poet. For in those two years immediately following college, I discovered my own forms and began writing some of my best poems, "For My People," "We Have Been Believers," and "Southern Song." It is one thing in college to study the creative process by reading Aristotle's *Poetics* or Brewster Ghiselin's *The Creative Process* (1952), but quite another to discover for myself the kind of thinking that makes a poem or the way to organize any imaginative writing.

Students are taught, but they must also discover what they are constantly told about the relation of thinking to writing. It is here that the teacher is only a guide. The teacher's basic job is to inspire the student to think. The English composition professor must instruct the student on how to think to understand what creative thinking is all about.

What is creativity? I think it is originality, talent, innate ability to make something distinctively of artistic worth and individually different, the God-given ingredient in artistic production; that which is neither taught, bought, nor conveyed from one person to another. These aspects or factors are: (1) the creative personality, (2) the creative process, and (3) the creative product. These factors are all interactive: acting upon or reacting from the thing created, the person creating, and the method of creation. We are, therefore, involved with both nature and art, the fire of imagination and the craftsman who hammers out the creation on the forge of his own intuitive self or his own intelligence, as well as the thing in itself which is being created.

Perhaps, if it were possible to blend all these into one composite whole we might have demonstrated creativity. There is, however, something involved here which is intangible and ephemeral. Despite all our vocabularies, it defies definition, description, or adequate distinguishing from the tangible which is explicable, and involves no special mystique or mystery. Creativity cannot be considered inspiration, conception, organization or realization of the artistic thing expressed, but it partakes of all of these. And yet, it involves a power defying all three. Creativity is, in fact, that special power to blend all three and also transform human experience and chaotic phenomena into a work of art which we call creativity.

Who, then, are poets? They are the creative personalities who seem especially endowed with what Samuel Coleridge calls the esemplastic power: that power to transform or change the shape of raw experience into a work of art. This work of art is a whole, new creation partaking of beauty, truth, and affecting both our emotions and sensibilities.

Poets, however, are no different from their fellow creatures in physical or mental attributes. They have the same physical apparatus for seeing, hearing, and feeling. Furthermore, they use a common language. According to Coleridge, they share fancy and primary imagination, yet do not share the secondary imagination. So, they share quality, but not quantity. For in their capacity to evoke the recurring image, poets are more sensitive and intense. They see the same daffodils, the same waterfall, the same lark on the wing, the same red clover bloom as the poet, yet non-poetic people would not make a poem. These conventional individuals do not suffer the same quantity of intensity in the recurring image; William Wordsworth would often refer to this state as being "recollected in tranquillity." Therefore, poets are makers. To make, create or fabricate are the poets' special concern. Like nature, poets are creators, cooperating with the creative energies of the universe and using the total personalities to accomplish this fact.

Moreover, everything the poet *is* goes into the creation of poems. What makers see, hear, think, and believe are a part of what poets or makers create. Can it be otherwise? The integrity or the wholeness of the poets' personalities are in some measure a part of what they spawn or bring to birth. The poem is part of the self out of which it has come. They cannot be inimical or strangers to each other. Poems are more than the handiwork of poets, they are an imprint of selves seen in the style, language, image, music, and meaning.

The philosophy of the poet is, therefore, in the poem. The ear of the poet catches the rhythmic music in the sounds of the world around him. The eye of the poet grasps the beauty of the natural landscape without and within them. What they perceive or what they conceive is all the same, and this is what is in the poem.

The poet, then, should be a sensitive instrument for the sounding and testing of raw sensory experience. Yet, they must be more than a creature of sensuous experience. They become a creature of mental activity, as well. They are busy transferring the image or the concept to the written or spoken word, the series of images and concepts into expressed thoughts, the figurations and configurations of ideas into meaningful metaphors and similes that comprise this figurative and poetic language.

The poet is a juggler of words, a dreamer with spoken dreams, a fire-maker who blows the sparks into flame with magic bellows. Every day of his or her life, the poet is becoming a personality sensitive to this creative task and destiny. Actions, thoughts, observations, and dreams are the raw experiences that go into the laboratory for this selective process and creative function.

Accordingly, the poet's personality should be developed into a well-honed, finely tuned sensitive instrument on which they play the music of their universe and transform dross into gold, silken thread into shimmering cloth, sounds of hummingbirds' wings into melodies, and harmonies to be sung in celestial choirs. The poem is really no greater than the poet's personality; for it is their expression and creation, although sometimes the poem seems the sumtotal of the poet's potential. Only then, it expresses more than the poet has thus realized either consciously or unconsciously with themselves. When poets suddenly rise to the heights of their time and personalities, they may sometimes lift us beyond ourselves and our mundane world into a society of the sublime and noumenal universe. Thus, poets, like prophets and priests, serve a social function and enhance our day with the luster and brightness of their own creative spirit. They may, perchance, open the door to the future and give us one brief ecstatic glimpse into a secret and sacred place.

How do we make a poem? What happens when the poet creates a work of art? The creative process begins in creative thinking. Creative thinking begins as all thinking, either from the thing perceived outside the physical self or conceived within the physical self. Perceptive and aperceptive thinking, or perceptive and conceptual thinking, mark the beginning of any creative thought, idea, or venture. The daydream may also lead to creative thinking which in its highest expression and development leads on to new knowledge and invention. William Wordsworth demonstrates the creative process from the romanticist's point of view with his poem, "I Wandered Lonely as a Cloud," both in this particular literary piece and in his preface to the lyrical ballads. Because this is a personal, subjective, emotional, simple and natural approach, it works well with the lyric:

> I wandered lonely as a cloud
> That floats on high o'er vales and hills,
> When all at once I saw a crowd,
> A host of golden daffodils,
> Beside the lake, beneath the trees,
> Fluttering and dancing in the breeze.
>
> Continuous as the stars that shine
> And twinkle on the milky way
> They stretched in never-ending line
> Along the margin of a bay:
> Ten thousand saw I at a glance,
> Tossing their heads in sprightly dance.
>
> The waves beside them dance; but they
> Out-did the sparkling waves in glee:
> A poet could not but be gay,
> In such a jocund company:
> I gazed—and gazed—but little thought
> What wealth to me the show had brought.

When he saw them they caused a rush of spontaneous emotion and he looked on them, drinking in their beauty, color, movement, and massed effort, and then he went home thinking little of what an impression they had made on him nor how often they would recur in his memory:

> For oft when on my couch I lie
> In vacant or in pensive mood
> They flash upon the inward eye
> Which is the bliss of solitude
> And then my heart with pleasure fills
> And dances with the daffodils.[1]

The same spontaneous emotion recurs as when he first saw them and this emotion, image, meaning, movement, and beauty all reoccur. They are "recollected," as he says, "in tranquillity."

How do I make a poem? Sometimes, in the same way. Yet, perhaps I am thinking about a subject I have seen or read in a history book or someone has told me a story about a person, a folk-story, or I am walking and I suddenly think of a line:

> What am I bid for this face?
> Or
> What is the price of her face?
> Or
> What will you pay for my face?
> Or
> How much am I bid for this girl?

I may not use all or any of these lines but I know exactly what I want to do, write a poem about a young slave girl, only seven years old, put on the auction block and sold. In ten years, she would be famous for her poetry imitating Alexander Pope and in 1773, she would be publishing the first book by a black person in America, two hundred years ago—before the Declaration of Independence.

I am deliberately planning a poem, perhaps a set of poems, lyrics, free narrative verse or dramatic monologue? What will I do? An occasional poem? Is it the same? Almost always my poetry comes out of my thinking, sometimes out of my feelings as well. It begins with a mere color, a sound, a place, an idea, and it grows.

Sometimes this creative process goes on unconsciously in the mind of the poet until the whole poem takes shape there: initial idea, development, and share of form and complete resolution. Then, the poet struggles to bring it forth as the mother in travail brings forth her child. Nothing must go wrong in that birth process or the child comes out wrong, ill-formed, and damaged. The poem, too, must come out whole and as it was conceived, and if it is truly as the poet would have it, then the readers will experience a similar emotion and satisfaction every time they read that poem. We do not always think the same things about a poem nor feel the same, yet if in the aesthetic reaction to that poem, the total personality responds in some way to that poem, then the poet has truly succeeded. This is creativity.

Throughout the ages, various poets have offered their theories about this thing, creativity. In prehistoric man, all the arts of music, painting, and tale-telling existed. Tribes of people developed their own artistic culture following a natural and simple process of creativity. In ancient Africa, India, China, Persia, Greece, Rome and in the great Mayan cultures of South America, Mexico, and Central America, people were creative, and there are evidences of this creativity today. Throughout these countries, we find their ancient carvings, sculptures, musicians, and poets preserved in stone and marble, in pyramids and tombs of their great kings, their written hieroglyphics or cuneiform or language in characters still unknown to the Western world.

We, also, have evidence of this creativity in the recorded literature of the ages. Consider the stories of Aurelius and his golden ass, of Aesop and his fables, in Plato's Phadrus an explanation of this very creative process, Aristotle's theories of tragedy and classical form, and in the Old Testament or Hebrew history stories of the prophets, and the priests with their visions and smoke-filled altars over which they prophesied, the beginning of theories of inspiration—in all of these are records of the creativity of humanity.

Italian Renaissance artist Michelangelo and German musician Beethoven move us with their masterpieces every time we see and hear them. These men created their art from definite creative ideas. They were purposely planned from conception through organization and development to the realization. The greatness of the works depended first upon the greatness of their conception. The power of the artist varies with her ability to bring the art she has conceived into reality. Music, painting, architecture, poetry, and drama must all have great conceptions to arrive at great realizations or creations. The artist, moreover, must have tremendous power and artistic stamina to see works through to their logical conclusions or realizations.

Genius, then, is the greatest degree of creativity expressed in the human mind. Every artist is clearly not a genius. Every person works within the scope of their own creativity. They learn and develop a craft that becomes automatic, yet has nothing to do with their artistic creativity. Their creative talent challenges them constantly to find methods and processes suitable to develop their creative ideas and emotions and to bring the conceptualizations they are capable of expressing into fulfillment.

Creative thinking is, of course, the key to creative writing, and all teaching must be creative and conducive to this highest kind of thinking. Once poets have learned to think and write in images, rhythms as well as with meaning, they crave an audience. For many years, Harriet Monroe's magazine, *Poetry*, printed in the back cover Walt Whitman's admonition, "To have great poets, there must be great audiences too." And so creative writers generally crave to see their work in print. Of course, there are those few like Emily Dickinson who is presumed to have had no such yearning, but those are special cases whom I have never met.[2] From the time I was sixteen until the present I have been meeting other poets and like them I sought to publish. Oddly enough, I have not published a great deal of poetry—not nearly as much as I have written—because I had some notion instilled in me early about printing only the very best and not being satisfied easily. With short stories my agony has been even greater and *Jubilee* took half a lifetime.

When I teach creative writing I do only two things: teach the business of thinking and reading, and insist that writers practice their craft and art by writing. Nothing succeeds like success and the only way to learn is by doing. I do encourage an imitation of the masters; read the best, but write what you know and imitate what you like and think is best. Professors E. B. Hungerford, Stephen Vincent Benet, Paul Engle, and Norman Holmes Pearson were some of my teachers in three great universities, and they all were practicing writers.

Verlin Casill and Vance Bourjaily were professional fiction writers and they taught me how to write fiction. Anybody who tells you that writing is easy is trying to fool you. I know a lot of people who think anybody can write. I do not believe that either. I know writing well is not easy. My creative adventure has taken a lifetime and perhaps, I have yet to learn all my lessons. Each day brings a new problem, and every day has something new to teach me in my great escapade.

Each age may produce many painters, dramatists, poets, musicians, yet only one great master may emerge. This, too, is a question of genius, destiny of creative personality, and the sources brought to bear upon that creativity, for it is not a matter of craft, training, or education at all.

In the antebellum United States, black slaves brought their creative proclivities and predilections from Africa to the New World. Here they were stripped of their language and culture; nevertheless, they made music which consisted of black songs that still stir the world with their pathos, poignancy, and artistic purity. Folk music such as the spirituals form a collective expression of faith culture. John Lovell, author of *Black Song* (1972), says that the spirituals were hammered out of the creativity of black slaves on a forge of suffering and with a flame of beauty, religious faith and truth together with their indomitable will and integrity. This is creativity.

All artistic creation and productivity must, therefore, be understood as developing in this same way. Individuals and groups develop creative talent and express their creativity in this manner. All the creative energies of the creative personality strive toward a universal and, therefore, immortal expression of beauty and truth.

All of this creative expression is, therefore, derived from the integrity or wholeness of the creating personality as these creative energies or forces are brought to bear on the raw materials of human experience and chaotic physical phenomena. They are transformed, according to William Blake, in the fires of Los, hammered into shape on a forge of esemplastic power and driven with a flaming touch of creative fire, and then in shining raiment and blazing with gems of beauty. These creations come forth to delight and instruct us, to entertain and give pleasure to all those fortunate enough to behold these works of art. Creativity is a gift that cannot be taught or bought. It is part of the divine itself, power to create and to transform. Yet, every person is born with their own spark of this divinity. For the creative artist, this is creativity.

Notes

1. William Wordsworth, *The Poetical Works of Wordsworth*, revised and with a new introduction by Paul D. Sheats. Boston: Houghton Mifflin, 1982.

2. The idea that Emily Dickinson did not wish to be published is a myth; she was discouraged from publishing by her male mentor, Thomas Higginson.

The Writer and Her Craft

I SPENT FOUR YEARS in the Writers' Workshop at the University of Iowa where I learned so much that I have ever afterward been in praise of all creative writing programs. Even now I have difficulty assessing the influence my advisor, Paul Engle, had upon me; finding the wherewithal was his specialty. He irritated me into writing almost every day. Consequently, I found myself in several ways. Years later, when I discovered I knew almost nothing about the novel form but was still determined to write one, I went back to the Writers' Workshop in Iowa, and again Paul Engle encouraged me.

I believe that the writer can be taught many things—chiefly their craft, structure, and the elements of fiction. However, they cannot be taught the art of fiction. There is a distinct difference between craft and art. This blending of talent, creativity and technique into a work of design is what we call artistry, and this alone the writer must do for herself.

After all is said and done, the only tools the writer has are words. Insofar as one is able to control language, the writer succeeds with the craft of writing and the art of fiction. Teaching writing merely means inspiring the writer toward his own creative thinking, helping him manipulate words, and showing how the language may be controlled effectively.

It may seem trite to say the only business of language is to communicate, but then that is all the writer is trying to do—communicate ideas and emotions. We have to use the language as we know and understand it. Everybody knows that language is a changing thing because it is a living and palpable thing.

I once heard a creative writing instructor say that he had difficulty as a white person relating to a young black writer. I appreciated that kind of honesty. But does one have to be black to understand black humanity? I ask myself, what is it about words or language that I can teach the white writer? After all, I have also had this education in white universities superimposed on my southern black origins and schooling. My teachers were white as well as black, and if I succeed as a writer it must be with this black idiom that is me. Black writers, like white ones, must be themselves; a natural-born woman or man writing about a world we sometimes understand, interpreting ourselves as Africans in a hostile white land, trying to make the society in which we live less inhospitable. We seek understanding, liberation and reconciliation through the mere manipulation of words.

Furthermore, educators incur this dubious problem across the country. Instructors are frequently unable to communicate with black youth who tend to be distrustful, and not only of the white instructor. They are also skeptical of the black teacher who they feel may be whitened as well. Young Black America views this professional as one who is under the influence of white education or the European, and they want no part of this. Where these attitudes are concerned, we are in an extreme place. The answer is in arriving at the common ground of humanity that is in the basic understanding of people as human beings.

I never had a feeling of leeriness around my teachers because they conveyed their interest in me. I felt that these people were trying to do something for my good. However, I had a shocking experience at Yale when a professor, whom I greatly admired, told me that black people were acceptable as long as they remained primitive and did not imitate white people. I was aghast. Then I realized that what African Americans have experienced in this country is an insidious form of institutional racism that we still feel. This is because the history is overladen with racist implications. For one thing, black people are acutely sensitive to persons who believe that they are from a savage land and maintain what they call "primitive instincts." Many white people continue to be ignorant of an African culture in which there are highly sophisticated people, civilization, and traditions. Another time a white woman in Illinois asked me, "Are you bitter because you are black?" She could not comprehend that that is completely outside the realm of understanding. Not being able to conceive of me as another human being, she simply thought that being black should give me an inferior feeling. It is that sort of thing black youth are fighting. I am not sure that anybody has the answer because the panacea is beyond our immediate reach, insofar as I understand it.

When we consider the impact of race in this country, we are involved with layers of mores and patterns of our culture. Contrary to some opinions, it has nothing to do with whether we are an invisible people who cannot be seen because no one wants to see tradition and a European education that has done so for a compelling reason. Their writing was never accepted in the traditional American literary world unless it was imitative, servile, or compromising, and this was never intellectually honest.

Young black writers are doing their own thing. They speak to the African American world, express the black experience, and create their own system. They want to follow their own tradition. A tradition, but an oral one. Hence, we have the Black English controversy.

Although anything created by African Americans is just as American as a brainchild of whites, I wish to state for the record that there is no such thing as Black English. There may be a black idiom in the American language, and I am sure there always has been and will continue to be. However, Black Americans who are people of African descent speak an American language. It is a language not merely adopted, but adapted daily to the changes of a people oppressed and repressed, yet never suppressed. We have had much to do with keeping the English language rich, vital, dramatic and as varied as all the nuances of our black experience.

Stephen Henderson's *Understanding the New Black Poetry* (1972) discusses black speech and music as reference for the new literature. This great oral African and African American tradition has not been understood, whether it was in the folk speech of the ballad, jazz music, the blues or rap. It has been ignored. The young African American is quite cognizant of this fact. Because I am not one who denies the cultural heritage of either the European or the African, I have always felt that one of our great problems in America is understanding the equal value of these two traditions.

We have a great potential in this pluralistic society; however, there is an obstacle for most of us. African Americans are more conscious of it because we are the ones who suffer. People who do not endure it are not even aware of what the culture has done to them. They are not conscious of how this affects their thinking. It has become an unconscious part of our society.

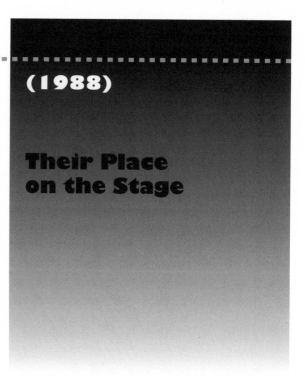

(1988)

Their Place on the Stage

ELIZABETH BROWN-GUILLORY has ac-
complished three major tasks in this very important and absorb-
ing book. She has first of all given a historical overview of black
women playwrights in this twentieth century; second, she has
analyzed and assessed the works of three major examples: Alice
Childress, Lorraine Hansberry, and Ntozake Shange; and third,
she has given some objective thought to the general structure
and criticism of drama as a whole, with particular emphasis on
black drama.

It is good to remember that American drama has really come of
age in the twentieth century, that plays on the American stage in
the eighteenth and nineteenth centuries were really little more
than glorified minstrels, farces and melodramas. Eugene O'Neill is
the first great name in the Hall of American Playwrights and following him there may be about a half-dozen great names: Maxwell
Anderson, Robert Sherwood, Edward Albee, Tennessee Williams,

This essay originally appeared as the introduction to *Their Place on
the Stage: Black Women Playwrights in America* by Elizabeth Brown-
Guillory (Westport, Conn.: Greenwood Press, 1988).

Arthur Miller, and Lillian Hellman. So it is not surprising that black theater in America has its real beginnings with the Harlem Renaissance and in that famous group at least four women wrote plays. They were May Miller, Georgia Douglas Johnson, Alice Dunbar-Nelson, and Angelina Weld Grimke. Since Johnson was the most successful of these four with her *Plumes* (1927) appearing off-Broadway, Brown-Guillory chooses her as her first example, showing the tradition out of which subsequent black women playwrights have come.

Between the Harlem Renaissance and the black arts movement of the 1960s are three decades, the thirties, forties, and the fifties. While the Chicago Renaissance of the thirties and forties produced few playwrights, mostly men, hardly any women appear until the decade of the fifties, when three important examples emerge. They are Beah Richards (1950), Alice Childress (1955), and Lorraine Hansberry (1959). Brown-Guillory deals with two of these in detail.

The civil rights movement and the women's movement exploded in every direction, and the three decades following the fifties have been replete with black women playwrights. Sonia Sanchez is an early example of revolutionary black drama, combining the two revolutions: the Negro revolution led by Martin Luther King, Jr., and the black revolution led by Malcolm X. During the past twenty years (1968–88), Sanchez has written eight plays which have been published and produced. The most famous of these are *The Bronx is Next* and *Sister Sonji*, both of which appeared in the late sixties (1968 and 1969) off-Broadway and on college campuses.

At the end of the sixties and the beginning of the decade of the seventies, black women playwrights exploded all over the country. J. E. Franklin's *Black Girl* (1971) led the group. Adrienne Kennedy's *Funnyhouse of a Negro* (1962) was a good example of the new Theatre of the Absurd. But the most explosive of these new women playwrights was Ntozake Shange at the end of the seventies with her choreopoem, *For Colored Girls Who Have Considered Suicide/ When the Rainbow is Enuf* (1976), and *Spell #7* (1976).

The decade of the eighties is truly the decade of the black woman in American literature, whether in fiction, poetry, drama, or non-fiction. Three black women are examples of this luxuriant flowering in drama. They are Kathleen Collins with *The Brothers* (1982); Elaine Jackson with *Paper Dolls* (1983); and P. J. Gibson with *Brown Silk and Magenta Sunsets* (1985). It is this decade in which Brown-Guillory belongs with two plays produced and published in the eighties: *Bayou Relics* (1983) and *Snapshots of Broken Dolls* (1987). Shirley Hardy is an upcoming new playwright in Chicago.

With these successful black women playwrights, we have run the gamut of the century. These are serious craftswomen. They understand the form and structure of drama. Frequently, the major conflict centers on race or family. They understand the social implications in black drama, and they are aware of our African heritage of myth and ritual. Brown-Guillory further explains these as they apply to African American drama and precisely to these women exponents of this particular form of literature.

Black women have undergone an age-old struggle to find their place on the American stage, and these examples indicate that their heroic struggle has not been in vain. When the twentieth century is written in history, these names shall shine in the heavens and maybe they shall lead all the rest.

(1975)

Chief Worshippers at All World Altars

AFRICA IS MORE than the cradle of civilization and the birthplace of all mankind along the shores of ancient rivers; she is also the mother of man's cultural expressions, whether language, art, music, or religion. Man's earliest religious expression is animism from which all religions have developed, and animism may still be found in the heart of the great mother continent, Africa.

Animism consists of two major tenets: (1) all matter is animated by spirit, and (2) spiritism or the belief in spirits is indigenous in all spiritual belief. Whether man has developed his religious expression in pantheism or all nature gods, polytheism or many gods, theism or one kingly god, monotheism or one God, these have all proceeded from animism.

One of the earlier nations to develop cosmogony, cosmology, and mythology was Egypt, and she developed pantheistic, polytheistic, and monotheistic systems of ethical and religious thought. Her coffin texts in the great pyramids and her epic—*The Book of the Dead*[1]—all attest to her ancient concern with religion. A great body of belief encompassed all life and death in relation to the sky—heaven—the earth, the Nile River, and the underworld.

All tribal belief throughout ancient Africa extended beyond mere dogma or religious bodies of thinking into the communal life of the village. This life was inextricably bound up with two factors—nature or the natural world around mankind and the human life cycle which was obviously part of nature and the natural world. Men and women lived according to the cycle of life and death seen around them—birth, puberty, courtship, marriage, reproduction, and death. Each followed the seasonal, lunar, and solar cycles of spring, summer, autumn, and winter or full moon and new moon and the yearly overflow and flooding of the Nile River. All of these natural facts became a part of the religious socialization of man and woman. Thus hunting and fishing, crafts and arts—whether of the drum, dancing, weaving, painting, or wood carving—all had and still have religious and sexual and therefore sacred meaning.

One more simple story should illustrate this ancient beginning of religious belief. The highly evolved and developed system of African magic or juju, homeopathic or sympathetic, must also traced to its earliest religious beginnings in Africa. Because early or primitive mankind feared natural forces of sun, wind, fire, thunder, rain, mountain, and desert, he named gods for them and offered sacrifices to them to appease the fury or the anger of these gods. Thus from superstitious fear came witchcraft and religion simultaneously. The priests and medicine men were the mediators—even the creators of symbiology and systems of ceremony, ritual, dogma, and sacrifice doctrine. Therefore, the satanic powers of evil and the benefic powers of good were intertwined in the minds of believers so that they moved in various directions— toward Chaldean embryonic astrology, Persian Manichaeism, Chinese mysticism, or African mesmerism and hypnotism.

During the heinous years of human slavery in which Europeans and Americans cooperated in the African slave trade, many Africans were transported by means of the horrendous Middle Passage to the islands in the Caribbean Sea, as well as South and North America. Although the preponderance of Africans was made slaves in the colonies that became the United States, large numbers of black people carried the religious culture of black Africa to numerous islands of the West Indies, notably Jamaica and Haiti. In Jamaica, the Rastafari, and in Haiti, Vodu (Voodoo), African worship of the Loa of gods, are the most enduring.

During the height of slavery in the southern cotton-kingdom states, Christianity was deliberately used to convert the "heathen" African to docile, humble, and "Christian" slaves. White southerners continued to use Christianity during segregation to subdue the so-called Negro by all kinds of subtle means. It is not by accident that white Southern Baptist churches carry the subtitle, SBC, Southern Baptist Convention, while black Baptist churches are subtitled Missionary Baptist churches. The Methodist church had an even tougher racial problem—it was driven to division over the slavery question. Southern white Methodists formed a southern church, and even in 1939 when unification was again attempted, a segregated black jurisdiction was declared. Now under a mandate to integrate, the church has continued to drag her feet and has failed as has all other White America to meet the challenge.

The white Anglo-Saxon Protestant church in America has maintained a zealous concern for converting the foreign black heathen while manipulating the church at home to conform to the political whim and economic system of capitalism in all its racist manifestations.

While the Ku Klux Klan, the John Birch Society, and the Americans for the Preservation of the White Race all declare themselves as patriotic Americans to be devout Christians, the Black Church has maintained for three hundred years a militant, revolutionary, and black nationalist role and position. During slavery it was the black preacher who was frequently the conductor on the Underground Railroad. He was the literate black leader who preached freedom in the year of Jubilee and frequently was the only person to lift the slave consciousness to the role of the Union army and the United States government in the struggle for emancipation.

Despite a long period of apparent apathy, Uncle Tomism, and preachings of the status quo and the virtues of the Republican Party, the Black Church has fought the black man's fight and has continued to struggle through the abject prejudice and morass of Jim Crow toward the civil rights movement and black liberation.

Most of the leaders of the civil rights movement were Baptist preachers—a few were Methodists and Congregationalists—but they represented the Black Church. The Black Church differs widely from the white Christian church. The two are as distinctly different from one another as is the status quo from revolutionary change, as is the orthodox establishment of a hierarchical church from a boldly new revolutionary ministry, as are the teachings of the eighth-century prophets from the break that the Nazarene made with an old order.

Black women are a basic part of this revolutionary and militant black church. Even in such orthodox faiths as Roman Catholic, black women are part of change.

Many unorthodox churches, cults, and sects are led by women. The Holiness Pentecostal sect has a tradition of women workers. The Islamic world has been freed of purdah, and Islamic women no longer wear face veils, but they are certainly not part of the movement for women's liberation.

Religion is fundamental in black life, and black women have been the chief worshippers at all world altars. From the earliest recorded times they have been priestess and prophetess. Isis was not only wife and sister to Osiris, she was one in a long line of earth mothers and goddesses of love. Black goddess of Egypt, she is followed by Astarte, Astoreth, Aphrodite, and Venus.

In black churches all over the world, black women have kept the candles burning on the altars whether in orthodox churches or unorthodox cults. In the Christian churches of the United States, black women have been bedrock, foundation, basic in fundraising and financial support either by means of domestic service or the washtub or as actual professional leaders of the congregation.

In every orthodox church black women have roles as leaders and followers. They are leaders in storefront churches and faith healing cults. They are board members of the YWCA and missionary societies. They are ordained ministers and theologians. They are teachers and students in schools of divinity. They are Catholics, Anglicans, Methodists, Baptists, members of Holiness Pentecostal sects, Christian Scientists, Muslims, Buddhists, Jews, and members of Yoruba cults, worshipping Shango.

Some of these women are more prominent in religious circles than others. Clarie Collins Harvey is a past president of the national organization Church Women United, having served three years and with the distinction of being the first black woman so honored. She has for years been active in the United Methodist Church on all levels and is also a successful businesswoman. Theressa Hoover has served on the board of missions of the United Methodist Church. She has been active in this denomination for a number of years. A native of South Africa, Brigalia Bam has been the chairperson of Unit Three on Education and Renewal in the World Council of Churches, with offices in Geneva, Switzerland, and in New York City. A member of the Anglican Church, she has been active both in the Province of Natal and in Zululand. An active member of the World Council of Churches, Jean Fairfax has been a member of the Central Committee and the United Church of Christ, a member of the staff of Legal Defense and Educational Funds, and notably has also been on the commission of the Program to Combat Racism. Professor of education at Herbert Lehman College, State University of New York, Dr. Olivia Pearl Stokes is a Baptist and ordained minister. A previous member of the World Council of Churches, Stokes, a world traveler, is the author of two books on Africa: *Why the Spider Lives in Corners* (1972) and *The Beauty of Being Black* (1971).

Other women in various denominations are Valery Russell, who has worked with the YWCA at New York City's Riverside Church and especially with urban or metropolitan missions and the division of education in relation to black colleges; and Dr. Thelma Adair, the wife of a Presbyterian minister, mother of three children, and a professor at New York's Queens College, who has worked in the division of education concerned with the support of the Presbyterian church for predominantly black schools. Dorothy Height, long connected with the work of the YWCA, has worked at international and national levels. President of the National Council of Negro Women and past president of Delta Sigma Theta Sorority, Height's major interest has remained with the religious commitment of the YWCA. Emily Gibbs is another Presbyterian woman who has worked in her church at the national level. In September 1973, she became the position of associate general secretary of the National Council of Churches. Jessie Pratt is involved with Church Women United. Bessie March is a social worker whose husband is a YMCA secretary and whose interest has followed community service.

Black women in the Roman Catholic church have encountered the same problems of racism as those in other denominations. Two black women who have been catalytic agents in the Roman Catholic Sisters Movement for Social Change in the black community are the former Sister Martin de Porres Grey, who has left the Community of Sisters of Mercy based in Pittsburgh, and Sister Teresita Wynd of Holy Angels Church in Chicago. An effective organ in the Catholic world is *Freeing the Spirits,* published by the National Office for Black Catholics in Washington, D.C.

Two orders of black nuns exist in America—the Oblate Sisters outside Baltimore, Maryland, and Sisters of the Holy Family in New Orleans—but black women have always encountered difficulty when attempting to enter traditionally white orders or sisterhoods.

Perhaps two facts should be made clear. First, black women in orthodox churches work within the system of traditional Christian institutions for reform, renewal, and significant social change. Second, black women in unorthodox churches express their religious convictions in the same direction of black liberation.

Economically or politically, the crisis of the old order is clearly a racial concern. As the Arab world threatens, even promises, and aligns itself into a new world order that is in no way like the Western world of capitalism, the black woman finds herself challenged by three major world religions—Christianity, Judaism, and Islam—regardless of sect or denomination. Moreover, in the international women's year, 1975, the black woman moves from the shadows of a deprived, outcast status to a role in which she determines the destiny in a new world order. All over the modern world the African diaspora is dynamic and energetic, from Africa to the United States to the islands in the sea. The black world is in motion. It has always been a religious world. Basically, the black woman still is religious.

Note

1. Walker is referring to *The Book of the Dead: The Hieroglyphics Transcript of the Papyrus of Ani,* an early black Egyptian text translated by E. A. Wallis Budge (New York: Gramercy Books, 1995).

(1973)

Phillis Wheatley and Black Women Writers, 1773-1973

IN OCTOBER of 1972, I was on my way by train to Dayton, Ohio, for the centennial celebration of Paul Laurence Dunbar. I rode the train from Jackson to Effingham, Illinois, and would have to spend a day's layover before taking the "Spur" to Dayton. There in the Holiday Inn, I conceived the idea of a Phillis Wheatley Poetry Festival to be celebrated in 1973 on the bicentennial occasion of the first book published by an American woman. Dunbar was one hundred years old in 1972. Mary McCleod Bethune, the great educator and founder of Bethune Cookman College in Tallahassee, would be one hundred years old in 1975. What else would be more fitting in 1973?

A year later, the idea of a Phillis Wheatley Poetry Festival was a reality. Twenty-six outstanding black women were invited to share with Jackson State College (now Jackson State University) in celebrating the bicentennial of *Poems on Various Subjects,*

Margaret Walker organized the centennial celebration of Wheatley's first book of poetry with support from the National Endowment for the Humanities and Jackson State University.

Religious and Moral by Phillis Wheatley, the first known book published by a black in America. Twenty-three women actually came.

It is a unique experience in the life of any college to bring to its
campus an array of creative individuals such as those who were invited for this occasion. In this case it was also a prophetic experience. Little did we know that this unique event should be the spark
that lit a prairie fire—only a few years later, those women would
be the very ones to proclaim a new renaissance in belles lettres,
and black women's writing would go on to rise to unprecedented
heights.

In 1973, only a few of the women who came were known:
Marion Alexander, Linda Brown Bragg (now Linda Beatrice Brown),
Carol Gregory Clemons, Lucille Clifton, Margaret Danner, Mari
Evans, Sarah Webster Fabio, Nikki Giovanni, June Jordan, Audre
Lorde, Naomi Long Madgett, Gloria C. Oden, Carolyn M. Rodgers,
Sonia Sanchez, Alice Walker, Malaika Ayo Wangara, Vinnie
Burroughs, Margaret Burroughs, Paula Giddings, Ida Lewis, Dor-
othy Burnett Porter (now Dorothy B. Porter Wesley), Doris Evans
Saunders, and Etta Moten Barnett. Three other women who did
not attend were Johari Amini (Jewel Lattimore), Julia Fields, and
Gwendolyn Brooks. Miss Brooks was kept away by a previous
commitment to attend the centennial of Willa Cather in Kansas,
which is also her native state.

Three events during the festival deserve notice: Nikki Giovanni,
"the black princess of poetry" in the 1960s, gave a concert reading
backed by a gospel choir from nearby Tougaloo College; the late
Sarah Webster Fabio gave a reading accompanied by a family jazz
trio with a solo dancer and vocal soloist; and Alice Walker wrote a
special piece for the festival, "In Search of Our Mothers' Gardens."
That piece, which would appear in MS magazine in 1974, has now
become a classic. Every woman poet present at the festival had published at least one book of poetry, but several went on to distinguish themselves in the field of poetry and fiction, including Alice
Walker, June Jordan, and Audre Lorde. Now, looking back twenty
years later, I realize how historic that occasion was. If Phillis
Wheatley had only known what she had started.

Charlayne Hunter-Gault's special to the New York Times may
well have been the first official recognition that there was a new
"movement." In her article, Hunter-Gault notes the celebratory

tone of the event, but pointed out how "the festival raised many questions . . . and ended with the examination as a public policy issue of the exclusion of black women from the textbooks of America." Ironically, that exclusion has been turned around somewhat and today black women writers are in vogue. This seems to suggest that we have had an impact. The Jackson, Mississippi, festival was only the beginning of things to come.

The most important reminder for us is that it is indeed a woman who was the best-known black writer of her period, and when today, black women writers become as well known as Toni Morrison or Alice Walker, we are simply continuing a tradition begun by Phillis over two hundred years ago.

Born in Africa about 1753 and brought to Boston at the age of seven to become the personal maid of Mrs. Suzanna Wheatley, Phillis Wheatley entered a world in which women wrote and spoke in a very different tongue. The world in which Wheatley lived was different, one which we should not take for granted.

The religious awakening in England, and the Methodist revival in America led by the Wesley brothers, had a tremendous influence on frontier and pioneer America. As a matter of fact, it had a great influence on the cultivated eastern shore. Reverend George Whitefield, a black man to whom Phillis Wheatley dedicated one of her poems, was a part of this revival, and he rode the circuit of churches in rural America with the Wesley evangelistic team. America's literature was tinged deeply with religious philosophy and fervor. The Puritans were noted for their long church services and their delight in long sermons which became part of the literature of the day. We are not looking at the very earliest literature, that is, of the seventeenth century; we are looking really at the literature of the early eighteenth century. If you know the story of American literature, you realize that there was very little published at first in America; that books were published in England and shipped to America; that literature consisted largely of promotional tracks, of diaries, of sermons, and of letters. There were no novels; they were taboo, and the poetry was largely of hymn-like quality. This religious influence seeped down through the early American white households to slaves and servants. They were truly marked by this early piety. Phillis Wheatley's verse was saturated with this religious fervor which she was taught in her master's home.

Apparently the Wheatleys discovered the quickness or the sharpness of the young African girl, and she was taught to read the Bible and to develop an appreciation for history, astronomy, geography, and the Latin classics. In 1770, her first poem on the death of Reverend George Whitefield was published in 1773. When she was manumitted, she was sent to England for her health. She showed early in her life a tendency toward ill health. She married a free man and obviously her life was not any better in freedom than it had been as a slave. In fact, it seemed to have been worse. Her children died in infancy, and she was too proud to let the family for whom she worked know of her hardships. It is said that she died in a rooming house in New York in her early thirties.

The first book of Phillis Wheatley's poetry was published in England because that was the usual thing in the eighteenth century; even well into the century, a poet was published in England. She was well known throughout the colonies, and in the northern section of the country she was quite honored. The trip abroad brought her a great deal of honor and the thing that happens is that she fell on unfortunate circumstances after her marriage. The marriage was not a good marriage, bore several children, all of whom died in infancy. Her life in the end was tragic.

How are we to assess the women who come after Wheatley? What is the relationship to the literary culture? In short, what are we to make of Phillis's "relatives?" The list of black women poets following Wheatley is impressive, although few have been as well known or as widely published until recently. In each period, there seems to be only one whom America is willing to claim. In the nineteenth century, it was Frances E. W. Harper whose long and active career made her a household name for over fifty years in America. Black women poets in the early decades of the twentieth century are only now coming to be known, but their work forms an important part of the output of the early and middle years of the Harlem Renaissance. Ann Spencer, Alice Dunbar-Nelson, and Georgia Douglas Johnson are among those who extended the rich tradition of black women's poetry. One black woman poet has won the Pulitzer Prize—Gwendolyn Brooks in 1950—a sure indication that black women's writing, poetry in particular, has come of age.[1]

It should not be surprising that those earliest writers of the black women's renaissance were poets. The earlier period of the black arts movement had revitalized poetry. Not only was it seen as one of the most expressive, but also the most public of the art forms. Writers like Sonia Sanchez, Nikki Giovanni, and Mari Evans could pull large audiences and gave new meaning to the performance of poetry. As the major houses began to tap this new resource, women writers increased in abundance. Alice Walker started her career as a poet and only later turned to fiction as did Linda Brown Bragg. June Jordan and the late Audre Lorde, however, continued to keep the tradition of poetry alive.

I like to think that our coming together in 1973, ostensibly to honor and celebrate the first among us to raise her voice within mainstream America, challenged us to give shape and form to a movement which permitted even more voices to be heard. It is not significant that the site for this movement's nurturing, if not its beginning, was the South, at a historically black institution, in a state where black people had for a long time been the majority of the population. Mississippi could indeed contribute the richness that had kept Phillis Wheatley's spirit alive. Wheatley took from her New England culture a very muted sense of the slavery that enveloped her and of her own oppression as a woman—one who died sick and destitute. She opted more often than not for a literary style that utilized the heroic couplet made famous by Alexander Pope. She excelled because she had talent and training, and because she wrote on subjects that interested both the eighteenth and nineteenth centuries, keeping her own feelings about slavery and freedom closely guarded. Her readers no doubt preferred her thoughts expressed in a poem like "Imagination" because it reminded them of Philip Freneau's "Power of Fancy"; they could embrace her well-known "To the Right Honourable William, Earl of Dartmouth" because she is toadying to Tories. We hear the other Phillis coming through in her own quiet way in "On Being Brought from Africa to America" or "On Liberty and Peace."

When black women celebrated Phillis Wheatley in 1973 in Jackson, Mississippi—in their poems or in a performance such as that done on the life of Wheatley by Vinnie Burroughs—they were acknowledging the power of her work and its continuing impact. It was the still small voice of Phillis Wheatley, as constrained as it was, that enabled us to remember how important it is to write out of our own cultural and historical moment and to tell the truth as

we see it. Fortunately for black women in the 1970s, some powerful new truths had begun to emerge, truths which forced a new
space to accommodate the very telling of them. All of this, we owe
to Phillis Wheatley.

Note
  1. In 1993 Rita Dove became the second black woman to win the
     Pulitzer Prize.

(1983)

Reflections on Black Women Writers

MANY PEOPLE IN AMERICA may know that African Americans have been publishing literature in the United States since colonial days. They may know the name of Phillis Wheatley, the first person of African descent to publish a book in the United States, but they may not know she was not the first black poet. That honor goes to Lucy Terry. Perhaps fewer Americans, black or white, know the history of fiction by African American women or realize that the first and third novels published by black people in the United States were written by women.

Despite these startling facts, it is little comfort to know that across a century of fiction writing by African Americans, less than two dozen black women have written and published novels that were considered creditable or otherwise. Who are these women? What are the titles of their nearly twice as many books? What are their problems? What is the continuing problem of the African American woman novelist? How do they measure up to the standards of the craft of fiction? Can any of these works be considered artistic successes? What has been the critical reception of novels

This essay was written for *Black Scholar* in 1983 but was never published.

by black women? How do they get published and where? Do these books sell? Does anybody read them?

First, we should state that black women belong squarely in the humanistic tradition of African American literature. They have written books to depict the life of African Americans. These volumes express the African heritage, and what we sometimes call the African diaspora. Here are publications that seek to find a common ground in humanity, speak of our pursuit of love and justice, truth and beauty, freedom and human dignity.

Second, it should be clearly understood that black women in the United States are categorized under two traditions of American fiction: the gothic and the sentimental. The major difference between the gothic and sentimental lies in the quality of imagination.

Those who write in the gothic tradition and deal with the supernatural, macabre, bizarre, and the grotesque are, nevertheless, writing out of the same values as those in the sentimental tradition who have neither tragic vision nor gothic imagination. We usually identify some of the features of the gothic novel as magic, mystery, chivalry, gray castles or dark and empty old mansions. Certainly these are the trappings of a horrific environment, but that's the point. On the other hand, the sentimental novel usually consists of melodrama, or an overindulgence in emotion. This inducement of emotion is frequently used as a tool by writers to accomplish artistic goals, regardless of the tradition she is writing in.

One of the ways we can look at the writings of these women is to ask questions about her work. My training in formalism guides my thinking. First, I would ask the author's intention. What was her purpose in writing this novel and telling this story? How well does she succeed?

I would then move to more specific questions about form and structure. What is the theme of this novel? What is the methodology or method of organization and characterization? How well does she create action, drama, or scene? How well does she control the language? What is the tone? What kind of style? Does this bear a relationship to her times? Is the novel a period piece? What about the question of universality? Of immortality? How shall we distinguish between craft and art? Is she a virtuoso, a clumsy amateur, or an artist? How well is her craft wedded to her art? Is this true to the black experience? Do you like the story? Why? What is her contribution to American literature? To African American literature? To world literature?

I begin with *Iola Leroy; or, Shadows Uplifted* by Frances E. W. Harper, published in the "gay nineties," 1892. Harper was already known as a successful poet who had published several volumes of poetry and prose before the appearance of her novel. An antislavery poet born free in 1825 and educated in Baltimore, she was also a popular lecturer working with the abolitionist movement, the Underground Railroad, and the Women's Christian Temperance Union, as well as the African Methodist Episcopal Church. In addition, Harper was perhaps the first female (certainly the first black female) teacher in Ohio at the Union Seminary in Columbus.

Her first two volumes of poetry were best sellers which sold at least fifty thousand copies. *Iola Leroy* enjoyed favorable critical reviews upon its appearance. Yet, black male critics panned her novel as inept, dull, pious and influenced by William Wells Brown's first novel *Clotel* (1853). The theme of *Iola Leroy* was miscegenation, or the tragic mulatto, and appeared at a time when educated Negroes were trying to efface their African heritage, instead of showing pride in it. It spoke to its diverse audience in a language of assimilation and a strong desire to refute stereotypical images of black people that ran rampant during the Reconstruction period due in part to plantation fiction. The book is typical of the times and must be considered interesting if for no other reason than it is one of the first from an African American woman.

A teacher, editor, Phi Beta Kappa scholar, and the author of four novels, Jessie Redmon Fauset wrote almost entirely of the black bourgeoisie. Although she was writing in the 1920s during the middle of the Harlem Renaissance and was associated with W. E. B. Du Bois at *Crisis* magazine, she reflects the ideas, philosophy, and psychology of the Victorian Age. For her novels read much like that prolific period in English and American literature. Fauset's writing calls to mind the great white women novelists of the Victorian period such as Jane Austen, George Eliot, and the Brontë sisters. I have no doubt these were her models and ideals. What Fauset's writing lacks in blackness, she makes up for in competence. *Plum Bun* (1928), which was published in 1929, is considered by many to be her best work, although she also wrote *There Is Confusion* (1924), *The Chinaberry Tree* (1931), and *Comedy, American Style* (1933).

Just as Jessie Redmon Fauset's themes are similar to her literary foremothers, Nella Larsen patterned herself after Fauset. They were both interested in miscegenation and the social phenomenon of "passing," or blacks trying to be white and moving because of their color into "white" jobs and "white" living. Nella Larsen differs from Jessie Fauset in that technically, she moves closer to the twentieth-century novel and is not like her predecessors still dealing with the nineteenth century. Larsen understood her craft better than Harper or Fauset, yet she is not read any more widely. Her work has experienced a recent critical resurrection, however, as scholars such as Thadious M. Davis, Deborah E. McDowell, Cheryl A. Wall and Lillie P. Howard reassess *Quicksand* and *Passing*.

Rita B. Dandridge classifies all male critics, black and white, as either apathetic, paternalistic, or chauvinistic when it comes to the fiction of African American women. Her straightforward article, "Male Critics / Black Women's Novels,"[1] brings to the forefront one of the major problems facing black women novelists. These writers are seen first as black, then as female. They attempt to triumph as artists under the double socially induced burden of race and gender. White male writers find it easier to be published and receive critical recognition than white women. Congruently, black male writers experience difficulty getting published and recognized, yet even they are more likely to attain acknowledgment than black women. Here is a major problem for African American writers.

The first great black woman novelist, in my estimation, is Zora Neale Hurston. She is our greatest forerunner and my favorite mentor. Armed with a thorough understanding of her craft, she writes of black southern life with genuine authenticity. This excellent story-teller uses her knowledge of black folklore as a trained anthropologist with consummate technical skill. Her work often includes humor to the point of raciness, love interests, and use of superstitions. I firmly believe that her novel *Their Eyes Were Watching God* (1937) is a work of art. Having loved everything Hurston has written, I read her with relish over and over again. And this is, perhaps, the greatest yardstick of artistic success.

Hurston absorbs her reader, for there is never a question as to whether the reader will turn the page. One is often sorry when she sees that the book's end is at hand, wishes there were more, and reads Zora again. Although Hurston hones her craft admirably in *Jonah's Gourd Vine*, other books such as *Tell My Horse* (1938), *Mules and Men* (1935), *Moses, Man of the Mountain* (1939), and *Seraph on the Sewanee* (1948) have a definite fascination. She later wrote an autobiography, *Dust Tracks on a Road* (1942). These books of folklore which never claim to be fiction highlight Zora's masterful touch.

However, Hurston fared badly, particularly during the Harlem Renaissance, from such confreres as Langston Hughes, Arna Bontemps and Richard Wright in later years; and even more recently from a chauvinistic essay by Darwin Turner. What is often lost on Zora's critics is the fact that this African American woman belongs to the twentieth century; she has the ability to create drama, to effect scene after scene, to develop tension, and best of all, to reveal character. I do not know of a black or white male writer who understands the folk novel better than, if as well as, Zora. She obviously had a profound influence upon Richard Wright and others who claim they have never heard of her.

Yet, Hurston suffered great pain and trauma due to the milieu of race and gender. She was falsely accused of sodomy, and though later acquitted, it was not before her reputation had suffered greatly. Not surprisingly, Hurston's popular success followed suit. Before this particular time of peril, Zora's books were highly regarded and sold well; unfortunately, personal financial success eluded her as she never received much money from these sales. She died broke and filled a pauper's grave, unmarked and unnoticed until a modern disciple, Alice Walker, found and placed a handsome tombstone on her resting place.

Hurston never received her Ph.D. in anthropology at Columbia simply because she was a black woman and not because she was not a brilliant student of "Papa Boaz." She was neither Ruth Benedict nor Margaret Meade. They were white.

The problem of the black woman novelist is perhaps best illustrated in Zora. Her marriage failed chiefly because of her career. Being a black female of great brilliance and talent, she felt the sting of racism and prejudice even among her own. She was criticized and belittled by her male peers who certainly were not one whit smarter nor more talented. The Langston Hughes feud[2] is well known, and Arna Bontemps's opinion was not much better. Personally, I think they were more than jealous of her; they hated her.

The black woman novelist, therefore, faces a dual impediment to success. Her dilemma as a writer is reflected in the treatment of African American females in the fiction by black and white male writers. One has only to look back at *Scarlet Sister Mary* (1928) by Julia Peterkin and Margaret Mitchell's *Gone With the Wind* (1936) to see the demeaning role of black women in American fiction. This practice is repeated in the fiction by black men such as Richard Wright and Chester Himes. This negative treatment in fiction and criticism by male writers of black women is only a reflection of her status in society and the role she has encountered from the days of slavery through segregation. Her foes are racism and sexism. These are her problems. How do we overcome them?

Three women of the 1930s and 1940s assist African American females with the scaling of the literary wall, before other novelists would later emerge to take center stage as artists whose skills matched and out-ranked prominent black and white male authors. These literary titans are Ann Petry, Dorothy West, and Paule Marshall. Ann Petry, winner of a Houghton Mifflin Literary Fellowship, has more than competently written four books of fiction. *The Street* (1946) was called a naturalistic novel after the school of Richard Wright, but *Country Place* (1947), *The Narrows* (1953), and *Miss Muriel and Other Stories* (1971) could not be stigmatized. These books were excellent by any literary standard. This novelist knows her subject and understood her craft. Petry handles the language with skill and artistry. Certainly one of her strengths is the ability to psychoanalyze her characters, seemingly becoming one with them. Yet, her popular period during *The Street* faded into oblivion, and she is virtually unknown today. Sadly, *The Street* did not break into the mainstream of American literature nor experience world acclaim as *Native Son* (1940) did. Fortunately, *The Street* has been rediscovered by black feminists and Petry once again enjoys but a fraction of her due.

Phi Beta Kappa scholar Paule Marshall is the author of some of the finest fiction in the English language. A careful and talented craftsperson, she chooses material from the Caribbean world that is authentic to the black experience as well as universal. *Brown Girl, Brownstone* (1959) deals with a young girl, *Soul Clap Hands and Sing* (1961) is based on an old man and the tensions of the aged, *The Chosen Place, The Timeless People* (1969) tells the story of an island family, and *Praisesong for the Widow* (1983) illustrates a middle-aged black woman's self-discovery. Marshall produced three novels in the decade between 1959 and 1969. I am not aware that she has garnered special literary prizes or great sales, but then she is a black woman. Nevertheless, Paule Marshall is a great person of letters, regardless of race and sex.

Gwendolyn Brooks speaks deprecatingly of her only novel, *Maud Martha* (1953), but it is, nevertheless, a sensitive portrayal of a young adolescent girl who happens to be black but might have been of any race. *Maud Martha* examines the plight of a dark-skinned black female who seeks fulfillment as a wife and mother in American society. It touches upon many issues pertinent to blacks, among them self-hate and intra-racial prejudice. Brooks's skill as a poet is evident in her prose style, and it is, perhaps, a pity that she has not written more *Maud Martha*s.

Rosa Guy has written more than seven novels, including *Bird at My Window* (1966), *The Friends* (1973), and *A Measure of Time* (1983). She is perhaps our most political of the women writers. Although Guy has a slant from the left, she does not write propaganda. This craftsperson is true to the black experience, writing stories of poignancy and wistfulness. Most of her fiction concentrates on impoverished young black adults living in Harlem, and so she is known as the author of young adult fiction. Nevertheless, we should know this strong and compelling voice.

Sarah Wright and Louise Meriwether have each written one novel, but each book is one the reader will remember and hate to put down. They remind us somewhat of Dorothy West, the last living writer of the Harlem Renaissance, who wrote *The Living is Easy* (1948) much later. Wright is the author of *This Child's Gonna Live* (1969), while Meriwether's novel is *Daddy Was a Number Runner* (1970).

In 1952 we had the pleasure of inviting to the Jackson State University campus for the Seventy-fifth Anniversary Literary Festival a young woman who had just burst upon the literary scene with a story in *Ladies Home Journal*, "See How They Run," which was made into a movie, "Bright Road." She was Mary Elizabeth Vroman and now, regretfully, she is long dead, but not before she wrote a successful novel, *Esther*, in 1963. Nobody can guess what Vroman might have done if she had lived longer. Understanding the art and craft of writing, she will be remembered like the flash of a bright meteor across our darkened sky.

The three most distinguished black women practicing the craft and art of fiction today are Alice Walker, Toni Cade Bambara, and Toni Morrison. Each of these women thoroughly knows and understands the craft of fiction.

Toni Morrison demonstrates an equal knowledge of the art of fiction in her first two books. *The Bluest Eye* (1970) and *Sula* (1973) are both masterpieces. Both are examples of a gothic imagination and a tragic vision. Yet, *Song of Solomon* (1977) does not hit me in the solar plexus in the same manner, not because it is not well written, but because I find it almost too pat and formulaic for success. Certainly, it deserved the National Book Award, although her two preceding books were better. The manner in which Morrison handles the problem of evil as it becomes entangled with the dilemma of race and racism cannot be superseded in its excellence.

I am, perhaps, partial to women characters; however, there are better expressions of the black experience than *Song of Solomon*. The use of fantasy or insanity as symbols of our American experience can be taken as either black or white, and therefore, its ambiguity relieves it of the stigma of race. This is why *Song of Solomon* could win a National Book Award, whereas *The Bluest Eye* and *Sula* could not. These two novels speak directly to the experience of the black woman, for both novels explore female friendship. *The Bluest Eye* concentrates upon society's racial bombardment of three girls growing up in Ohio and its effect. Whereas, *Sula* juxtaposes the lives of two black girls who also grow up together, yet choose different paths in adulthood. Interestingly enough, they both end up in the bosom of the black community in radically different positions. The greatness of this book lies in tracing the reasons for the choices made by the black women in this novel and their ramifications. The reading of Morrison is an exercise in the grotesque and psychoanalytical as one delves into the folkloric roots of storytelling. But then Morrison should know her craft; she has taught English composition and was an editor in one of the large American publishing houses. Morrison understands what is required. She has also served as editor for another gifted and current black woman novelist, Gayl Jones, whom we will discuss later.

Toni Cade Bambara was a special African American woman novelist. She published three books of fiction that must be considered excellent by every standard of craft, art, and the trade. Being gifted in relating her work to the black experience and understanding the street culture as an avenue and vehicle of folklore, Bambara speaks in a language from an African American environment that is expressive of life and indigenous in black culture. Her three books—*Gorilla, My Love* (1972), *The Sea Birds Are Still Alive* (1977), and *The Salt Eaters* (1980)—one collection of short stories and two novels, respectively, are so original that they are innovative. No black men can claim to be her major influences, although they may have taught her the realities of black male prejudice and female envy.

Bambara captures Black America with a style that is as haunting as it is lovely. She regards the pathos, humor, tragedy, and the brutality of African American life in all its variegated, kaleidoscopic wonder. *The Salt Eaters* is about cult life among black people and is much more authentic than anything our television news has had to offer.

More socially conscious and politically aware than most of her black sisters, Bambara's prose follows suit accordingly. She has a global perspective which helps her interpret world events and deal with Third World issues in a telling and powerful manner. *The Sea Birds Are Still Alive* is an excellent kaleidoscopic view of black female life, for it vividly, as well as adroitly, portrays her point of view, sensitivity, and bruised humanity. In *Gorilla, My Love,* which sounds almost as gothic and paradoxical as anything in literature, Bambara examines the unbelievable fidelity of African American women to the beauty and ugliness of their love lives and men.

I cannot help but compare Alice Walker with two white women novelists who are also natives of the state of Georgia. I hope the comparison will not seem odious; it is not meant to be. Carson McCullers, Flannery O'Connor, and Alice Walker seem to have a great deal in common. They are extremely talented and prolific writers who have the same vision, type of imagination, and virtuosity. Whether they are to be considered great artists still remains to be seen. There is no question as to their ability to handle the craft. Having tragic vision and gothic imaginations, they write of the macabre, grotesque, supernatural, and violent. Certainly, a bizarre commonality arises out of being born within miles of each other in the same violent white Southland, for they write out of the welter of southern life and culture.

As an African American woman, Walker dishes out the same medicine to black men that they have dealt to their female counterparts. They have harshly accused her of putting "them" (all black men) down. Alice has been luckier than many of her black sisters. She has had something of the white success, perhaps, due in part to an education at a white women's college (although she began at a black women's college), marriage to a white man by whom she bore a daughter, and for a while she was the darling of the *Ms.* magazine crowd.

Kristin Hunter is a singular example. She has no equal. Author of more than six novels, *The Landlord* (1966) was successful enough to warrant and get a movie made from it. *God Bless the Child* (1964) was also thematically interwoven into that movie. *The Survivors* (1975) is little known, while her last and best, *The Lakestown Rebellion* (1978), has been slow to catch the eye of the general public. A serious writer, Hunter sometimes seems the exception that proves the rule about black women novelists. Not only did her writing force critical attention upon black women writers of the 1970s, but she also spoke to the experience of the black children and adolescent reading market with appearance of novels such as *The Soul Brothers and Sister Lou* (1968) that contain messages of strength and didacticism.

Carlene Hatcher Polite published *The Flagellants* in 1967, partly autobiographical, but not proficient technically. She is also not as successful in depicting time as Dorothy West in *The Living is Easy* (1948). Nevertheless, she is an innovative voice in literature.

One of the constant complaints of the male critic is the way the woman novelist handles sex. There are two current novelists who completely refute this accusation. Gayl Jones has written two novels, *Corregidora* (1975) and *Eva's Man* (1976). Since I have promised not to moralize or make ethical judgments, I will refrain from calling her books sordid or even shocking and sensational, but I will say she is most explicit sexually. Jones develops the thesis that black men have brutally driven their women into exploring varied forms of human sexuality, including lesbian relationships. Now Jones declares herself to be one who is particularly interested in relationships that develop character. This does not exclude bisexual, homosexual, or any other type of sexual encounter. However, she is no more explicit than Richard Wright, John O. Killens, and James Baldwin.

Another current novel which explores an interracial love affair between two women is Ann Allen Shockley's *Loving Her* (1974). This book is far more explicit than the first white book of its kind, Radclyffe Hall's *Well of Loneliness* (1928) or D. H. Lawrence's *The Fox* (1923). While it may not be as subtle or as full of symbols, it is sensitively accomplished. The craft and techniques are sure. Again, it remains to be seen whether it will become an immortal work of art. Frankly I do not find myself eager to re-read these books. I am repelled by some of the scenes in sexually explicit books, but never let it be said that women, particularly black women, cannot write them as well as men.

In handling love, sex, and the black male/female relationship, few of these women have fallen into the stereotypical and negative depiction of African American love life and sexuality as their male counterparts who certainly have aped the white society. Black women find themselves puzzled by the ongoing expression by black men that their wives, sweethearts, mothers, and sisters are enemies.

As mothers, wives, daughters, and sisters, we have felt constantly that they feel we owe them more than our lives. "Ain't no need of working so hard, I got a gal in the white folks yard." We are to nurse their hurts, salve their bruised pride, and heal the castration daily placed on them by their white brothers, yet we deserve no tenderness, no consideration, not even respect. This is what we find in the literature and literary criticism: apathy from the white male world, paternalism from both white and black males, and most of all, a brutal chauvinism from our African American brothers.

And that brings me to a few brief remarks about my own novel, *Jubilee*. The worst reviews that *Jubilee* received were from black men.

While the white press, with few exceptions, was generally kind to *Jubilee*, the black press was not. One male critic said, "*Jubilee* was not well written and had every stereotype including the kitchen stove." Another lesser-known critic writing in a black magazine said, "The story was no good, not even interesting, not well written, and not worth the reader's time. It had no sex in it and was not worthy of a poet's reputation."

Despite the fact that *Jubilee* has been sold around the world and translated into seven foreign languages, only two or three black male critics have been generous and kind enough to say it had minimal worth. One of those critics was Richard Barksdale and another was Sterling Brown. A possible third was Nick Aaron Ford. It is, therefore, quite clear that the problem of the black woman novelist is one of discrimination. In my case, I have suffered on at least four counts of discrimination: first, I am black; second, I am a woman; third, I am southern; and, fourth, I am not rich.

In my estimation, the greatest black woman novelist of our time is a woman born in 1937 in South Africa who lived and died in exile in Botswana. Bessie Head published *When Rain Clouds Gather* (1969) and *Maru* (1971) in London and *A Question of Power* (1973) in the United States. These books are masterpieces. She is an artist as well as craftsperson of the first order. Her themes are freedom, love, and power. Head's books are moving and memorable. Whether it is the fact that she comes out of such horrible oppression and poverty and is so eloquent, her genius is unquestionable.

Clouds Gather and *Maru* invite re-reading over and over. *A Question of Power* is more difficult and obscure, but will command your attention. When I was recounting to a fellow countryman, who was a native South African and a male writer, how much I liked and respected her, he was patronizing and chauvinistic. He replied, "Oh, yes, she is a feminist writer." I wanted to add, her work is better than anything you have ever done or could do, but I restrained myself. So these sexual politics go back in black literature as sexual discrimination persists along with racism in white American literature.

Notes

1. Rita B. Dandridge, "Male Critics / Black Women's Novels," *College Language Association Journal* 23 (Spring 1980): 1–11.

2. Langston Hughes and Zora Neale Hurston wrote a play called
   Mulebone, which became the source of bitter antagonism between
   them and caused difficulty with their common sponsor, Mrs.
   R. Osgood Mason. According to Hughes's biographer, Arnold
   Rampersad, Hughes discovered Hurston had copyrighted *Mulebone*
   in her name, without his knowledge. Based on information
   received from Hurston, Mrs. Mason discontinued her financial
   support of Hughes.

Part II

Discovering Our Connections

African Heritage, Southern Culture, and the American Experience

Symbol, Myth, and Legend

Folk Elements in African American Literature

NOTHING IN African American literature springs like Athena grown from the head of Zeus. Neither does it begin hydra-headed *in media res*. Before such Greek myths were invented, the African myths of creation, death, and the resurrection, races in the family of mankind, languages, super-gods, and their lesser divinities lived in the dust, air, fire, and water of black Egypt, and flourished along the banks of the Nile River some five thousand or more years ago. Since the seed of all literature as well as religion may be found in myth and since such symbols continue to exist through legend, we must look for the beginnings of African American literature in our African past. It is in this African background that we will find the indigenous black idiom in all authentic African American cultural expression. We must further study the process of acculturation in America throughout the periods of slavery and segregation in order to understand the black experience in America and see that experience reflected in African American

This essay was originally delivered as a classroom lecture at Jackson State University in 1976.

literature for more than three centuries of literary expression by black folk.

This earliest black folk expression is, like all historic and epic literature coming from people shrouded in anonymity, neither designated by author, time, nor place. But we are familiar with a small residue from the possibly thousands of folk poems, tales, and songs that embrace the dark beginnings of African existence during human slavery in the Americas. These we know today as spirituals, animal folk tales and anecdotes, and seculars, prison hollers, aphorisms, and even recorded minstrel routines. Like the blues, and the limbo, the folk literature expresses a constant social comment on black life expressed in the vernacular of the black people. The basic components of this literature—symbol, myth, and legend—are all expressed in folk terms; the unit of the language or the word is a symbol for the concept or mental figuration of a physical picture thus creatively perceived. This is always couched in folk terms. The imaginative unit or myth, like the religious concept of heaven as a big fish-fry (which is not a black concept, it must be noted) is, nevertheless, an example of folk myth; and the tall tales of black strength, sexual prowess, and magic powers all belong to this folk body of legend.

A clarification of the folk elements according to definition includes folk speech, sayings, or corruptions of English and American language into broken speech, slang, idiomatic changes, and varieties of pronunciation according to geographical location. Frequently this has erroneously been labeled Negro dialect rather than southern speech, since dialects are basically and technically categorized by geographic areas rather than racial labels; most folk expression, however, is a corruption of the language of both dominant and subculture, and this is what has happened with the descendants of black Africa in White America. Second, folk belief, which includes pithy gems of black philosophy, is derived from a parent culture and couched in earthy, racy, but quite realistic folk terms. These folk beliefs are generally regarded as superstitious, and they are tied as much to religious myth as they are tied to literature. They are spread over a range of ideas and systems of thought known as witchcraft, voodoo, faith healing, conjuring, and confidence workers. Folk ways, in the same fashion, are based on mores, customs, attitudes, and actions developed over a long period of time and, though based on folk beliefs, are again the result of a process of acculturation or adjustment of people of one culture to another. Folk ways are inevitably tied to the natural life cycle—birth, puberty, marriage, reproduction, and death. All of these folk expressions are translated in the literature as symbol, myth, and legend.

There are five major periods in African American literature when leading exponents of this folk art have skillfully and imaginatively used these folk elements in their poetry, fiction, and drama. These periods are first, the post–slavery periods of the 1880s and 1890s until after the turn of the century. Key writers for this period are Paul Laurence Dunbar and Charles Waddell Chesnutt. A link or bridge between this period and the next is the towering literary figure, James Weldon Johnson. The second period is the decade of the 1920s and the Harlem Renaissance with such major exponents as Zora Neale Hurston, Langston Hughes, and Sterling Brown. Arna Bontemps and Wallace Thurman, author of the novel *The Blacker the Berry* (1929) also belong to this period. The third period is the decade of the thirties and the decade of the forties. Black writers in this depression/war period were known as writers of social protest. Richard Wright, Margaret Walker, Gwendolyn Brooks, Owen Dodson, and Melvin Tolson belong to this period. The decade of the fifties, or the fourth period, includes James Baldwin, Chester Himes, John O. Killens, William Melvin Kelley, and Ralph Ellison as well as the poet LeRoi Jones, or as he later became to be known, Imamu Amiri Baraka. The young black arts movement of the sixties led by Baraka and Larry Neal spun off such poets and meteorites as Carolyn Rodgers, Sonia Sanchez, Nikki Giovanni, and Mari Evans. There were many young dramatists, too, such as Ed Bullins, Lonnie Elder, Ron Milner, Douglas Turner Ward, and Richard Wesley, all following the playwrights of the fifties: Lorraine Hansberry, Loften Mitchell, and Ossie Davis.

In a special category of prose writers appearing in the sixties are Ernest Gaines, Alice Walker, Louise Meriwether, and Sarah Wright. One of the geniuses of folk expression is already deceased, Henry Dumas.

Now let's look at some examples. The first major black poet to use the black idiom and other folk elements in his poetry was Paul Laurence Dunbar. He used this material with great imagination and consummate skill. Dealing equally well with pathos and humor, he employed comic and tragic modes. Unhappy because his white public applauded his "jingles in a broken tongue," Dunbar nevertheless made a major contribution to American literature with his "dialect" poems.

It is significant that Dunbar appears on the literary scene in the post–Civil War period. His parents were ex-slaves who migrated north to Ohio. Born there in 1872, Dunbar heard the plantation dialect from his parents. More than that he captured the authentic folk speech, belief, and folk ways together with the feelings of African slaves. He obviously belongs in literature to the plantation tradition which we will discuss later in some detail. Although Dunbar wrote a number of prose pieces, short stories, and even novels, his prose is not nearly as successful in his utilizing of folk elements in his poetry.

Contemporary with Dunbar and equally adept in the use of folk elements was the prose writer Charles Waddell Chesnutt. His short stories and novels were based almost entirely on black folklife, folk expression, folk ways, and to a great extent on folk beliefs. "The Gophered Grapevine" and "The Wife of His Youth" (on the theme of race and miscegenation) are only surpassed by his novels *The Marrow of Tradition* (1901), *The Conjure Woman* (1899), and *The House Behind the Cedars* (1900). Chesnutt must be read and understood technically as belonging to nineteenth-century American fiction, and as such, his fiction measures up to a high standard of technical efficiency and facility. Plot, character, and language are blended with folk feeling in a simple style that all reflect a knowledge of black folklife and culture together with the racial tensions and contradictions or conflicts of the American society. Chesnutt's elements like Dunbar's are clearly in the tradition of the southern plantation. A study of group actions, beliefs, and mores or customs as they move from an African village to a southern slave plantation in the United States would provide an interesting backdrop and parallel study for an understanding of Chesnutt, especially in *The Conjure Woman*. Here we are not merely concerned with folk speech, but clearly with folk beliefs and folk ways. Sociology of religion, sociology per se, and anthropology are all most relevant here.

James Weldon Johnson was born one year earlier than Dunbar but like Chesnutt, he outlived Dunbar by many fruitful years. He does not, however, belong in any way to the plantation tradition.

Rather, his use of folk elements—speech, beliefs, and ways—as symbol, myth, and dogma in *God's Trombones* (1927) all reflect his interest in the Black Church or religion and the tradition of the black preacher as expressed in the folk sermon. Here these folk elements may clearly be seen as symbol, myth, and dogma, and moreover they coincide singularly with an Americanized as well as folk version of the Christian myth of redemption. Poems based on creation, the lawgiver, prophets, immaculate conception, epiphany, temptation, crucifixion, and resurrection are all structured here within a folk frame and the myth is unmistakable.

During the decade of the 1920s, three masterful innovators in the use of the black folk idiom appeared on the scene. The leader and grand dame of them all was none other than Zora Neale Hurston. Natural storyteller in the African griot tradition, trained as an anthropologist and therefore skilled in fieldwork, talented to the point of genius, Zora Neale Hurston was absolutely great. Fifty years later we know that everybody sat at Zora's feet and learned from her. "Papa Boaz" taught her well. When you read those opening italicized lines from Richard Wright's "Big Boy Leaves Home," remember he got them from Zora! "Yo mama don wear no drawers. . . ." Langston Hughes, Arna Bontemps, and Richard Wright never gave her lines of credit, but I don't need an educated guess to know how much they learned from Zora. Since there is another lecture scheduled on Zora's use of folklore, I will restrict myself to a mere listing of her books as well as expressing her knowledge and use of black folklore. Begin with the first novel, *Jonah's Gourd Vine,* and study it again in terms of symbol, myth, and legend. Then the rich studies in anthropology—*Tell My Horse* and *Mules and Men*—plus religious symbolism and magic in *Moses, Man of the Mountain.* The second novel, *Their Eyes Were Watching God,* is a masterpiece, and even the names of characters like Tea-Cake are rich in folk feeling and symbolism. *Dust Tracks on a Road* is her autobiography couched in folk terms, and the final published work, *Seraph on the Sewanee,* again shows her use of folk elements in fiction. Regardless of the genre, Zora Neale Hurston's work is steeped in folk elements. Her work is fascinating and richly entertaining. If, after reading her, you are not impressed, tell me she is not the greatest!

Langston Hughes is the first poet after Dunbar to introduce a new and authentic black idiom into African American literature with his blues-jazz rhythms. The publication of his first volume, *The Weary Blues*, in 1926, just fifty years ago, marked more than the beginning of his illustrious career. It was the beginning of a new age immortalized in song and poetry—the Jazz Age in more than musical fact. Langston Hughes captured the urban speech of Harlem and all Black America. Until the twenties, it is significant to remember that most black life and culture was rural. He caught the rhythms of jazz and blues, and he expressed the whole gamut of black world and life in the street culture. Jesse B. Simple is a folk character from that culture or tradition. So is Madame Alberta K. Johnson in the Madame poems. Langston knew and understood the whole psychological makeup of the zoot-suiter, the jive talk, the hep cat, and the new swing music. As a versatile and talented craftsman, he mined the ore of Negro folklore and used all the folk elements, speech, beliefs, and ways in three literary genres: namely, poetry, prose, and gospel folk drama. He used them as symbol, myth, and legend, incident, dogma, and ritual in every conceivable way. Sometimes consciously, sometimes unconsciously, Langston Hughes reveals black folklife in nearly all the eighty-six volumes he wrote and left to posterity—poetry, short stories, novels, gospel plays, autobiographies! Langston Hughes and Arna Bontemps have even collaborated on a large collection of Negro folklore.[1]

Arna Bontemps used very little of the folk elements in his hauntingly beautiful poetry, but he used a great deal in prose and various anthologies, for example *God Sends Sunday* (1941) and *Golden Slippers* (1941).

The third most significant writer to use folk elements during the decade of the 1920s and who suffuses most of his poetry with black folklife—ways, speech, and beliefs—is Sterling Brown. Master of the ballad form, he writes about the roustabout, the railroad hand, the blues singer, the legendary heroes of strong men, and super-human workers.

Briefly recapitulating, black folklore is no more than a welter of source material indigenous of the group-cultural expression of black people. It is a body of folk sayings, beliefs, and folk ways developed through the centuries of American slavery and racial segregation in the Americas, and it is the basic source, root, and inspiration behind most of the imaginative writings of African Americans. That these imaginative writers have used this material in various ingenious or inventive ways is indisputable. The root of the matter is that this welter of black folklore is seen in the basic components of the literature as symbol, myth, and legend. To these the poet adds figurative language or imagery in his own individual arrangement all wedded to music and meaning, while the prose writer merely develops incident, doubling, quadrupling, or multiplying it, and the dramatist adds conflict and heightened dramatic interest.

Note
1. Arna Bontemps and Langston Hughes, *The Book of Negro Folklore* (New York: Dodd, Mead, 1958).

(1976)

Black Culture

OUR BLACK AMERICAN culture is deeply rooted in Africa. Thirty-five hundred years before the coming of Christ, Egyptian civilization had a highly developed religion, architecture, agricultural system, and a literature expressed in the coffin texts and the first great epic poem, *The Book of the Dead.* The great Sahara Desert, archaeologists and geologists now tell us, did not exist until some two thousand years ago so that there was obviously no interrupted flow of communication and transportation between what is now North Africa and sub-Sahara Africa. The entire continent of Africa, with remarkable cultures and civilizations, was in reality one black continent.

Black culture is, therefore, as old as mankind's earliest recorded literature, art, and religion, for black culture began in Africa more than five thousand years ago with Egyptian civilization. Even Herodotus, the Greek historian who came late in the parade of ancient empires, speaks of Egyptians as people with "burnt" faces.

This essay was commissioned for the 1976 Bicentennial and was later published as "A Bicentennial Pamphlet: Black Culture" (1981).

Egyptian art remains in the great coffin texts of the ancient pyramids as well as carved on the temples of Karnak and Simbu. The earliest conception of man's journey from life to death and the hall of justice in the underworld is recorded in *The Book of the Dead*, a pre-Homeric epic from which both Homer and Virgil conceivably could have learned the epic convention of a descent into the underworld.

Black culture has two main streams: a sociological stream— with which we are not here concerned—and an artistic stream, which commands our immediate attention. In this artistic stream, black culture has five branches. These are language, religion, art, music, and literature. Both religion and literature begin in the seed bed of myth. It is out of the mythology of ancient Egypt and Africa that all the great world religions of mankind have proceeded. Animism is man's earliest religion and from this is a simple belief that all matter is animated by spirit, whether dust of the earth, air, water, plant, or animal life, comes our belief in many nature gods, belief in one great spirit, and belief in the primacy of human personality. Thus, human personality which is essentially spiritual and potentially divine has a spiritual destiny. This is implicit in the beginnings of animism and spiritism, essentials in the black man's mind from the earliest recorded time.

Art, music, and literature grow out of this religious belief or whole body of belief concerning life. Life is divided into the cycles of nature. Birth, puberty, marriage, reproduction, and death are tied to the seasonal or cyclic change of the natural or physical worlds around us such as spring, summer, fall or autumn, and winter. Birth and puberty correspond to spring and the resurrection, marriage, and reproduction correspond to summer and fulfillment or burgeoning blossoms and flowers. The end of the reproductive cycle or middle age corresponds to autumn, fall, and harvest time, and death or the end of life from old age correspond to winter. Ancient poetry and music and paintings preserved on the walls of caves, tombs, and temples celebrated as rites of passage these epic cycles of life and nature—love and war and the meaning of all existence, and death as part of the life cycle.

Black culture is, therefore, the seed-culture of all civilizations which have benefited from the black diaspora. This scattering or dispersion of black people came after the religious waves of the

Middle Ages when the Europeans who had embraced the Christian religion from Asia and Africa and made it a Western world religion collided with the rising religion and culture of Islam and Mohammedanism in the so-called Crusades or wars of five centuries: ninth, tenth, eleventh, twelfth, and thirteenth.

All modern culture stems from this diaspora of Oriental and African-Asian culture transported to the West. The mathematics of Islam was one of the greatest achievements of Islamic culture. Reflected in architecture, the geometry, calculus, and physics of the Middle Ages laid the physical basis for our modern technology. Examples are the remnants of Spanish temples in Spain in Granada and the Alhambra. The new learning brought from the Orient by the crusading soldiers transferred the Greek manuscripts translated by Jewish and Moslem scholars. This was the basis for the new scientific inventions. A new concept of the universe ushered in the modern world.

West African sculptures of both religious and sexual symbolism influenced the modern paintings of Picasso, Brancusi, and Modigliani. The stylized form and elongated faces, the blocks of cubism, and the surrealism of modern abstract art all come from these West African sculptures. African rhythms have influenced modern music whether Calypso, Spanish dance and guitar music, or black American jazz. Modern syncopation has a black African base. This is to say nothing about the influences of blues and all folk music on the speech and literature of Black America.

Many people falsely assume that the black American past is rooted in slavery and segregation just as many Europeans falsely declare a short African past of colonialism. Black America is rooted in ancient Africa, and Africa is as old as the Nile.

Our Black American culture is, therefore, as W. E. B. Du Bois has declared, two-fold. It is African, and it is American. As black people exiled from black Africa, we have continued our cultural development and expression despite slavery and segregation. White American slavery attempted to stamp out all evidence of African culture in the African slave. But this attempt failed. This cultural heritage is still expressed in our religion, language, music, art, and literature. All these cultural expressions have more than a folk base of speech, rhythm, color, and feeling tone which are ours indisput- and which are indigenous to our land, culture, and heritage.

All these cultural expressions are rooted in the spirit of our mind and cosmos of black Africa. And we have brought them from Africa to the new world during the diaspora. Even as we are historically descendants of Africa, we are also sociological and artistic reflections of our American environment. Wounded by American racism and tried like gold in a fire of racial suffering throughout the centuries of slavery and segregation, we exist today as a nation within a nation, ostracized and stigmatized by the very sociopolitical and economic forces which we have been forced to help in order to build America.

Slavery was not, as is commonly thought, the result of only one part of Africa. The West Coast of West Africa, the Bantu and Zulu in South Africa, the people in Sudan and Congo in Central Africa, people in Madagascar on the East Coast, as well as the great tribes from the Ashanti, Ife, and Fulangi in West Africa, were all transported to and from the West Coast at the hated slave islands and prisons of Goree and Alamari. In America, slavery destroyed the national and cultural ties of Africa. Religion, language, and tribal customs were all deeply affected but not completely effaced. Families and tribal communities were separated. Pestilence, war, famine, exposure, and brutal treatment, all common in slavery, gravely affected black people and seriously threatened black culture. But our culture survived. Historians now have and tell the records of slaves as to the attempt of white slave traders and slave holders to stigmatize, ostracize, and dehumanize black people and the great culture of which the white man was totally ignorant.

When the founding fathers of this nation conceived their documents of independence and liberty—the Bill of Rights, the Declaration of Independence, and the Constitution of the United States of America—black Americans were already a real presence in the growing revolution. The Black Church under Richard Allen, founder of the African Methodist Episcopal Church; Jarena Lee, wandering woman preacher; and Absalom Jones, the first black American Episcopal priest; the black poet, Phillis Wheatley; the black soldiers, Crispus Attucks and Barzillai Lev of Bunker Hill, and the black slaves of Jefferson who are credited with many of his patented inventions like Benjamin Banneker, inventor and free man, who later completed architectural plans for the city of Washington—these black exponents of African culture were American revolutionaries despite the denial of White America and their failure to recognize them.

Slavery could not submerge black culture despite its cruel oppression, for the great spirituals and work songs survive to this day, as a testament of black culture. African language lost its integrity, but words that are vestigial survivals are part of American language today. Gumbo and okra are perhaps most familiar and specific examples. Dr. Lorenzo Dow Turner has made a remarkable study of Gullah preserved in the Sea Islands off the Georgia coast. The shouts and songs in our Protestant churches and unorthodox cults are evidence of the persistence of African customs and mores in our Black American religious expression.

As for music, art, and literature, these are the most celebrated artistic expressions of black culture. From the black tragedian, Ira Aldridge, to Paul Robeson and James Earl Jones, the greatness of black actors has been witnessed by all America and the modern world.

The history of literature written in America by black people coincides with the history of the bicentennial of the nation. The first book published by an African American and the second by a woman was *Poems on Various Subjects, Religious and Moral* by Phillis Wheatley at age twenty in London, England, late in the year 1773. Phillis Wheatley was brought from Senegal as a small child and educated by John Wheatley, a wealthy merchant of Boston. Three black poets belong to the era of the revolution, and their works were printed during that time. In addition to Phillis Wheatley were Lucy Terry and Jupiter Hammon. Miss Wheatley wrote a poem to General George Washington. She must have also witnessed the death of Crispus Attucks, a black freedman, who was first to fall and die in Boston in the American Revolution.

Across these two hundred years, these black poets, playwrights, and novelists have won nearly all, if not all, the significant prizes America has offered. Yet, the literature has remained separated and obscure because of institutionalized white racism. In the twenties, thirties, forties, fifties, sixties, and seventies, these black poets, novelists, and playwrights won such prizes as the Harmon Award (Langston Hughes), Spingarn Medal (Langston Hughes, James Weldon Johnson, Richard Wright, and Gordon Parks), Yale Award for Younger Poets (Margaret Walker), Pulitzer Prize (Gwendolyn Brooks and

Charles Gordone), the Obie Award (LeRoi Jones or Imamu Amiri Baraka), and Houghton Mifflin Literary Awards (Ann Petry and Margaret Walker). Ralph Ellison received the National Book Award for his remarkable *Invisible Man* (1952), and at least a dozen writers have had best sellers including the antislavery poet, Frances E. W. Harper, and the Harlem Renaissance poet, Georgia Douglas Johnson. Fenton Johnson, John Matheus, and Arna Bontemps won *Opportunity* prizes for plays, short stories, and poetry. Dozens have had plays on Broadway since Willis Richardson first appeared in 1923. The latest successes include the plays "Anna Lucasta" and "Pearlie Victorious" by Ossie Davis and the black musical "The Wiz" with Geoffrey Holder as director. Famed black movie actor, Sidney Poitier, won the coveted Oscar or Academy Award while numerous black thespians have won the Emmy or television award, and the Grammy Award for having a million records or gold records published. These are too numerous to mention.

African American literature in its humanistic and realistic expressions runs like a chain from Phillis Wheatley and William Wells Brown through Charles Chesnutt, William Edward Burghardt Du Bois and Paul Laurence Dunbar to James Weldon Johnson and the giants of the Harlem Renaissance, namely, Langston Hughes, Countee Cullen, Claude McKay, Arna Bontemps, Zora Neale Hurston, Jean Toomer, Wallace Thurman, Rudolph Fisher, George Schuyler, Eric Walrond, Nella Larsen, and Jessie Fauset. This great humanistic tradition is maintained through the thirties, forties, fifties, and sixties by such major writers as Richard Wright, Ralph Ellison, and James Baldwin, followed by the near-greats John Oliver Killens, William Melvin Kelley, Ann Petry, Gwendolyn Brooks, and LeRoi Jones or Amiri Baraka. A new school includes Cyrus Colter, Toni Morrison, Nikki Giovanni, Carolyn Rodgers, Sonia Sanchez, Toni Cade Bambara, and Don L. Lee (Haki Madhubuti).

The late James Porter, artist, teacher, and author, has given a beautiful legacy to us with his history of black painters or graphic artists and sculptors from Edmonia Lewis and Meta Warwick Fuller, to Richmond Barthe, Elizabeth Prophet, Selma Burke, Augusta Savage, and Elizabeth Catlett and painters from Henry Ossawa Tanner to Jacob Lawrence, Romare Bearden, Charles White, and William Artis.

Black music is perhaps the most acceptable of our black culture.

The modern world is willing to accept the unique character of African rhythms and the language of the drum. White America, in general, reluctantly admits that black American music is *the* American music and most indigenous to our culture. In every category or classification of music, moreover, Black America has achieved monumentally. With a broad base of folk music—spirituals and gospel music, seculars (blues, work songs, prison hollers)—individuals have risen in notable achievement in classical, popular, and various forms of jazz. From Black Patti to Marian Anderson and Leontyne Price, the great black American singer has gained worldwide eminence. Roland Hayes, William Warfield, Todd Duncan, the late Ellabelle Davis, Dorothy Maynor, and Mattiwilda Dobbs are notable black artists known the world over. Our blues singers like Bessie Smith, Ma Rainey, and B. B. King; folk singers like Leadbelly, and the greats like Louis Armstrong, Jimmie Lunceford, and Count Basie; great composers like Scott Joplin, Eubie Blake, Charlie Parker, and the incomparable Duke Ellington are significant contributors to the modern world and all represent the undeniable genius of the black American musician.

Individual achievement, while part of our general cultural picture is not all. It is in language and religion that Black Americans as a group have made a significant contribution to the national fiber of American life and to the modern world. As spiritual creatures we have shown through unmerited suffering that we have a sense of humanity that can enrich the moral fiber and contribute to a new world ethos. Our black culture is aware of human needs and human values. Handicapped as we have been by a racist system of dehumanizing slavery and segregation, our American history of nearly five hundred years reveals that our cultural and spiritual gifts brought from our African past are still intact. It is not only that we are singers and dancers, poets and prophets, great athletes and perceptive politicians—but we are also a body of charismatic and numinous people yet capable of cultic fire as seen in our black churches and still creative enough in intellect to signal the leap forward into a new and humanistic age. We are the authors of the new paradigm.

As a new world of the twenty-first century emerges around us with a new alignment of political and economic theories and actions, new world systems that no longer value "white" money and

Western industry as the only capital leading the planetary world, as black people see a resurgence of liberated and independent Africa, Black Americans must understand as all Americans should that black culture is a springboard for new world achievement, new world understanding and philosophy, world peace and freedom, and a greater dignity for all mankind.

What is the nature of black culture? How is it developed, and in which way is it disseminated?

The nature of black culture is both spiritual and humanistic in its philosophical depths, romantic in content—change the world, give us freedom, celebrate love and nature, honor honest toil, and keep earthiness in our speech, are all romantic subjects. Black culture is realistic in structure or form. Black culture touches universal chords and response and partakes of the timeless or eternal as well as the universal. The aesthetic nature of black culture is evolutionary in that it has existed from ancient times and continues to be deeply related to, rooted in, and an outgrowth of black existence. In beauty and value, black humanity is the standard, the ideal, and the measure. Whether the vision of the black artist is tragic or comic, the authenticity of his compositions is always determined by its revelation of the black experience regardless of its location in the black diaspora. That location may be Africa, the islands in the Caribbean or North and South America. Wherever the black man has gone in the modern world, whether as slave or free man, he has taken with him his rich gifts of creativity and spiritual values to enrich the land and culture where he dwells.

As W. E. B. Du Bois has also stated, in *The Souls of Black Folk* (1903), our gifts are three-fold, "a gift of story and song . . . the gift of sweat and brawn . . .[and] a gift of the Spirit."[1] African melodies and rhythms are in our music and poetry, our drama and our dance; and our African idioms are in cultic worship and rituals, ceremonies for our dead, and folk customs for our living. Therefore, our culture is artistic in nature, spiritual in depth, and buttressed by vitality, reality, and the stamina of those who have survived human suffering, those who have survived the Middle Passage, the auction block, the shackles, and the coffle, the bloodhounds and chain gangs, and the lynch mob, the bayonet, and the bullwhip, the fire hoses and the police dogs.

How has this culture developed, and what sustains it? From the

ancient world and earliest existence of men who dwelt beside the
River Nile to the Amazon River, the Mississippi River, and the Caribbean Sea, we developed first as the great anthropologists tell us—
not merely as emperors and kings, soldiers and tyrants, tribal chief
and mercenaries, but also as hunters and farmers and fishermen—
as craftsmen who learned to carve wood and stone; as tellers of tales
who recited our history—as singers and dancers who sacrificed and
celebrated birth, marriage, and death—as men working and dancing and laughing on the planet earth who reveled in the light of sun
and moon and stars—as simple human beings who cradled the life
of God and the universe within our hearts. Our culture is as old as
this universe—an integral part of the earth on which we live. And
as the family man has evolved, so has this black strain of humanity
reached ever upward toward our divine and spiritual destiny.

Social justice has been our theme in America. The search for
freedom, peace, and human dignity has been our constant quest, and
this theme may be found as gospel in our religion, theme in our literature, and form in our graphic artistic expression. The ideals of
the American Revolution were ours, too. The freedom and belief in
universal brotherhood of man, fatherhood of God, dignity of honest
labor, rights of the human individual, and the fulfillment of the
dream of equality were all on paper, documents but not realities.
This same social justice is what the black man continually seeks—
what he has always sought: participatory democracy in a land of
democratic ideals which have been negated by racist realities.

At every turn, Black Americans have found our culture repressed, suppressed, and oppressed. Even as we have been stigmatized and ostracized by slavery and segregation, and by mechanistic
men, even as White America has sought to dehumanize, de-person-
alize, de-spiritualize Black Americans by economic deprivation and
political denial of all human and civil rights, even so has our artistic expression been denied national and international exposure in
all America's social institutions and relationships. In education, for
example, black children have been denied equal opportunities with
whites and both whites and blacks have been miseducated about
human nature and the artistic and spiritual values of black culture.

These problems of deprivation and denial did not begin recently
or even suddenly; there are deep and subterranean causes in our
American society and the history of our socioeconomic and politi-

cal system that explain these irrational and inimical forces t
war against black people and consequently against black culture.
Granted the rationale for white racism, institutionalized and anach-
ronistic, is a very irrational one, it is predicated, nevertheless, on
real and devastating theories or facts.

It is significant from a historical point of view that racism or
race prejudice and all the proliferations of race prejudice both ca-
sual and effectual did not exist as social phenomena in ancient and
medieval times or ages. Racism as an issue and social phenomenon
belongs exclusively to the modern world and is a direct outgrowth
of Western world capitalism, colonialism and neocolonialism, and
financial as well as territorial imperialism.

Five hundred years ago, when the modern Western world was
merely in embryo, the Europeans began expansion toward the new
world for many reasons, but chiefly economic and political as well
as social. They found a need for cheap labor to develop the natural
resources which were discovered in such abundance in America—
North and South. The African slave trade was their solution, and
in Africa they found not only human resources but a vast continent also rich in natural resources. Thus began the rape of African
lands and people by the Europeans and human slavery for Africa's
black masses of peoples resulted.

But how did white Europe explain away the horror and shame
of human slavery? The Middle Passage, the shackles and the coffle,
and auction block, the whipping post and the bullwhip, to say nothing of all the maiming and killing of black people during slavery
and segregation? First, by ignorantly declaring these black slaves
were not people, not really human beings—they were property and
were considered animals—inferior to whites and, therefore, fit only
to be their slaves and real property. These were cannibals and hea-
thens or savages who worshipped wood and stone and needed to be
converted to Christianity so that they would be "good, humble,
docile, and useful servants in their inferior and menial or servile
place." Therefore, they rationalized their inhuman act of using human beings as inhuman property. This was the white apology for
slavery and the beginning of racism, or the myth about race.

Illogical in its ramifications, this exploitation and oppression
sometimes was not limited to black people—when it suited the ex-
panding economy of American capitalism, race was not the only

factor—class was the additional measure. Poor whites came in masses from Europe, from jails (debtors' prisons and others) and the cities to make their fortune in America. America was supposed to be the land of economic opportunity, the land of political freedom, the land of religious tolerance. But it never promised racial and cultural freedom. The land was raped, confiscated, and taken from the Indians by battle, subterfuge, for a few dollars, and by actual cunning and then the land was cultivated—tobacco, corn, indigo, and finally cotton—by the agricultural experts of Africa who had cultivated crops beside the Nile since the dawn of time. Thus, as black slaves, they were designed to make their white masters rich.

As factories, mills, and industrial empires rose in America's northern cities, more and more white Europeans migrated to the new land. Thus, poor whites were exploited, too, as they joined the labor class or work force of America. Not until the nineteenth century did this labor force begin to organize unions for its protection and advancement, but as early as the Industrial Revolution of the nineteenth century this free labor began to clash with slave labor in America. The result was the Civil War and emancipation from chattel slavery for black people. But segregation was quickly designed as a substitute for the slave system, and this substitution was largely for economic reasons. Money was the desired objective, and black people had to be relegated to the bottom of the class system in order to be exploited for further economic gain by whites. Since the political system is based on the economy, the laws of the government were used to make these systems of dehumanizing slavery and degrading segregation legal and binding. The social position of black people was therefore that of a pariah and outcast not only because of race or color but to maintain a system of economic exploitation. The questions of morality and ethics were buried under the rationale for racism, rationalization, and irrational thought and action. Thus, America has had a cancer at the root and heart of her society. Moral and ethical evil have eaten away at justice and cultural understanding or unity.

But Western world capitalism and its financial imperialism have reached their peak and systematic conclusion. The system has come full circle and is now moribund. A new and vital socialism is stemming the tide of twentieth-century revolution all over the planet earth, and a new world order is already being aligned.

Western technology is completely mechanistic and its techno-culture has no humanity—no spiritual value and no moral value, ethical, or cultural viability. But if money is no longer the supreme value and returns to its true nature as only a bartering agent—if American industry can no longer control all the nations of the world—obviously black culture can hope to be rid of the shackles of exploitation, oppression, and repression which capitalism has forced on black people in order to maintain its vicious ascendancy. Free enterprise has been anything but "free," and the monopolistic character of the system has had a stifling effect upon human culture.

If anyone questions whether a new socialism will be more tolerant of black culture, the answer is it cannot be any worse than capitalism has been.

Socialism, whether the earliest form of African socialism or Ujamaa, whether Utopian of first-century Christianity, whether Fabian as Sydney and Beatrice Webb have expounded it in England, whether scientific as Marxism has derived it from dialectical materialism, socialism is obviously the economic and political ideology of the twentieth century. Black culture is a warm and earthy expression of black people, humanistic and endemic to all that is natural, free, and real. There is no doubt that the new world order has great implications for black people and therefore for all human culture.

Somewhere we must return to the world, the whole planetary globe to its humanistic center—to a knowledge of the oneness of all life, the unity of all knowledge and all mankind, neither fragmented by color, class or creed, but united with all nature and the spirit of the universe in man's search for freedom, peace, and human dignity. This is our human and spiritual destiny. This, too, is the vindication and fulfillment of the true goals and nature of black culture.

Black people did not accept the cruel, dehumanizing, and humiliating aspect of slavery or segregation. Many blacks killed themselves and joined those who died from unbelievable subhuman conditions and oppressive inhuman treatment during the Middle Passage rather than accept slavery. But Gustavus Vassa or Olaudah Equiano (African name) survived to write an authentic historical account of that abhorrent occurrence. This simple account became a great document in our history and in the humanistic tradition of our literature.

In America, where their fate seemed hopeless, black slaves not only refused to be slaves, they continued to rebel, revolt, and develop insurrections. Although these insurrections were never successful, they grew in power and significance, and although there were probably hundreds of plots not recorded for posterity, many of them are known today. The most prominent were lead by Denmark Vesey, Gabriel Prosser, Nat Turner, Cinque the Amistad Mutiny (the most successful leader), and John Brown at Harpers Ferry.

Black people used the Underground Railroad to escape slavery, and the famous Harriet Tubman was a guide. Frederick Douglass gave real leadership to black people as an abolitionist and a leader after the war. Frances E. W. Harper, a literary figure of prominence and the writer of best sellers, a lecturer on the platforms of abolition and temperance, was also very active before the war as an antislavery poet and after the war as a worker for women's rights. Sojourner Truth, that dynamic figure and perceptive woman, was also a leader in the forefront of the rights of black people and women's rights. These are again examples of how we have never accepted subjugation and repression, oppression, and suppression of our lives and culture.

At the turn of the century, our greatest leader for a century appeared, W. E. B. Du Bois. He has not only written the Bible of our culture, *The Souls of Black Folk*, prolific, and prodigious as he was, but he fathered a movement designed for our liberation and to secure justice in the courts—the Niagara Movement—which led to our National Association for the Advancement of Colored People. A leader in the struggle for human rights, especially for peace, freedom, and human dignity—Dr. Du Bois is, himself, a product and a producer of black culture. He had a seminal mind akin to the other great architects of the life of the twentieth century: Freud, Marx, Kierkegaard, and Einstein. There is no one like him before nor after him, since he predicted the problem of the twentieth century to be the color line. In both streams of black culture he has created, projected and achieved monumental works for our emulation. Educated in three great universities of the world—Fisk, Harvard, and Bonn—he is the first great sociologist of the century to understand completely the complexity of the social phenomena of race in the modern capitalistic world, understanding the struggle of black people to rise above the bottom layer of the American economy and to achieve political rights and social equality as human beings. Poet, novelist, historian, sociologist, and prophet of a new age, Dr. Du Bois never accepted the racist apologia of inferiority and dehumanization. His interests in world peace, Pan-Africanism, and universal social justice are still beacons for all black people in the world.

Since the turn of the century, black people and black culture produced great leaders for every crisis. The social, economic, and political challenges to our lives and culture have always been met with human, moral, ethical, and spiritual responses. In the form of black nationalism the response has come from Marcus Garvey and Malcolm X. In the great drive toward integration in the American mainstream the response has been led by Dr. Martin Luther King, Jr., and the Black Caucus in the Congress of the United States. As black people strive toward a piece of the American political pie, black people always have and always will meet the challenges of each successive crisis.

But all these pale before the new and onrushing socialist order of the twenty-first century. America marks the bicentennial of the American Revolution in 1776 even as we look in 1976 toward the socialist revolution already shaping in our world and promising to bring a greater measure of freedom, peace, and human dignity to all mankind in the twenty-first century.

Because Black Americans live in a repressive and hostile system always antagonistic to black culture, it is extremely difficult to maintain a high level of understanding on the part of Black Americans about the efficacy and spiritual value of black culture. This is even more difficult for White Americans to understand. During the past decade and a half, Black America has gone through a number of changes amounting to a kind of cultural revolution moving toward greater understanding, racial tolerance, and complete social emancipation. As a result of the two revolutions beginning in the late fifties and going through the sixties, not only have we seen some social changes within the American society and capitalistic system, we have also witnessed a cultural-nationalist explosion designed to raise the consciousness of masses of black people if not equally exploited poor white people. Thus, we have witnessed in effect a cultural revolution with an explosion in the arts. There are new schools of young black poets, novelists, painters, sculptors, actors and playwrights, musicians, and composers—all growing in black awareness and identity. They are moving to change the masses of black people, too, into a conscious revolutionary nationalism out of which can be developed not only a new world view or Weltanschaung, but a fulfillment of the role black humanity must assume and control in our dawning world order.

How then has black culture been disseminated and kept alive? Black culture has survived in the black institutions of Black Americans. In the black family, the Black Church, the black school, the black press, the black nation, and the black world. This is where our black culture has survived and thrived. This is where it must continue to grow. The ground of common humanity is not yet a reality in the modern world but when it comes as it must in the twenty-first century, Black Africa, and black humanity must be as always the foundation on which it stands and from which it logically proceeds.

One world of international brotherhood does not negate the nationalism of black people. It only enforces and re-enforces our common humanity.

Note
1. W. E. B. Du Bois, *The Souls of Black Folk* (New York: Fawcett Publications, 1961), 189–90.

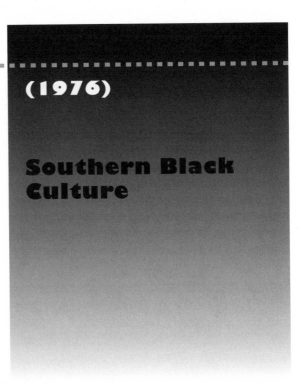

(1976)

Southern Black Culture

SOUTHERN CULTURE AND black culture are almost synonymous. They seem to be the same because they partake so much of each other. When the European came to America and began to appropriate the land of the Native American, who in turn had crossed the land bridges from Asia and Africa, the European began a melting pot of various European nationalities which today are simply referred to as the White American. This melting pot did not include nonwhites who became a part of the American myth about race—those divided into the master race were white and the slave race was black and thereby designated as superior and inferior for various social, political, and economic reasons. The European found it necessary to exploit the African continent, its land and people, and thrust the Africans into a night of slavery, colonialism, and neocolonialism. Their purpose was to create a Western empire of land and money and people. Slavery was a necessary component of this Western capitalism, which emphasized a class soci-

This essay was originally delivered as a speech for the Sojourner Truth Festival in Fort Worth, Texas, in September 1976.

ety based on color, caste, and race. To these were added Western Christianity as a world religion to buttress the economic and political aspirations. Therefore black people came to America in chains. They lost religion, language, and all other outward manifestations of culture. Those ancient and medieval civilizations, which were rich in all the arts, were thrown aside under the guise and misnomer of primitive, savage, and backward. They were taught to despise their worth and accept the forced culture of another continent, namely Europe. Black and white Americans have therefore been educated away from our African heritage and forced to undergo a re-education in the acculturation of black people that is neither historically accurate nor sociologically sound. This acculturation process of slavery continued for some four and a half centuries so that the true African heritage would seem to be lost in antiquity and forever forgotten by African Americans or descendants of Africa and citizens of White America. Cultural patterns, however, developed over long centuries of use and development, are not so easily lost. What has happened in America has been the development of an American culture that is as much African as European with the contributions of all classes, races, and nationalities to the fabric of American life. In language and religion, in music, art, and literature, in fashion and design, in cooking, dance, and architecture the African heritage can still be discerned, for it remains first preeminent and all pervasive so that Europe herself bears the mark of African civilization in all her arts and other cultural manifestations. American culture and particularly southern culture is replete with our African heritage of music in jazz or folk music, in cooking or southern culinary arts, in religion, in language, and even in architecture and dress design. The mark of Africa is on all modern American culture and the heritage of Africa is not lost. It has merely been assimilated. The American experience of slavery and segregation, while so degrading and demeaning as to be anti-human, nevertheless remains the acculturation process through which African culture has become a part of American culture, and southern black culture is its deepest manifestation.

Now is a fascist time when we are under great oppression, repression, and even tyranny, when the American economic system is obviously defunct and moribund, when the political system so dependent on that economic system is also in great disarray and

confusion, now when the conservative and rightist forces are determined to establish a world fascist system of military force and tyranny of money and imperialism, now when the enemy forces of
humanity fight again in terms of race and religion, it behooves us
to take a backward look and understand the roots of our southern
black culture in our African heritage and the acculturation process
of our American experience. This will give us a true understanding
of southern black culture. It is important to make this historical
analysis and synthesis in order to educate our children properly,
understand our present-day society, and prepare for a more humanistic world in the twenty-first century.

Africa is the mother of all humankind. Human life began first
in Africa. The earliest civilization and culture began around her
rivers and the rivers of Asia, around the Nile, the Tigris and the
Euphrates, the Yalu, the Yangtze, and the Ganges. Black culture,
like black humanity, is our first culture and our first humanity. The
Fertile Crescent, as James Henry Breasted called it, is the home of
man's first language, religion, trade, artistic accomplishments, and
artifacts.[1] That Fertile Crescent circles a Mediterranean world and
that Mediterranean Sea touches North Africa, Asia Minor, as well
as the ancient Aegean worlds of Greece and Rome. These are the
sources of your earliest and most ancient empires of recorded history. First is Egypt, African as she can be. Next is Babylonia and
Assyria, in the Arab worlds of Asia Minor. Third is ancient Persia,
now known as Iran. Fourth is the Greek Empire of Alexander the
Great, son of Philip of Macedon. Fifth and last in the ancient world
of empires is the Roman Empire of the Caesars from which the
Western world claims to have sprung.

Deep in the heart of Asia stands the isolated civilization and
culture of ancient China. All these preceded European culture and
the empires of the Western white man. History tells me that as
each civilization and culture grew more powerful in arms and material things, it became more corrupt morally, spiritually decadent,
and it became prey and the weak victim to new and stronger empires. Europeans introduced African slavery first into the southern
part of the American continent, in the Caribbean islands and along
the coast of that Caribbean Sea in South America, in Venezuela and
Brazil, and on the North American continent in the southern colonies. Millions of Africans were brought to these Southern places,

supposedly because the climates were closer to their own tropical or sub-tropical African countries. Millions died in the Middle Passage, so horrifying an experience that only the strongest with the greatest will to live could survive.

Although some northern places also had slavery, the largest numbers of black people were slaves in the Southlands. The American colonies underwent a revolution one hundred and fifty years later and the United States of America, declaring herself independent of Great Britain's empire, embarked on an adventure supposedly liberal and progressive enough to be in search of a democratic dream and the ideal of a republic that would include a commonwealth or a nation of the common people, with freedom or liberty for everyone as the cornerstone. This Declaration of Independence and Constitution of a free republic, however, did not allow for non-whites as free citizens. They were declared not to be human beings nor persons. They could not bear arms save in the protection of their masters, and they could not buy whiskey even if they were free and had money. Each white landowner gave himself one vote for every five slaves or "niggers" he owned. And the great adventure continued for nearly another hundred years with a nation half-slave and half-free.

Then as the social, economic, and political forces of an Industrial Revolution and a rising capitalistic system threatened to inundate the medieval, agrarian and feudal system of human slavery, the fratricidal war of the American United States tore the Union of States asunder and resulted in the end of human beings as chattel slaves. When slavery ended in the United States some thirty years after it had ended in the Caribbean islands and other parts of the world, black people found themselves wanderers in an alien land. Some went west, some migrated north, some even found their way to Canada or Mexico, but the majority of these homeless and penniless freedmen remained in the southern U.S.A. and tried to eke out an existence from the southern soil and the city streets. Three stages of Reconstruction ended with the substitute system of segregation taking the place of chattel slavery as a control mechanism in the hands of the dominant and ruling class or culture, the White Americans. Jim Crow became legal and mob violence or lynching the law of the land. The U.S. government gradually gave way to the southern demand that segregation have the tacit consent of the government. And so, we came to the end of the nineteenth century shackled and oppressed by a system that was equally as demeaning and dehumanizing as slavery had been. There were three factors in this oppressive system that determined our lives. One was disfranchisement, or the loss of the right to vote, which had been guaranteed by two amendments to the Constitution. Second was the establishment of a dual system of substandard education designed to keep the black people ignorant and semi-literate. Third was the high degree of job discrimination which prevented economic advancement. Thus, social, political, and economic progress were all impeded by this demoralizing form of human oppression called segregation. For one hundred years this system prevailed. Violent white racism became institutionalized and a part of American culture. The society is today sick with this virulent disease.

This, then, is the history of American culture. No wonder black people have lost the knowledge of a great African heritage and must now learn our role in perpetuating our greatest contribution to American life, our southern black culture. When segregation was thus established, black people were thus set back to a more subtle but equally egregious slavery, we began to meet the challenge of our environment and circumstance with a creative response both positive and productive. Forced within the system of segregation, we developed our own institutions and provided channels to continue the survival of our own culture. Even in slavery this creative response continued through all the means of cultural survival. Thus Africans continued the great oral tradition of our forefathers and in song and dance, tales, and religious feeling-tones, we continued the unbroken line of great African culture. The Brer Rabbit and other animal tales told in slavery, the great spirituals and ring games, the dances from the limbo to the Charleston and the struts of turkey trot, shimmy, the dark-town strutters ball, and above all the shout songs in our Protestant churches that became gospel, all of these are evidences of a long-ago far-away African culture. What is not as evident is the unmistakable African element in southern cooking mixed with the Native American, the Spanish, and the French influences, which of course is what Southern cooking is all about. Gumbo, like okra, is African, and what we did not bring directly from African shores we brought from the West Indies islands where there was a seasoning of slaves between Africa and North America.

In segregation, we built our great institutions of the church and the school, the benevolent societies, and continued to strengthen our greatest asset, the family unit, so grievously assaulted by white racism and racist institutions. The family unit is the tribal unit of African society and government, and the black family has endured despite malignant and gross neglect on the part of the ruling classes. Even in the darkest days of slavery our creative arts of music, painting, literature, and theater flourished. Just as our religious expression flourished, our language influenced the motley polyglot of Americanism with the slang and street talk, and just as our sense of flamboyant color in dress and our flair of rhythm and verse in the dance, so did our creative expressions in every cultural manifestation find meaning in the absurdity of American racist and fascist oppression. Pantomime and irony slipped through the vestiges of minstrelsy and entertained our enslaved forefathers with a secret amusement that helped them ridicule their oppressors.

And we had great leaders too. Every time we were challenged, we responded with personalities who rose to meet the challenge and the crisis. In slavery, there were the conductors of the Underground Railroad, Harriet Tubman an example of one intrepid leader. Sojourner Truth was another. Frederick Douglass was our first great mass leader fighting slavery and leading us afterward. W. E. B. Du Bois was born and educated in those early years after slavery, and he was one of the greatest minds of his age, prophesying what our life in this twentieth century would be. He was one of the great architects of Pan-Africanism, a philosophy for black people all over the black world. He understood our great gifts of brawn, of song, and of spirit, and he wrote about them in *The Souls of Black Folk.* But we are stepping now into the twentieth century, and there is too much after 1900 to concern us. There is an overabundance of cultural richness that belongs to our present time. Remember our first poets in the eighteenth century when America was just flowering culturally: Phillis Wheatley, Lucy Terry, and Jupiter Hammon.

We had great singers and instrumental musicians too, Black Patti and James Bland among them. Frances E. W. Harper must be remembered as a best-selling poet in antebellum days, and George Moses Horton, Alberry Whitman and James Whitfield as antislavery poets who lived before the Civil War. The Black Church and the black college began in the dark days of slavery, but they increased a hundred- to a thousand-fold in segregation. Fighters for freedom have always existed among black people, but it will remain for a later discussion of the twentieth century to see the beginnings of our great protest movement and our challenging mass leaders who storm the walls of segregation.

For a long time after slavery, we begged the question of our humanity, slavery enslaved our minds, as well as our bodies, and nearly a century would pass before we began to speak not only with pride but with protest. The unfinished revolution of the Civil War would await the years of mid-century in another century before we could see its completion and the end of legal segregation. Only when we had trained leaders, men and women, trained in the law and medicine and theology, trained even in the crippling schools of segregation but deeply imbued with a great race pride and spirit, could we hope to finish the revolution that the Civil War began. Now we are in another age, turning another corner. Integration has failed, and our most creative response to violent white racism has been a program of black studies educating our youth in their great heritage and their greater destiny. We must turn the pages of the twentieth century before we can assess how far we have come. Then we will know how much farther we must go to reach our goals of freedom, peace, and human dignity.

Note

1. James Henry Breasted (1865–1935) was an American archaeologist and historian whose works included *A History of Egypt* (1905) and *Ancient Times: A History of the Early World* (1916).

(1972)

Agenda for Action

Black Arts and Letters

BLACK AMERICA STANDS today at the crossroads of destiny for the future of all our people in the world. This is not a time of joyous freedom, but a crucial time of unmitigated tyranny. An age of technological tyranny. Not a time of tranquillity, but a stormy tie of senseless war and killing. Militarism is the weapon of politicians and the lives of men have become a political football. There is no lull of mercy in the oppressor's brutality, as we move closer each decade toward a police state. Starvation and suffering exist in the midst of affluence and waste. Spiraling inflation ticks off the hours of economic instability. Death and destruction control all the nations while we fight against evils of injustice. Most people recognize the assassin's bullet and the racist's rhetoric as belchings of a sick society. We are threatened with annihilation of an entire planet because of the greed and short-sightedness of one race in

This essay was originally delivered as a speech at the Black Academy's Conference to Assess the State of Black Arts and Letters in the United States, sponsored by the Johnson Publishing Company and the National Endowment for the Humanities, Chicago, 1972.

the family of man. A cancerous sore of white racism eats at the heart of all American life. Five major issues daily headline the news! First, racial enmity and hatred generating violence; second, a perpetual foreign war dating from the beginning of the century; third, industrial contamination of all nature, earth, water, and air; fourth, the extreme dilemma of urban life with the new controlling economy of crime and drugs; fifth, political chaos and economic collapse, for the two go hand-in-hand. Witness the three-ring circus of political primaries in White America, while the faltering, fluctuating stock market is sick enough to die and prove it. The twilight of the Western world has come. This is the state of our society. What is the state of black arts and letters in the year of 1972? Alive and well, doing fine, and improving every day, struggling to thrive and survive in a hostile society. It is as if we were some kind of paradox, a strange anachronism, the handicapped horse that wins the race. For black art seizes on this time of oppression and repression and makes us use our art functionally for the people. Not art for art's sake. Art cannot exist in a vacuum. What is the hope for black people? How can we talk about life tomorrow for our children unless we dare do something today to shape that life? There is no question but that worldwide societal revolution is a fact of our times. It is not a question of whether we want revolution; as one of our young black poets says, "there is nothing we can do to stop it. . . ."[1] What then can we do?

In this death struggle for freedom, for peace, and for human dignity, the black artist and the black scholar must see and understand their role as scholars and as artists. We must first see the state of our world which our art and actions must reflect, and we must understand our role as thinkers in the struggle. We must begin to use the black mind as a tool for black liberation, not as yoga to liberate a single individual but to liberate an entire people. Then we can accept the challenge of a thinking black world whirling into action. We must understand that the masses of our people expect and need, no, more than that, demand, from a black mind a new paradigm, for the shape of our borning society. That society is not waiting for the first day of the twenty-first century to be born—it is converging upon us now.

It becomes the awesome duty and destiny of black people to

bring about complete societal change because we are the slave that must throw off the yoke of oppression. He cannot expect the oppressor to condemn the chains of his slave. We black people can—and must—accept the challenge and the task because we have the creative minds, and the spiritual strength to do what must be done. We are the myth makers and the timeless dreamers with a vision for the world. We are the priests and the prophets with the cultic magic to bring the creative fire and energy of imagination to the inanimate and transform the dust of things and ideas into living action and spirits of power. We must put on our thinking caps and decide the shifting shape of our utopian world that is already emerging. There are only two pillars left under this toppling house, political and economic, and every day we are watching them crumble into decay. "Lawd, if I had my way, I'd tear this building down."

Recently I read what seems to me to be a serious tactical mistake. One of our black brothers, Amiri Baraka, said, "The problem of rebuilding society is Whitey's bag, not ours." I think that is going back through the same revolving door we used to come outside. Why should we expect Whitey to do better for us, when we consider the mess his industry and technology have already wrought for him? We do not wish to rebuild this society as Stokely Carmichael said, but we wish to create a better one.

Man should be the master of money and machines and not their slaves. The white man has used the black man's mathematics and the black man's labor to build his technological universe, but it is against us and destructive to all life, rather than for us and constructive of life. How do we turn these cybernetic automatons into vehicles for man's good? Where are our black engineers? Human relations cannot become positive when the moral values are subject to the power of money and machines. Black people have the creative and spiritual power that is not depleted nor wasted by the western diaspora, because it is rooted in the earthy, natural, realistic and humanistic welter of our African and Oriental heritage. The black scholar and artist is challenged as never before to tap the roots of this creative and spiritual power and name the paradigm for our past revolutionary society. Before all the concrete action and change that is necessary takes place, there must be a bona fide paradigm. What kind of paradigm do we want to create for our new and borning society? What is the nature of the world we want for our children?

You may answer: first, a different economy and a new political system. Does anyone doubt that the old paradigm has failed, is collapsing, and chaos exists in its place? Before there can be a new paradigm there must be a malfunctioning of the old, a crisis of purpose or philosophy and a crisis of function. The social scientists, namely the economist and the political scientist, know that such a crisis now exists. The mass problems of unemployment in a war economy are clear evidences of malfunction of the system. We need a new paradigm. Is socialism the answer? Of one thing we are sure, black people must remember that whatever form the new economy and political system may take, they must be fashioned by us, for our own particular problems in this dying Western world! Hence, we know that neither Russian, nor Cuban, nor Chinese, nor Algerian communism will work for Black America. Black America needs its own special brand and system of its own making. That is why we must name the paradigm.

In every age of mankind's history and recorded progress, the scholar, whether scientific inventor, philosopher, or political scientist, has come forth with a new paradigm when a scientific revolution has changed the concept of the universe. Such a time is now. The Einstein revolution has changed man's concept of the universe. We live in an illimitable universe where everything is relative, where there must be unity in diversity, and where the space/time continuum challenges man to the outer depths or limits of space. And yet, this is only evident in physics and mathematics, not in the social sciences and the humanities. The family of man has not yet learned to live with the beneficial and peaceful uses of atomic energy, and with the social, moral and spiritual implications of this nearly century-old scientific revolution. We need a new socioeconomic and political paradigm. Black mankind is no less creative and inventive than those in other ages have been. We are a charismatic, numinous people of the black experience caught in a vortex of this time of crisis. Destiny declares that the responsibility is ours.

We sorely need and surely want a new religious belief for our new universe. Institutionalized religion in White America has broken down under the challenge of racial integration while the Black Church has been revitalized during the civil rights movement as a revolutionary instrument for social change. Today as a separatist institution, because it's always been segregated, the Black Church looms large in prophetic power with its cultic strength from blood and fire serving the needs for emotional catharsis within the oppressed black community as seen in the fervor of the gospel music and shout songs that flow directly out of the streams of our folklife and direction. What this welter of black emotion needs is channeling and direction. Most local black churches are lacking in harnessing these dynamics. A new religious belief will challenge the highest sense of deity and divinity in human personality, while at the same time more than encouraging religious tolerance for all world religions, as it is respectful of all world cultures, languages and spiritual entities of all human beings. Such a spiritual philosophy of humanism is destined to prevail.

We expect black people to continue to conceive of new uses for education, so that old curricula such as the liberal arts college, long since outdated and obsolete, will disappear and more relevant, productive and creative schools will develop. There will be less emphasis for the young child on the cognitive and more on the affective aspect of learning. Our black institutions will relate more closely to the black communities that inspire and support them. Sociological studies of the black family, the black community, and all other black institutions will focus themselves largely on our folk history, life and culture, rather than watered-down theories of outmoded white racists. The black scholar must provide more than the white rhetoric that he has learned from his white education. We must stop aping the very racism that oppresses us. Change is the name of the game, and dedication to the struggle for black people's complete emancipation into a new world of thought and action is what the black artist must be about.

The masses of our people are pleading, therefore, for the word. They want to know the name of that new paradigm. They have handed down a mandate for freedom. We have heard a new declaration for independence. Oddly enough it is not the black intellectuals who have come out of white universities with our monstrous degrees who are filling this need for intellectual leadership that the black masses demand. There is a new young black intelligentsia. They are truly a prophetic generation. They have the dreams of a man and the words of a God, and they have been spawned largely from the horrible oppression of the prisons. Whether it is poetry, painting, or pure intellectual constructs, they are coming from the prisons. They are not only vocal and articulate, they are terrible in their majesty and splendor. It behooves all black artists and scholars to listen to what they have to say, for these young men and women are like the veterans of a foreign and unholy war. They have lost all fear of death. They are desperate people who have had much time to think and are not afraid of action. They do not feel that they have anything to lose in action, violent though it may be. They have had a baptism of fire, and they preach a vision of rebirth to the entire world.

I'm not here this morning to reiterate what a famous young black writer said in 1937 in his "Blueprint for Black Writers."[2] For the state of black art and letters is not in such a bad way today. I believe we are on our way to a greater height than ever, despite oppression and despite repression, for we have come through a cultural revolution designed to blackenize our mind. Dr. W. E. B. Du Bois said, "The blacker the mantle, the mightier the man!" In 1933 at the Rosenwald Economics Conference held in Washington, D.C., Dr. W. E. B. Du Bois spoke on the subject "Where Do We Go From Here?" He said then that we are facing revolution. I quote this: "The other matter, and the matter of greatest import is instead of our facing today a stable world moving at a uniform rate of progress toward well-defined goals, we are facing revolution. I'm not discussing a coming revolution, I'm trying to impress the fact upon you, that you are already in the midst of war. That there has been no war of modern times that has taken so great a sacrifice of human life and human spirit as the extraordinary period through which we are passing today. Some people envision revolution cheaply as a matter of blood and guns, and the more visible methods of force, but that after all is merely the temporary and outward manifestation. Real revolution is within. That comes before or after the explosion. Is a matter of long suffering and deprivation. The death of courage and a bit of triumph of despair. This is the inevitable prelude to decisive and enormous change and that is the thing that is on us now. We are not called upon, then, to discuss whether we want revolution or not; we have got it. Our problem is how we are coming out of it." And he continues—in the next section—by saying, "This matter of world depression and revolutionary changes in social life and industry is not primarily the problem of the American Negro." This is what he's saying in 1933, "and just because it is not our problem, we have plain proof of the thing that I have said before. Namely that we are not, in reality, a part of this nation. We stand even in its greatest crisis at one side . . . only partly connected with its remedies, but dumb victims of its difficulties and by just that token because we are outside the main current of the country we have got most carefully to ask ourselves what we are going to do to protect our past and to insure our future." And that's the end of his quotation. Now, when we have experienced all the revolutions brought on by the electronic revolution, all except political and economic, and we are facing more political and economic upheaval despite repression and fascist totalitarianism, military and financial imperialism. Now, again, we should ask ourselves, where do we go from here? Let us stop and take stock, where are we now? Where do we wish to go? How can we get there?

We can be eternally grateful for the revolutionary decade of the 1960s for a cultural reawakening to the worth of our heritage and the great potential of our people's destiny. What we inherit from the civil rights movement and the black revolution of racial consciousness are gems of inestimable worth. What have these social events done for us? They have given us renewed pride and dignity and a greater sense of mind and spirit. For we no longer possess a mass slave mentality.

Culturally we have watched a renaissance of the arts mushrooming across the length and breadth of this land. We have been inspired by all our martyred men—Medgar, Malcolm, and Martin— and all our poetry, music, drama, painting and sculpture powerfully attest to this fact. When this century is over some of the greatest literature, painting and music America has ever known will prove to be a product of black genius. Looking back across the centuries, we reaffirm the humanistic tradition, African American literature and art, the search for freedom, peace, and dignity, for social justice and for truth. This pervades all our cultural achievement. The world will recognize this great black genius despite White America's racist rejection. Because the world will recognize and identify the universality of human experience in the products of this black genius. We have constantly hewn to the line of the spiritual and manifold destiny of man, and it is manifest in our art.

And now about this renaissance across the land. From New York to Texas, from California to the Carolinas, our cultural art centers dot the entire nation. Our young poets, painters, musicians, actors and playwrights are legion. It is time we made a record of this. It is time we pledge our support to them. We see black art forms of every description—film, theater, poetry, poets, groups of poets, painters, and painting. We have an exhibit upstairs from the prisons. But they need support. The black community must sustain and support as well as generate its forms of artistic and cultural expression. The white man is not about to support us. The black community must support and sustain the great—black— renaissance and explosion of the arts. The organization of the Black Academy means more than a list of distinguished names. It should mean a bulwark of strength, to nourish both the old and the new— the established as well as the young black artists who are coming on. One of the items on the "Agenda for Action" at this conference is to do just this thing, to consider the support necessary to maintain the substance of black art in the black community. To prepare a directory of cultural centers and move toward building a resource bank of our cultural assets. Moreover, we need to compile a directory of all cultural activities in the black community, and I think it's past time that we get a synchronized calendar of events, listing these conferences, conventions and all national meetings concerning black art, artists and scholars in order that there will be no further conflicts. The Black Academy can serve as a clearing house for this. Already to my knowledge there are black art centers in Chicago, New York, Boston, in San Francisco, Atlanta, Houston, Miami, Newark, Philadelphia, and Detroit. But these are only a handful in less than a dozen cities. Other cities with the potential for art centers where our young people are clamoring for artistic activity are Washington, D.C.; Nashville; Memphis; Durham; New Orleans; Jackson; Birmingham; Los Angeles; San Diego; and Milwaukee, to mention only a few.

One of the goals of the Black Academy should be to identify such centers and establish others so that we build a network of these centers across the United States where the cultural activities include painting, sculpture, poetry, reading and writing, theater, jazz institutes, film festivals, et cetera. This conference is therefore called to find out the facts of our black art and artists; locate and establish these centers in order to compile a directory of cultural activity in the black community; and prepare calendars of these cultural events. The business of these centers shall be the total development of these young artists: to teach craft to our young people, so that they may learn the difference between craft and art, between technique and artistry. We must continue to encourage them and to provide new outlets and avenues for their talent. Of what value is this? This seems to me of immeasurable worth to our black struggle and our black communities where the new concepts of education are just beginning to sprout. We are seeding the future of our children. Another generation will reap the harvest. There is a real intellectual ferment in the black community today, and this ferment touches all black life on all fronts: political, economic, social, educational, and above all aesthetic or artistic. The black scholar must seize on this black ferment which is a natural raw material of his artistic and scholarly productivity, and we must direct the tide on which we ride, until we come to the overwhelming flood of success to the highest of all our endeavors.

The Black Academy must promote and support this rising tide of black art and letters. Black unity is the watchword and the rallying cry of our struggle today. The black artist must remember what our brother Floyd McKissick has written in his article "The Way to a Black Ideology":

> It is the task of black intellectuals to provide the cohesive philosophy which will propel the black-led revolution, which must happen if justice is to be achieved in America. We must not wait for others to lead the attack. Ideas are the key to organized action. And the intellectual must not be guilty of the proverbial indecision and reluctance to act.[3]

I like very much the definition of the black scholar which appears on the inside cover of that illustrious publication: "A black scholar is a man of both thought and action. A whole man who thinks for his people and acts with them. A man who honors the whole community of black experience. A man who sees the Ph.D., the janitor, the businessman, the maid, the clerk, the militant, as all sharing the same experience of blackness, with all of its complexities and rewards."

If we are to meet the challenge of our crucial times, if we are in truth to define the paradigm for our children's tomorrow, we cannot afford the pussyfooting, infighting, and petty jealousy that ape the white world and divide us between town and gown. If we are to take seriously the mandate of all black people for freedom in our time we must solemnly go about our business of creativity, expressing the highest essence of black art and intellect, that which is most authentic and germane to the black experience, for in doing most what we do best we serve with our greatest devotion our people's most glorious cause.

I do not stop writing to join the activist in the struggle, *I am* in the struggle when *I am* writing.

And now in closing I would like to read two poems by two black poets, one a black man whose name we honor and revere and who died five years ago this month,[4] my great mentor and friend, Langston Hughes:

Note on Commercial Theatre

You've taken by blues and gone—
You sing 'em on Broadway
And you sing 'em in the Hollywood Bowl,
And you mix 'em up with symphonies
And you fixed 'em
So they don't sound like me.
Yep, you done taken my blues and gone.
You also took my spirituals and gone.
You put me in *Macbeth* and *Carmen Jones*
And all kinds of *Swing Mikados*
And in everything but what's about me—
But someday somebody'll
Stand up and talk about me,
And write about me—
Black and beautiful—
And sing about me,
And put on plays about me!
I reckon it'll be
Me myself!

Yes, it'll be me.

And the other poem by a black woman who continues in the great humanistic tradition of African American literature, partaking of our African heritage and our black American situation and experience. As black scholars and black artists let us remember above all what Mari Evans admonishes us in her splendid poem, "Speak the Truth to the People":

Speak the truth to the people.
Talk sense to the people.
Free them with reason.
Free them with honesty.
Free the people with love and courage and care for their being.
Spare them the fantasy.
Fantasy enslaves.
A slave is enslaved;
Can be enslaved by unwisdom
Can be enslaved by black unwisdom
Can be re-enslaved while in flight from the enemy
Can be enslaved by his brother whom he loves,
His brother whom he trusts
His brother with the loud voice
And the unwisdom.

Speak the truth to the people.
It is not necessary to green the heart
Only to identify the enemy.
It is not necessary to blow the mind
Only to free the mind.
To identify the enemy is to free the mind.
A free mind has no need to scream
A free mind is ready for other things—
To BUILD black schools
To BUILD black children
To BUILD black minds
To BUILD black love
To BUILD black impregnability
To BUILD a strong black nation
To BUILD.

Speak the truth to the people.
Spare them the opium of devil hate
They need no trips on honky chants
Move them instead to a BLACK ONENESS
A black strength which will defend its own
Needing no cacophony of screams for activation
A black strength which attacks the laws
exposes the lies disassembles the structure
and ravages the very foundation of evil.

Speak the truth to the people
To identify the enemy is to free the mind
Free the mind of the people.
Speak to the mind of the people.
Speak Truth.

© Evans

Notes

1. The young black poet Walker refers to is Nikki Giovanni.
2. See Richard Wright, "Blueprint for Negro Writing," *New Challenge* 1 (1937): 53–65.
3. Floyd McKissick, "The Way to a Black Ideology," *Black Scholar* 1 (Dec. 1969): 16.
4. Langston Hughes died in 1967.

(1972)

Humanities with a Black Focus

RHETORIC IS THE business of the English composition teacher. Literature is a figurative and mythological commodity. We would like, however, to spare you the rhetoric and cut through the myths and figures of speech to give you the bare necessities. We wish to get down to the "nitty-gritty." On the other hand, trite expressions and clichés, despite their obsolescence and hackneyed usage, sometimes may meaningfully serve our purposes of communication as well as fresh and vitally stimulating images.

I believe the teaching of literature in an interdisciplinary program of Humanities with a black focus answers the need at this historical point for a black paradigm in education which the masses of our people are desperately seeking. Two of the basic principles in literature and literary criticism are analysis and synthesis. Students of literature are frequently asked to analyze a particular literary genre, but how many teachers of literature are asked to develop

This essay was originally published as "Humanities with a Black Focus: A Black Paradigm," in the Institute for Services to Education's *Curriculum Changes in Black Colleges III* (Washington, D.C.: U.S. Department of Education, 1972).

a synthesis of subject matter for fields as a basic plan for the teaching of literature? Humanities with a black focus calls for a black synthesis.

We tell our students that they have come to college to become highly literate: to read and speak effectively, to think and write creatively, and to express themselves in an organized fashion. To do this they must read the recorded history, philosophy, and literature of the world. If the freshman composition teacher's job is mainly to stimulate and teach the freshman college student how to think— and that is precisely his job, to teach the student how to think— then the sophomore literature teacher's job is to teach a half-dozen different subject matter fields through the form and content of literature and by the precise method of analysis and synthesis. Rarely does any one person have the broad interdisciplinary training to handle all the subject matter fields necessary in the teaching of the humanities. A broad understanding means more than a knowledge of the particular literature; it includes a knowledge of the social sciences and the natural sciences. The philosophy of science of the theoretical scientist bridges the gap between the humanities and the natural sciences. Consequently, there must be team teaching. The various departments must pool their skills, their most brilliant teachers, their library resources, and all multimedia aids.

Literature cannot be effectively taught, therefore, in a vacuum. It is not enough to deal in analysis of literary form and content by the purely intrinsic approach. All literature requires an added extrinsic method and other disciplines. Philosophy, history, language, art, and music are absolute companion studies for a full understanding of literature. This is true regardless of the character of the literature—whether world literature, wisdom literature, African American literature, you name it. The teaching of literature is most effective when it is handled in an interdisciplinary program.

Let us take for an example, a humanities program. In a historically black college where the majority of our students are black, a humanities program dealing exclusively with white Western world culture is a tragic mistake. Teaching European art, music, literature, and Western civilization exclusively is a crime against all humanity and particularly against black humanity. It is altogether misleading. It demands in the first place a truncated world and a truncated civilization which, of course, cannot exist. It is like a worm with neither head nor tail, beginning in the middle of things. It divides the natural world into unnatural parts of East and West, then ignores and eliminates the oriental world and all its ancient significance. An adequate humanities program which in essence is nothing more than the study of man begins with man's beginnings and with the beginning of his world.

Humanities then obviously begins in Africa with black humanity. World literature begins with the ancient Egyptian *Book of the Dead* which predates all the epics of Homer and Virgil and obviously influences the Rhadamanthus legend from the beginning of recorded literature to Ralph Ellison's *Invisible Man.* We proceed from Egyptian to the Babylonian epic of *Gilgamesh,* to Hindu and Chinese literature, to Hebrew and Arabic literature to Persian, Greek, and Roman literature. An excellent example of ancient synthesis of oriental tragedy is found in the Hebrew book of Job which scholars claim includes fragments and influences from the Egyptian, Babylonian, Hindu, and Arabic, all later revised by the Hebrew writer. And with these, we are touching only superficially the body of ancient world literature. Handicapped by a lack of knowledge of ancient oriental languages and only recently having deciphered enough to make translations possible, a racist white world has perpetuated ignorance and cultivated intolerance of all man's earliest activities and his ancient role of human existence on this earth.

An adequate humanities program, therefore, concerns itself with three major premises and demands a core of three fundamental subject matter fields. The three major premises are first, the chronological order of man and his world, man in the ancient world, man in the Middle Ages, and man in the modern world. These concern themselves with his knowledge of himself and his world, his awareness of nature and the growth of awareness of himself and his world, his concept of the universe, his definition of his purpose of living, and his creativity expressed in his human response to the challenging changes of his universe. The second premise is philosophical and has to do with the unity of all life, the recognition of the relationship between all mankind and all living things, the nature and purpose of physical existence, the constant dangers that threaten that existence, and all the problems of the human condition. The third premise is intellectual and deals with the unity of all knowledge or the relationships between all subject matter fields of knowledge. In philosophy this is not concerned with being as the first premise, not with ontology and teleology as the second, but rather with epistemology, logic, aesthetics, and all the natural and social sciences, and the humanities as language, literature, music, art, and the correlation of all this knowledge and these subject matter fields. The three subject matter fields that form a core for the study of the humanities are philosophy, history, and anthropology. If you are fond of diagrams, draw a wheel and let these three form the hub. From these form the spokes of the wheel with literature, art, music, religion, et cetera.

It seems further necessary that a humanities program be concerned with the history of ideas and a history of culture. Running through a good humanities program should be a set of ideas, whether of a religious, socioeconomic, or historical nature. For example, it is impossible to understand the religions of the world without a knowledge of animism and the endowing of matter with spirit or seeing all the substance as spirit. Animism is man's first religion, and it is found in the heart of black Africa. All the religions of the world—pantheistic, polytheistic, monotheistic—have grown out of it. One of the basic and intrinsic values to be derived from humanities with such a core of ideas would be tolerance of all world religions based on knowledge and understanding.

Physical and cultural anthropology also take us back to black Africa for the skulls of prehistoric man and the cradle of civilization. Studying the history of language as well as religion provides the student with cultural tools. A study of art and the roots of music springing from Africa (including discovery of the earliest musical instruments) as well as a thorough understanding of the oral traditions from which all literature has proceeded depend upon a basic foundation in cultural anthropology.

All systems of political government stem from the family unit or tribalism. These facts may sound quite simplistic and not at all the profundities you may wish to hear. They are, nevertheless, the unvarnished truth.

The black student has a right to know how the black diaspora has affected the entire planet earth. He must be taught the three moments in historical time when black people were cut off from their mother country—Africa—by the Roman Empire, by the religious wars of the Middle Ages, and by the colonialism and slavery inflicted upon us through European domination at the beginning of their modern civilization. A suitable philosophy of history must also be chosen and should consider how the challenges of life and human society must inevitably engender a human response. This response must be traced through the various cultural and scientific expressions whether in music, art, literature, or scientific invention. They must then be linked directly to the philosophic principles or body of ideas which have produced such a response.

It is therefore imperative that the student be equipped with a body of related knowledge—a knowledge of the history of civilization from man's earliest life on the planet earth and a knowledge of the history of ideas and culture, philosophy, and anthropology. This knowledge must furthermore be correlated with his study of art, music, language, literature, and religion. In other words, these basic ideas lead to the cultural implementation or development of all man's intellectual and spiritual constructs. Black students must have the awe-inspiring opportunity to see the role of the black man in world history and thereby gain a genuine respect for the intellectual constructs of all great black scholars, artists, and social engineers of world progress. White racism has tried for three hundred and fifty years to nullify the spiritual and cultural dynamism and initiative of black humanity, but we know that this is an impossible thing to do. Despite all negative efforts to brainwash us through a white racist education, black people are still charismatic. We still have numinous power and all of white technocracy has not yet succeeded in dehumanizing us.

But there is a real danger that the technological world in which we live, the completely industrialized and urbanized society which our people do not understand, is a white man's Frankenstein that will destroy us along with him unless we can and do re-educate our youth with a completely new humanistic philosophy and awareness. Time is running out, and if we allow this megalomaniac with his Frankenstein monster and his God-complex, he will destroy the planet earth and all life on it. Man should be the master of machines and not their slave. A new value-system must be based on our cultural heritage of spiritual and human values, not on money and industry. This is what we must teach our students, for in truth, it may be their destiny to lift us from this quagmire to lead and save this nation.

Too many of us are impractical dreamers and full of unchanneled emotion and imaginative fantasies. It is very important not only to know our heritage, but it is equally important to know how to make a practical application of our theoretical knowledge. We need to reexamine the uses of our education and strip ourselves of the unnecessary baggage clinging to our liberal arts education. We need to know how to do things well and with skill, first in order to survive, for pure survival; second, in order to liberate our people or actually accomplish complete social and intellectual freedom; and third, in order to entertain and occupy ourselves in times of leisure. These should be the meaningful goals of our education.

Black people have always been creative. That creativity must be channeled in various constructive ways. A study of humanities should teach our students the value of creative activity of body and mind; the dignity of human toil that touches earth and man and does not depend alone on machines such as the television or idiot box, the automobile, and the record player. What happens when the electric power fails? Can we survive on the land, the desert, the island, the mountain or in the forest? Can we rehabilitate a demoralized community? Do we know how to help sick children and old people? What is the true nature of our education? What are the uses and values of our liberal knowledge? What is the practical application? Is it a good thing to know how to read a book for information and for pleasure? Is it also a simple matter to follow the botanist through the woods? Can we apply our physics, biology, or chemistry? A technological universe has given our enemies the negative minds for destruction. Their mammoth machines are used to program us for mass ignorance, for automatons and helpless control, even for genocide. Jensenism, Schockleyism, Moynihanism, to name but a few control mechanisms, are designed for our racial destruction. A positive, constructive humanism is our only weapon. It is a powerful answer to racism, an antidote for poisonous hate. It may be our only chance for survival.

The team teaching which is so essential to a humanities program is an answer to many problems in education today. It copes first with numbers. It involves many uses of multimedia—overhead projectors, transparencies, tape recorders and videotape recorders, record players, film strips, slides, and teaching films—everything constructive and not including bugging private homes and tapping telephones and invasion of privacy like the no-knock laws. The program requires constant variety. Large unwieldy groups can be broken into interesting rap sessions. The student learns how to organize various kinds of papers: research or investigative themes, critical analyses, parallel studies, autobiographical and character sketches and other themes generally based on literature. Most importantly, a college career ceases to be a piecemeal hodgepodge or smattering of knowledge. The student moves into a major field of study after humanities with a solid background of general and scientific knowledge about the world within and without.

In the history of mankind, every recorded age of progress has been marked by revolutions or power or energy and intellectual constructs that meaningfully change man's concept of his universe. As his ideas of power and energy evolve, his imagination strives to make the leap forward into another age or era and to implement his physical and social changes with adequate cultural and spiritual experiences, products, and values. Thus artists, musicians, and poets follow the avant-garde of the philosopher, the theoretical scientists, and the social engineer. Insofar as archaeologists and anthropologists have been able to determine the scientific truth based on their experimentation and observation, man's intellectual and spiritual adventures began along the banks of seven rivers. If we follow the story of one river, the Nile, we shall discover an amazing story that will take us through the ages to the very hour in which we live.

It is a long distance from the days of ancient Egypt to the end of this century, but it is in the continuity of that open-ended time we must constitute the body of knowledge that we seek to impart daily to each student who sits in our classrooms. They have a right to know that all knowledge is related and that all life has a oneness, a natural oneness and a spiritual destiny. If the student knows that humankind's first religious idea is the warm earthy spiritism or animism that springs from our African progenitors, then he or she knows why our ancient culture was centered in nature and the physical world around us. That natural world was full of spirits, and ancient people named them gods who surrounded them and were present from birth till death and even beyond into the underworld. From the earliest Egyptian, Babylonian, and Hindu manifestations to the pantheon of Greek and Roman gods, the ancient world has evolved, one whose meaning, purpose, and rectitude were based on the concept of the universe that included earth, sky, and water, and the nether regions of the grave beneath the earth.

From the invention of the wheel and the discovery of fire to the days of water power and steam, and from the idea of gods and goddesses to the age of scientific invention, social institutions and cultural expressions of the people have followed the trial and error method of nature's challenge and society's response. Empires rise and fall, but society's progress follows the star of the imagination and the spiritual consciousness of an abiding faith in the prevailing goodness of a better future which we all hope and dream lies just ahead. Today we live in this technological universe where we neither glorify nature, god and spirit, nor ourselves, but worship machines, money, and the means of material production. We are faced with the Frankensteinian monster that threatens to dehumanize and destroy us. Our people are confused and deceived by this tyrannical age of technocracy in which scientific revolutions have outpaced human understanding and human relationships. An Atomic Age, a Space Age, or an Electronic Age—call it what you will—our educational institutions and their learning programs have become obsolete. Until mass education of all our people can lead to their understanding of the society and equal the power and control of technocracy, we are doomed.

In this century we have been awed by the spectacular nature of scientific and cultural revolutions spinning like meteors across our universe and effecting such rapid physical and social change and worldwide upheaval that we have been unable to grasp their meanings fast enough to implement the moral and spiritual values spinning away from them. During the past several decades we have witnessed, among countless other social phenomena, the realities of a black revolution. This revolution is of such cultural magnitude that the new young black intelligentsia is still busy spelling out the resultant artistic renaissance in all its dramatic, literary, musical, and graphic manifestations. What about black education? Black students in the late 1960s demanded a more relevant educational system in terms of our multiracial society, particularly in terms of the Third World, and an educational system modern enough to face the twenty-first century. Education is always the last of the social phenomenon and institutions to express the new theories that result

from a new concept of the universe. The Einsteinian revolution began early in this century and supplanted the Newtonian revolution.
It has been many decades since the Atomic Age began, and since
that time the electronic revolution, which is more and more evident in our society, has completely changed our concept of the
universe.

We live in an illimitable universe with a space-time continuum, a society of pluralistic nature demanding the principle of
unity in diversity. Just as we now recognize new principles govern-
ing motion, energy, light, and sound, so there must be in effect new
social and moral educational principles in the light of this new concept of the universe. We fly in machines that break the barriers of
sound and with the speed of light. We threaten to sweep the floors
of the oceans and reveal a new world of oceanography. We are also
threatening this natural universe and all human life on this planet
with death from the polluting acids of industry and from a society
that has gotten out of hand. When we consider the worldwide wave
of assassinations of men of good will during previous decades, the
mass murders, the billions spent perpetuating a century-old war,
the prisons overflowing with young black men, the political chica-
nery and social chaos and economic collapse, we cannot help but
think that the society has gotten out of hand. In the words of the
gambler, the joker is wild, man, the joker is wild!

Our problems today are human problems. They are spiritual,
moral, and intellectual problems. They cannot be solved merely
by mechanical instruments, by guns, bombs, and billions of dollars
at the expense of human life. Our problems are problems of peace
and freedom and human dignity. They are problems brought on
by automation and cybernation displacing the worker with the
machine, computers and computer systems. They are problems
brought on by mechanized farming, displacing the peasant on the
land with the cotton picker, the harvester, and the cultivator, send-
ing him into ghettoes and driving him to welfare rolls. Our problems are international brought on by war and greed for gain, decimating the peoples of the earth by bombs and gas and germs;
pitting man against man, man against nature, and man against
God. Our problems in the cities are problems of black people surrounded by wealthy suburbs where the white man has run from
the inner cities to avoid integration and where they drain us of la-

bor and money and continue to control the city with political and economic power and suck our blood to sustain themselves. Our people are suffering for food and adequate housing, for medical care, and jobs. We are sick from bad air, bad food, bad water, rodents or vermin, and subsequent disease. Everything is out of balance. Our very planet earth is threatened with destruction. Our children and our people are threatened with genocide. War, violence and crime are the political bedfellows of big money and big business, of syndicated world crime. And we seem powerless to help ourselves. Must we follow those who have lost their vision and spiritual power and have therefore forfeited their right to lead? Education may not be enough, but if positive, constructive re-education cannot help, then nothing can.

(1986)

Of Tennessee and the River

I REMEMBER as a small child in Alabama singing:

ALABAMA, ALABAMA
We will aye be true to Thee
From Thy northern shores where floweth
Deep and Blue Thy Tennessee.

Of course every American in these parts of the United States thinks of the Mississippi as "the River." Not only does it bisect the country into East and West, but it begins as a small stream in Ithasca, Minnesota, and empties into the Gulf south of New Orleans. The state of Tennessee forms the northern border of Mississippi, Alabama, and Georgia. Here in Memphis, the states—Arkansas, Mississippi, and Tennessee—meet at this juncture in the Mississippi River. I have crossed this river repeatedly from Ken-

---

This speech was delivered at the Tennessee Council of Teachers of English convention in Memphis, Tennessee, October 11, 1986.

tucky at Paducah and Missouri to Cairo, Illinois, and from Illinois
west to Iowa. The Ohio, Mississippi, and Missouri Rivers all con-
verge. Crossing the river from Covington, Kentucky, to Cincinnati,
Ohio, marks the old Mason-Dixon line from slavery to freedom.
Tennessee has an interesting and curious history. Here in Memphis
in this very neighborhood lived a rich white woman who was a
staunch abolitionist. In the community of Neshoba lived black
women she had bought as slaves to be set free at the first oppor-
tune moment. The Mississippi River is famous in story, song, and
fable. Many of our greatest American writers, poets and novelists
have immortalized this historic river. Abe Lincoln traveled down
this river from Illinois to New Orleans. Mark Twain (Samuel
Clemens) was born on the river at Hannibal, Missouri, and he opens
a great new chapter of American literature with his adventures of
Tom Sawyer and Huckleberry Finn, *Old Times on the Mississippi*
(1877) and *Life on the Mississippi* (1883). Thomas Wolfe probably
had another river in mind when he wrote *Of Time and the River*
(1935), but Langston Hughes in his great poem, "The Negro Speaks
of Rivers," written when he was only eighteen, speaks of the Mississippi. Listen:

I've known rivers:

I've known rivers ancient as the world and older than the flow of
human blood in human veins.

My soul has grown deep like the rivers.

I bathed in the Euphrates when dawns were young.
I built my hut near the Congo and it lulled me to sleep.
I looked down the Nile and raised the pyramids above it.
I heard the singing of the Mississippi when Abe Lincoln went
down to New Orleans, and I've seen its muddy bosom turn all
golden in the sunset.

I've known rivers:
Ancient, dusky rivers.

My soul has grown deep like the rivers.

Then there is that wonderful encyclopedic poet, Walt Whitman, whose words roll on like a river in that great poem, "Crossing Brooklyn Ferry":

Flood-tide below me! I see you face to face!
Clouds of the west—sun there half an hour high—see you also
face to face.

Crowds of men and women attired in the usual costumes, how
curious you are to me!
On the ferry-boats the hundreds and hundreds that cross, returning home, are more curious to me than you suppose,
And you that shall cross from shore to shore years hence are more
to me, in my meditations, than you might suppose.

The others that are to follow me, the ties between me and them
The certainty of others, the life, love, sight, hearing of others.
Others will enter the gates of the ferry and cross from shore to
shore,
Others will watch the run of the flood-tide,
Others will see the shipping of Manhattan north and west, And
the heights of Brooklyn to the south and east,
Others will see the islands large and small;
Fifty years hence, others will see them as they cross, the sun half
an hour high,
A hundred years hence, or ever so many hundreds years hence,
others will see them,
Will enjoy the sunset , the pouring-in of the flood-tide, the fall-
ing-back to the sea of the ebb-tide.

I too many and many a time cross'd the river of old,

On the river the shadowy group, the big steam-tug closely flank'd
on each side by the barges, the hay-boat, the belated lighter,
On the neighboring shore the fires from the foundry chimneys
burning high and glaringly into the night,
Casting their flicker of black contrasted with wild red and yellow
light over the tops of houses, and down into the clefts of streets.

Flow on, river! flow with the flood-tide, and ebb with the ebb-tide!

Cross from shore to shore, countless crowds of passengers!
Stand up, tall masts of Manhattan! stand up, beautiful hills of
Brooklyn!

Come on, ships from the lower bay! pass up or down, white-sail'd
schooners, sloops, lighters!

Thrive, cities—bring your freight, bring your shows, ample and
sufficient rivers,
Expand, being than which none else is perhaps more spiritual,
Keep your places, objects than which none else is more lasting.
You have waited, you always wait, you dumb, beautiful ministers,
We receive you with free sense at last, and are insatiate
henceforward,
Not you any more shall be able to foil us, or withhold yourselves
from us,
We use you, and do not cast you aside—we plant you perma-
nently within us,
We fathom you—we love you—there is perfection in you also,
You furnish your parts toward eternity,
Great or small, you furnish your parts toward the soul.

But Tennessee and the river have been celebrated in other literature and letters aside from poetry. George Washington Harris
wrote about Tennessee and the Tennessee River; Mary Noailles
Murfree, under the male pseudonym Charles Craddock, wrote of
her native Tennessee and celebrated the mountains of Tennessee
in her book *In the Tennessee Mountains* (1884) and her novel *The
Prophet of the Great Smoky Mountains* (1885).
    Perhaps the most intellectual and literary movement in Ten-
nessee began in the 1930s—more than fifty years ago—with the *Fugitive* magazine and the agrarians at Vanderbilt University in Nashville, Tennessee. A half-dozen of that group went on to national
and international fame while more than a baker's dozen remain recognized only by the region. One of the leaders of that movement
was Donald Davidson, a native Tennessean, student and professor

of English at Vanderbilt. He wrote a two-volume work, *The Tennessee* (1946–48), which appears in the series "Rivers of America." His work is recognized as being among the best of that series.

Alan Tate, Andrew Lytle, Robert Penn Warren, John Crowe Ransom, and Cleanth Brooks are the five other famous members of the agrarian group, also identified with the new critics and the modernists, or modernism, as it developed fifty years ago around T. S. Eliot, William Butler Yeats, the French symbolists, and Marcel Proust.

But we should continue that list to include other names familiar to any southerner with literary interests whether scholar, critic, teacher, or imaginative writer. This list includes Merrill Moore, Lyle Lanier, Frank Lawrence Owsley, John Donald Wade, Henry B. Kline, H. C. Nixon, John Gould Fletcher and Stark Young—John Gould Fletcher with his poetry and association with the Imagists, and Stark Young, the Mississippian, with his famous Civil War novel, *So Red the Rose* (1934). The last two share a wide circle of fame with the first six. Altogether there were twenty young agrarians in the Fugitive group, and for many years a whirlwind of controversy centered in the particular piece, "I'll Take My Stand." This revived old and raw wounds of the Confederate South as a defeated slave state struggling to survive against the rising industrialism and capitalism of the federal North.

To the black writer, scholar, or teacher, this was a hotbed of racism continuing an ostracism of black writers and all our creativity, the successful suppression of our southern literature and our substantial contribution to American culture in language, religion, music, art, dance and literature. The clear lines of racial demarcation almost obliterated the folklore such as:

> On top of old Smoky
> All covered with snow
> I lost my true lover
> From courting too slow

But there have been famous African American writers also associated with the great state of Tennessee. W. E. B. Du Bois, although born in Massachusetts, went to college here in Tennessee and graduated from Fisk University, also in Nashville. He spent his first teaching years in rural Tennessee before he went on to Harvard and the University of Berlin. He became a great leader of the Negro people—writing many books of history, sociology, fiction and poetry, and editing two major magazines of literary interest—*Crisis* magazine, organ of the National Association for the Advancement of Colored People, of which he was a founder, and *Phylon: The Atlanta University Review of Race and Culture,* which he founded teaching at Atlanta University. He is one of five seminal minds of the twentieth century and father of Pan-Africanism, a philosophy of unity and freedom in the entire black world. Du Bois spent nearly seven years in Tennessee—four years studying at Fisk and at least two years of teaching.

Richard Wright lived and worked here in Memphis for two years when he was a teenager, on his way from the southern state of rural Mississippi to the urban city of Chicago. His serious reading began here with Henry Louis Mencken, whose words were used as a weapon fighting prejudice and who inspired Wright to use words in the same way. Wright is perhaps the most important black writer of the twentieth century.

I do not see how any southern writer aware of the southern landscape can escape writing about rivers, especially southern rivers. In my own poetry, most of my images come from the southern landscape which I think is physically indescribably beautiful. I have grown up loving this physical landscape and hating the horror of the social climate. When my first book was published, I read my poetry in a New York town hall, and at that time, a woman asked me a question about my poem, "Delta." She wanted to know if I was talking about the Mississippi Delta or if my meaning was symbolic. I answered that the poem is both about the valley of the Mississippi River where we live and the valley of our spirits where my people also live.

All of you have read those famous words that the Delta begins in the lobby of the Peabody Hotel here in Memphis and ends on Catfish Row in Vicksburg. Here is my poem, "Delta":

I

I am a child of the valley.
Mud and muck and misery of lowlands
are on thin tracks of my feet.
Damp draughts of mist and fog hovering over valleys

are on my feverish breath.
Red clay from feet of beasts colors my mouth
and there is blood on my tongue.

I go up and down and through this valley
and my heart bleeds for our fate.
I turn to each stick and stone, marking them for my own;
here where muddy water flows at our shanty door
and levees stand like a swollen bump on our backyard.

I watch rivulets flow
trickling into one great river
running through little towns
through swampy thickets and smoky cities
Through fields of rice and marshes
where the marsh hen comes to stand
and buzzards draw thin blue streaks against evening sky.
I listen to crooning of familiar lullabies;
the honky-tonks are open and the blues are ringing far.
In cities a thousand red lamps glow,
but the lights fail to stir me
and the music cannot lift me
and my despair only deepens with the wailing of a million voices
strong.

O valley of my moaning brothers!
Valley of my sorrowing sisters!
Valley of lost forgotten men.
O hunted desperate people
stricken and silently submissive
Seeking yet sullen ones!
If only from this valley we might rise with song!
With singing that is ours.

II

Here in this valley of cotton and cane and banana wharves
we labor
Our mothers and fathers labored before us
here in this low valley.

High above us and round about us stand high mountains
rise the towering snow-capped mountains
while we are beaten and broken and bowed
here in this dark valley.

The river passes us by.
Boats slip by on the edge of horizons.
Daily we fill boats with cargoes of our need
and send them out to sea.

Orange and plantain and cotton grow
here in this wide valley.
Wood fern and sour grass and wild onion grow
here in this sweet valley.

We tend the crop and gather the harvest
but not for ourselves do we labor,
not for ourselves do we sweat and starve and spend
under these mountains we dare not claim,
Here on this earth we dare not claim,
here by this river we dare not claim.
Yet we are an age of years in this valley;
yet we are bound till death to this valley.

Nights in the valley are full of haunting murmurings
of our musical prayers
of our rhythmical loving
of our fumbling thinking aloud.
Nights in the houses of our miserable poor
are wakeful and tormenting,
for out of a deep slumber we are 'roused
to our brother who is ill
and our sister who is ravished
and our mother who is starving.
Out of a deep slumber truth rides upon us
and we wonder why we are helpless
and we wonder why we are dumb.
Out of a deep slumber truth rides upon us
and makes us restless and wakeful

and full of a hundred unfulfilled dreams of today;
our blood eats through our veins with the terrible destruction
of radium in our bones and rebellion in our brains
and we wish no longer to rest.

III

Now burst the dams of years
and winter snows melt with an onrush of a turbulent spring.
Now rises sap in slumbering elms
and floods overwhelm us
here in this low valley.
Here there is a thundering sound in our ears.
All the day we are disturbed;
nothing ever moved our valley more.

The cannons boom in our brains
and there is a dawning understanding
in the valleys of our spirits;
there is a crystalline hope
there is a new way to be worn and a path to be broken
from the past.

Into our troubled living flows the valley
flooding our lives with a passion for freedom.
Our silence is broken in twain
even as brush is broken before terrible rain
even as pines rush in paths of hurricanes.
Our blood rises and bursts in great heart spasms
hungering down through valleys in pain
until the storm begins.
We are dazed in wonder and caught in the downpour.
Danger and death stalk the valley.
Robbers and murderers rape the valley
taking cabins and children from us
seeking to threaten us out of this valley.

Then with a longing dearer than breathing
love for the valley arises within us
love to possess and thrive in this valley

love to possess our vineyards and pastures
our orchards and cattle
our harvest of cotton, tobacco, and cane.
Love overwhelms our living with longing
strengthening flesh and blood within us
banding the iron of our muscles with anger
making us men in the fields we have tended
standing defended the land we have rendered
rich and abiding and heavy with plenty.

We with our blood have watered these fields
and they belong to us.
Valleys and dust of our bodies are blood brothers
and they belong to us:
the long golden grain for bread
and the ripe purple fruit for wine
the hills beyond for peace
and the grass beneath for rest
the music in the wind for us
the nights for loving
the days for living
and the circling lines in the sky
for dreams.

We are like the sensitive Spring
walking valleys like a slim young girl
full breasted and precious limbed
and carrying on our lips the kiss of the world.
Only the naked arm of Time
can measure the ground we know
and thresh the air we breathe.
Neither earth nor star nor water's host
can sever us from our life to be
for we are beyond your reach O mighty winnowing flail!
infinite and free!

(1990)

Natchez and
Richard Wright
in Southern
American
Literature

THE SOUTH HAS suffered many names
and misnomers, including the Old South and the New South, the
Confederate South, the antebellum South, the solid South and the
secessionist South. But I speak here of the historic South—that is,
the South of history and fact—and the mythic or mythical South, a
literary South of fantasy mixed with reality or fact.

Southerners who live in this region rarely think of its dual nature—fact and fiction, reality and fantasy—and, if we are mindful
of this duality, we seldom, if ever, recognize or consider the effects
of the region on our lives and our personalities. Southern literature
illustrates this for us. The South is both a historical region and a
mythical place, at least in the literature. Southern American literature, like all great world literature, is grounded in myth. We have
only to look at Eudora Welty's *The Robber Bridegroom* (1942) to
see an illustration of this fact.

This essay was originally delivered at the Natchez Literary Festival in
June 1990 at the home site of Richard Wright, now a national landmark.
The speech was later published in *Southern Quarterly*, Summer 1991.

The historic events of the region are well known, but the elements of myth found in fantasy and taken from folk tales, legends, and gothic imaginations, frequently puzzle and confound us. We squirm under the label of the Bible Belt, yet we live every day in terms of John Milton's theology and many fundamentalist beliefs from the King James version of the Bible. Violence seems to be native to the region from the days of the frontier, when the Native Americans lived and fought here, through the violence of the Civil War, the scourge of the Ku Klux Klan in the days of Reconstruction with its pattern of lynching and mob rule, to the days of the civil rights movement of the 1960s. Segregation was declared legally dead and unconstitutional on May 17, 1954, but the economic and political support systems of institutionalized and entrenched racism still distress and disturb us today.

Natchez is a pivotal and historic point in the literary legacy that we now declare for the Natchez Trace. The nation of the Natchez Indians began the legacy; the black slaves imported from Africa built the antebellum mansions which the French architects designed; those same slaves escaped through the Underground Railroad by the Natchez Trace and the Mississippi River to the banks of the Ohio and free soil. The Union soldiers broke the economic back of the cotton kingdom and devastated the land. Despite a century of lynching and mob rule by the Ku Klux Klan, the civil rights movement of the 1960s dictated another social revolution to free the people, black and white alike.

These are the historic facts. What about the myths? John Pendleton Kennedy began the plantation tradition in southern American literature with his novel *Swallow Barn* (1832). The best examples of that tradition are Thomas Nelson Page with his trilogy of southern novels[1] and Margaret Mitchell's *Gone With the Wind*. In this tradition, slavery is romanticized and glorified and the Old South is given mythical qualities which in fact it never possessed. The system is seen as benign and beneficial to all involved. The Greek state is revived and glorified as a slave state and utopia; agrarian culture—or agriculture—is considered superior to industry and business. The architecture is that of Greek Revival. The War between the States was a crusade in which valiant knights went forth to rescue damsels in distress. But what about the slaves? According to myth, they were mindless pieces of property who loved their masters and never wanted to be free. As a matter of fact, the slavocracy included thousands of poor whites who hated the slavelords and the black slaves alike. Caste and class were as bitter a struggle as race.

If we read the books of secessionists and abolitionists, we see this battle going on between races, classes, and nations. *Natchez on the Mississippi* (1947) by Harnett Kane describes this place. Stark Young's novel, *So Red the Rose,* describes the society and the system. The beautiful white ladies in crinoline skirts lived in the mansions but behind the mansions were the slave quarters with the threat of branding, beatings, killings, and fires.

The Confederate generals in their gray and gold uniforms were leading thousands of not-so-rich white men to death in the dirt and carnage of battle. Richard Wright's grandfathers were slaves in Mississippi, in Natchez. One became a sharecropper on Travellers Rest plantation, and one was a Civil War soldier who never got his pension. There were two Mississippis which William Faulkner and Shelby Foote have recorded as fiction and history and another Mississippi in Richard Wright's *Uncle Tom's Children* (1938), *Native Son* (1940), *Black Boy* (1945), *12,000,000 Black Voices* (1941), and *The Long Dream* (1958). Today in Natchez we pay homage to the myth of Mississippi in all these great southern writers.

The poverty of the region also has had its effects. Until the mid-twentieth century, the Industrial Revolution did not exist in Mississippi. There was no heavy industry and very little light and diversified industry. Suddenly in the 1950s, the industrial and the electronic revolutions hit Mississippi simultaneously with mechanized farming and computerized technology. What was the effect from 1877 to the 1950s on the minds of the people? Political demagoguery, substandard education and housing, and religious fundamentalism affected us all with a psychic wound of racism. Richard Wright, who was clearly a genius, was born in Natchez in 1908, and spent his early childhood here. He suffered all his life from that psychic wound of racism. He wrote sixteen books, and the first four were written before he went to Paris. All four were influenced by Natchez and Mississippi. Only one book written in Paris was most affected by Mississippi, and that was *The Long Dream.* I used to wonder when I read his first books from whence came all the violence and the horror. Years of study and research taught me. They came out of his deep-seated anger, neurotic anger and realistic anger against the system of segregation and the violent white racism he experienced here in Mississippi.

Early in his career, Richard Wright was further influenced by four great American writers. All four were southerners: Mark Twain, Edgar Allan Poe, H. L. Mencken, and William Faulkner. Wright believed (and I sometimes think he was right) that all Americans suffer from a form of paranoia. Black people suffer from delusions of persecution, some based on fact, and some on fantasy, while white people suffer from delusions of grandeur, a kind of God-complex.

White Americans believe they can fix the world. If only everybody looked and thought like them, the world would be a perfect place. That's a God-complex. The poor white people in the Ku Klux Klan believe that when God made this southern land, it was a kind of Eden, a physical paradise, until sin, death, and hell came into the garden. That the serpent brought sin, death and hell into the garden and made Eve make Adam eat the apple and thus disobey God. They fell from grace and were punished, but the serpent also left children and according to the Ku Klux Klan, the children of the serpent were black people, Jews, and Catholics. How big a myth is that? They tell me the Arab or Moslem nations declare America is the Great Satan. That must be their myth. And the Black Muslims declare all whites are devils. Everybody's got his myth.

Faulkner made himself a system, but it was built on the myth of Christian redemption, and the New Critics have worn out that myth. Faulkner had more than a religious myth of Christian honor, he had a myth of racial superiority and inferiority which he grew up believing in Mississippi. It was a myth Richard Wright refused to believe. Their philosophies are diametrically different, but their symbiology is the same. The folk roots of their fiction are in Mississippi, but they develop their symbolism in a very different way. For Richard Wright, Mississippi was no Garden of Eden, it was a racial hell. Faulkner believed the South was a ruined world. Slavery, miscegenation and rising capitalism destroyed the pastoral paradise and ruined the Edenic South.

The world of fiction is one of myth, not history. Fiction blends fantasy with reality. Each enhances the other. Sometimes the fantasy of fiction seems as real as history, and sometimes the reality seems absolutely fantastic. When we read Ellen Douglas's fiction,[2] we are caught up and enthralled in the racial myth and the social horror that a pastoral land of beauty breeds before our very eyes. Douglas, like Wright, was born in Natchez. Clearly, the fiction of Eudora Welty[3] also illustrates the skillful blending of fantasy and reality, while we hear the speech of the Mississippi Delta and see the land of myth and legend that the Natchez Trace truly and historically is.

Southern writers, like all other writers, seek to reflect their life and living in their literature. Life, however, is chaotic, and the artist seeks to rearrange and order life into an artistic whole. Imagination works, therefore, with reality and creates a blend of fantasy and reality, thereby resulting in myth. When the artist is successful, the reader sometimes finds it difficult to separate myth and fantasy from fact and reality. This may be the greatest test, that fiction rings as true as fact. Southern American literature is a great component of all world literature. The great masters—Edgar Allan Poe, Mark Twain, William Faulkner and Tennessee Williams—stand shoulder to shoulder with the greatest. Not the least of these is Richard Wright, native of Natchez, Mississippi. Despite the obstacles of extreme poverty and little formal education, coupled with a broken home, religious fanaticism and the psychic wound of racism, Wright rose to world renown. He died thirty years ago in Paris, but today Natchez, the state of Mississippi, and the United States Department of the Interior honor this great author with a historic marker on the Natchez bluffs overlooking the Mississippi River. Wright leaves a proud literary legacy to his family, to his children's children, to his race—but most of all, to all humanity.

Notes

1. Thomas Nelson Page's trilogy of southern novels includes *In Ole Virginia* (1896), *The Old Gentleman of the Black Stock* (1897), and *Bred in the Bone* (1904).
2. Ellen Douglas's works include *A Lifetime Burning* (1982), *Can't Quit You, Baby* (1988), and *Black Cloud, White Cloud* (1989).
3. Eudora Welty's major works include *Delta Wedding* (1946), *The Ponder Heart* (1954), and *The Optimist's Daughter* (1972).

(1968)

Critical Approaches to the Study of African American Literature

THE STUDENT OF African American lit-
erature is confronted at the very beginning with a number of quite
controversial issues. Not the least of these is the name given to the
literature. Having begun as Negro literature, is it Afro-American
literature, Black literature, or African American literature? Why not
American literature? What is the historical context in which the
literature should be read? Must it be approached from the sociological or ideological viewpoint rather than always from the critical imperative of analysis and synthesis? Is there a separate and distinctly black American tradition or African American tradition as
distinguished from an Anglo-American or Anglo-Saxon tradition?
Does this literature pose different aesthetic problems for the cre-

This essay was originally delivered in 1968 as the keynote lecture at the
opening of the Institute for the Study of the History, Life, and Culture of
Black People in Jackson, Mississippi, one of the first Black Studies/Cul-
tural Studies programs in the nation. In 1989 the name was changed to
the Margaret Walker Alexander National Research Center for the Study
of the 20th Century African American and is supported with state and
federal funding.

ative artist and critic from any other literature? Do black writers develop their literature from a different kind of ethos and mythological background than the white writer? What about the separate worlds of East and West, of black and white? Which world does this literature represent and why?

The first task, therefore, is one of definition. It is necessary for the student to approach the literature with a knowledge of certain basic facts, an understanding not merely of certain terminology, but also with a definite methodology. The first approach is from the historical background in which context the literature has been written and should be read. This also extends itself to a social perspective or sociological knowledge of the world of which the whole body of African American literature arises. The second, and certainly not least in importance, is the critical approach through literary analysis of forms and content. Ordinarily, this second approach would be the only valid approach, but widespread ignorance of African American literature dictates the necessity for the first approach. The third, a theoretical approach, seeks to discover a relationship between the knowledge derived from the first two approaches: the sociohistorical context and the analysis of form and content. In other words, the theoretical approach often tells us how and why literature is what it is.

I

Thirty-five hundred years before the Judaeo-Christian world became known, there developed on the shores of the Nile River a cosmogony and cosmology out of which the first literature in the history of mankind was written. Like the literature of all ancient people, it was centered in nature. Nature gods named for the sun, moon, and all the elements of the physical world determined the destiny of every believing person.

This world consisted of the heavens above, the earth beneath, and the world under the waters and under the earth; it was mankind's belief that after death the soul journeyed to the underworld where it entered the Hall of Justice. There the heart would be weighed in the balance with gold, and, according to the life lived on earth, one would be allowed to enter the world of eternal life. The literary guide to this underworld the Egyptians called *The Book of the Dead.*

The epic convention of a journey to the underworld was first conceived thirty-five hundred years before Christianity, and long before the days of Greece and Rome. Subsequently, as the great empires of the ancient and Oriental worlds developed, they also developed a body of Wisdom literature—the Babylonians, the Hebrews and all other people in the Fertile Crescent, the Persians, the Chinese, the Indians of the East, and, finally, the Greeks. The Romans merely copied the pantheon of gods of the Greeks and imitated their literature.[1]

What can hardly be disputed is that this wealth of ancient oriental[2] literature flourished centuries before the Western world of Europe and North America developed its own empire. The Romans were only the transfer agents of this Oriental world to the Occident; they developed commerce with these people and later conquered them. Western society has only recently learned to read the languages of this ancient Oriental world and for centuries this lack of understanding and ignorance made its denial convenient. A view prevailed that all western culture began with the Greeks and Jews.

Black people are well aware that this is not true. Civilization began long before the culture that produced either Homer or Virgil. According to the Old Testament, when Abraham went out of Ur of the Chaldees and up to Haran to take the land of the Fertile Crescent he said God had given to him, he found people living on that land who had an ancient culture and civilization. His descendants have been fighting for possession of that land throughout all the centuries that have followed. That ancient world was neither Nordic nor Anglo-Saxon. It was a nonwhite world that was highly civilized with a highly cultivated society including manifestations of great art, literature, and music.

But what has this to do with black people living in America and writing a literature that is the product of a culture unrecognized and rejected by the dominant culture of White America? Black people have lived four hundred years in America and we are not native Africans; we are native Americans. Yet we are, definitely, descendants of Africa.

Three times, however, in the history of humankind, Africa has lost its ties with its western descendants. First, the world was split into East and West with the rise and fall of the Roman Empire. Rome conquered and destroyed the great cites of the Oriental world before she turned westward to what she named a barbarian world,

the world of European strangers. Second, when Rome became
Christian, she moved further toward splitting the world into two.
The Christian church also was split in two sections, Eastern and
Western, and Christianity moved westward while Mohammedanism
soon swept through Asia and Africa. We know the story of the Crusades and how the Europeans returned from the holy wars with rich
spoils from the East. Our history books tell us very little about that
Eastern world, but they do tell us that the soldiers brought sugar,
glass, tapestries, rich silks, precious gems, and sacred manuscripts
from the East. These were lost manuscripts from Greece that had
been translated and preserved by Jewish and Moslem scholars. Our
books also do not tell us how the so-called Dark Ages of Europe
and the Middle Ages or the medieval world ended when the culture
of the East and its civilization became the basis for the European
Renaissance and the modern world. And third, came the great Age
of Exploration when discovery and colonization resulted in the new
world of America and the beginning of the slave trade. Once again
Africa was raped, her great nations and civilization destroyed while
her land was parceled among European nations who, for more than
a hundred years, grew fat on her natural resources while subjugat-
ing her people. Not only were the black slaves in America cut off
from this Africa but they were taught to despise her as a heathen,
primitive, dark and backward land. No wonder Phillis Wheatley
wrote in such disparaging fashion about her native land, from
which she was torn at age seven. No wonder Countee Cullen could
speak in such a callous, almost enigmatic way, asking, "What is
Africa to me?" Black people in America became totally estranged
from Africa, from their cultural roots of language, religion, and art.

It is nevertheless a strange phenomenon, but true, that wherever Africans have lived as slaves or free people in Europe or South
and North America they have carried with them from Africa great
gifts with which to enrich any foreign land and culture they have
known. It is well known today, for example, that the rhythms of
Africa have influenced the music of the world; black slaves and
their descendants in America have left an indelible mark on music
in America with spirituals, blues, work songs, jazz, gospel music,
rap and all other evidences of African folk culture. African art and
sculpture from the Ashanti and Ife people of Benin have influenced
the modern art of Picasso, Modigliani, and Brancusi. The African

influence is also seen in the folk literature of African Americans. The folk hero, John Henry, is only one example. This is a natural part of African American literature, despite centuries of cultural estrangement. Black America is still tied to her African heritage in her physical and cultural manifestations.

II

But African Americans are more than descendants of Black Africa. Born in America, this literature is unquestionably as American as any produced in America. The only native Americans, indeed, are the tribes of red men who have survived the fate of massacre, annihilation, and assimilation. If descendants of Europeans are Americans, descendants of Africans are also Americans. Neither has more right than the other: by right of birth, by right of toil, by right of sacrifice. This is all to say that African Americans are a fusion of two cultures, African and American, one no less nor more than the other and, as such, we inherit much from Africa even as we are entitled to much from America. A sociological study of life as African Americans in this nation reveals some astonishing facts and these facts must be considered in the study of African American literature. The institutions of slavery and segregation have stigmatized African Americans and, therefore, every phase of our life and its manifestations has been stigmatized. Our literature has not escaped this ostracism.

In order to accommodate both slavery and segregation, White America was forced to develop a negative and antihumanistic philosophy of racism in which races of people could be categorized as inferior and superior. Without such a philosophy, human slavery and inhuman segregation would obviously be morally insupportable. If a person is a person for all that, then he or she is capable of thinking, can be educated, can create art, and can be self-governing. These are the tenets of democracy. If all of us are members of the same human community and the children of God, then we must recognize the primacy of human personality and we admit that every human being is potentially divine, that the destiny of all mankind is spiritual, and we do not insult or denigrate any human being based on the pain of our own spiritual destruction. These are the facts of Christianity. Our nation, America, claims to be democratic and Christian. Slavery and segregation demanded not only a denial of all human and civil rights to Black America, they demanded a false philosophy of racism. This racism further denounced humanity by declaring race to be worth more than humanity and evaluating ability and human worth or intelligence in terms of race. How could a racist society accept the literature, art, and music of a people denounced as racially inferior, incapable of thinking and, hence, incapable of creativity? If a race is mentally inferior, how can one accept the imaginative products of such people? This is the *only* reason White America has refused to include the literature of Black America in its textbooks.

Do you wonder why so few people know Afro-American writers? America has chosen to ignore her black citizens because her racist philosophy of white supremacy developed over three hundred and fifty years ago is otherwise completely untenable. This is the reason White America refuses to call this literature by African Americans "American literature." Like the people who wrote it, the literature is segregated, separated, and treated like an illegitimate child.

It is a historic fact, however, that black people in America have been producing a body of literature ever since colonial days in this country. Despite laws forbidding education for African Americans, black people learned the English language and early in the eighteenth century were writing and publishing their writing in this country. It is further true that this literature reveals similar intellectual trends in comparable periods, schools, or writers, but it is also true that this literature, while basically American in language, form, and technical and intellectual trends, is suffused with an emotive content completely different in tone and subject matter from that of White America. The humanistic, realistic, and emotive content is tied historically in tradition to the ancient Oriental world of literature, to ancient Africa and to everything racially indigenous to black people or nonwhite cultures everywhere in the world. This is the literature of an oppressed people, yet it is entirely different in emotive content from the Talmudic literature of persecuted Jewish people. Nationalistically, it is distinctly different from any national body of European literature. It may sometimes be Anglo-Saxon or Anglo-American in form, but never in content, tone, or philosophy, and always it is suffused with a revolt against artifice, sterility, self-consciousness, and contrived morality and pseudo-ethics.

It is not in the spirit of the white man's religious ideas or emotions as they have been superimpacted by European culture with racial cruelty, blindness, bigotry, and materialistic greed for money and power, but whenever one sees this black idiom at work in African American literature, as in all black art, it is antimoralistic, antiformalistic, and antirationalistic. It demands a certain verve, what Arna Bontemps calls a certain riff. Above all, at its best it reflects the ultimate of the black experience or the life of black people in America: a people oppressed, but who refuse to be suppressed; a people who refuse to be dehumanized or made into machines, who refuse to give up secular play, warmth, and gaiety of love and joy, or a continuous awareness of the deepest spiritual meaning of freedom, peace and human dignity; a people who have had to develop compassion out of suffering and who are passionately tied to all that is earthly, natural, and emotionally free.

As for a name, what's in a name? Many black writers have winced at the name Negro poet, black novelist, African American writer. Why not American poet, American novelist, American writer? This is as hard for a white American literary critic to say as it has been for our southern white brothers and sisters to say "Mr." and "Mrs." to a black person or to pronounce the word "Negro." Most white southerners say "Nigra"; and who wants to be called "Nigra?" They seem incapable of making the "e" sound, but this inability does not nullify the truth. Some black people today object to the word Negro ("El Negro" from the Spanish conquistadors and the Portuguese slave masters) because they say White America has used it for racist purposes, or for the purposes of slavery and segregation. They say that in American society it is used as a stigmatizing word which automatically relegates a man or woman to subhuman status. Hence, what some scholars at one time called Negro literature is now rejected because of the word Negro. African American recognizes the two basic cultures of Orient and Occident in African Americans. I know many people, close friends and even relatives, who object to being called "black." They would prefer to be known as colored, since they no more look black than white people look white, as far as skin tone is concerned. But in South Africa the word "colored" is also used to categorize people in a stigmatizing fashion. So you see what happens in a land where people are not people, but red, black, brown and white, all blood kin, and not speaking to each other. Our literature reflects this world, this divided world of East and West, of black and white.

III

Insofar as literature is created, evaluated, analyzed, and synthesized, black writers have produced a literature in America that can be considered in terms of form and content, language, style, and tone, as every other world literature. If one is aware that black writers are sometimes inclined toward an Anglo-Saxon tradition rather than our own African American tradition, then analysis of subject matter and form should not be too difficult. When we speak in the vernacular of our people; when we deal with folkways, folk beliefs, folk sayings; when we revolt against form and create new rhythms, improvise as the jazz musicians do, sing the blues, or dance the limbo, then we are dealing with an idiom that is indigenous to black people, always natural, freely experimental, always humanistic, and most of all authentic to what is most real in the black experience; we are following an ancient tradition that is definitely *not* Anglo-Saxon.

Two major facts have governed black life in America from colonial days to the present: most black people are working people and most black people are poor people. This labor and poverty have determined our lives and our lives have determined our literature. Whether as peasants on southern plantations or as laborers in northern cities, black people have remained at the bottom of the economic scale in America (the lumpen); as slaves or freemen, our people have been basically poor and the problems of poverty are the problems of our lives. Understanding the sociology of Black America should help all readers, black and white, to understand the literature.

We have experimented with all forms and with no form. African American literature in its most indigenous expression is not written in any Anglo-Saxon form but takes the form of all Oriental literature, which all western writers have copied or modified into free alliterative verse with the use of all such devices as one uses to get music into that free verse, including the key to wisdom, literature, parallelism and thought.

The folk ballad is not as Oriental as that free line of alliterative verse, nor is the sonnet, but the Arabs were masters of the nomadic song and the love lyric, as well as the song of praise. All Asia and Africa sang before the Saxons recorded their epics and romances. The black people in America do have a heritage, ancient as life and mankind's record of that life; and in a new land, in a strange land, even as slaves, songs have been sung in a new language out of which came a new art to express their pain.

Anyone who reads African American literature, particularly the poetry, will understand what is meant by this gift of song. They will discover the individual voices each speaking in their own tongue, the racial vernacular, and the adopted language to which they have contributed so much.

From the eighteenth century until the present, we can trace the problems of black people and see their suffering transmuted into song; not always a song of joy or love, not always a cry of pain, but sometimes a stern impassioned plea for justice, sometimes with a bitter note of anger, or sometimes the rousing note of social protest against slums and poverty, substandard education and housing, disease and war. But throughout the literature, there is a faithful record of what life has been for black people in America for four hundred years. It is also a remarkable affirmation of the human spirit that against all odds does *prevail.* It is not nearly so remarkable that God could make a poet black and bid him sing, as Cullen so aptly put it, for song is his gift. What is most remarkable is that this song can rise above the tragic world in which we all live and transcend our misery.

Notes

1. Walker's discussion of Africa as the original civilization and the source of humankind is in keeping with contemporary debates over the origin of the human species.

2. Oriental here refers to the ancient or traditional world of the East, Africa and Asia, i.e., the ancient non-white world. Occident is a historical term for Europe, or the West.

Part III

On Black People, Mississippi, and U.S. Politics

(1984)

On Money, Race, and Politics

     I COME TO THIS occasion ill equipped for the tremendous task before me. It is not as a speaker or writer that I feel unprepared because I have spent a lifetime speaking and writing. I am, however, neither a political scientist nor an economist; I am neither a politician nor a money expert. I come as a layman in the field, as your average American citizen, an everyday consumer of goods; a registered voter; a concerned person for the quality of life for all black people, and especially for black Mississippians in this crucial decade of the eighties. I speak to you today as a woman, mother and grandmother, a wife and daughter, sister, et cetera. I am that person who shops every week for groceries to feed her family, who finds the market basket costing more and more dollars to fill. I am the black woman who is insulted daily by the clerks and underlings who take my hundreds of dollars for escalating utility bills: telephone, electricity, water, and natural gas. At the gasoline pump or filling station, my dollar no longer buys a gallon of gas,

---

This essay was originally delivered as a speech supporting Leslie McLemore's bid for Congress from Mississippi.

and twenty dollars will not fill my automobile tank with unleaded gasoline.

My husband and I are retired and we live on a fixed income. What happens if we are stricken by catastrophic illness and need expensive health care and must pay exorbitant drug bills? When we are dead how much does it cost for a decent funeral and standard burial? Will the prices double next year or when will they reach a ceiling or bottom out?

I am that mother whose married children working and raising a family are appalled at the cost of building a house, an average house, any kind of house. I am a grandmother, and I wonder how much it will cost for my grandchildren's parents to send each one of them to college.

I am talking about the practical business of living; about our money problems, our economic dilemma, and I cannot promise to give you the professional theories for their solutions because I know you and I don't give a tinker's dam about their theories and their scientific ideas. We want to know what is going to be done about this *mess* we are in *now!* Who is going to help us get out of this jam, and how long are we going to be the victims of an evil system that works against us while it feeds itself upon us?

If all these problems are happening to me, what about those less fortunate than I am, the poorest of the poor, those living on welfare and food stamps and victims every day of the brutality of the white police?

Do you know that government is the master of our lives? Do you know that without a change, a far-reaching and radical social change, none of us can be saved?

There is a long history behind our poverty and our lack of power and our inability to control our lives and our destiny. We could begin with chattel slavery and proceed through the long years of segregation when the lynch rope, the bayonet, and the poll tax or the grandfather clause kept us intimidated, disfranchised, and demoralized. Dispossessed, disinherited, despised, and denied all human rights, we have spent more than a century protesting and fighting for our inalienable rights of life, liberty, and the pursuit of happiness. The civil rights movement of the sixties was a climaxing period of revolt against tyranny, and the civil rights acts and laws of 1964, 1965, and 1967 promised to guarantee the voting rights and all civil rights to us. Now we are faced with cruel tides of reaction, reprisal and repression that threaten to inundate us again. Our immediate answer is in the ballot box. Voter registration drives were and must continue to be coupled with voter education. It is very important, first, to vote, and it is important, second, to know who you are voting for, what you are voting for and why.

During the Republication administration of Nixon, Rockefeller, Ford, and Kissinger, the Western world of capitalism underwent a monetary crisis; manipulating money and rigging the price of oil, whether from Iran or Saudi Arabia and whether from OPEC or Wall Street, meant changing the economic order of the whole Western world. The Shah is dead, but the Shah's partners are alive and rich and well in these United States today.

Israel, South Africa, and Brazil have their heaviest foreign investments from American billionaires and their economies are the direct results of American banking interests. There is no doubt that these are contributing causes to an impoverishment of this country. The price of bread is no longer determined in the market by the price of grain but by the price of a barrel of oil. Our American domestic economy has changed, and the political system has been reeling and rocking and teetering back and forth ever since. If you don't believe me, believe inflation, unemployment, banking and business failures or bankruptcies and the rapidly devaluating currencies while the price of gold fluctuates and the stock market jumps up suddenly sky-high or plummets to the ground. The election four years ago meant Mr. Carter with more of the same or Mr. Reagan with worse. The present Reagan administration has written off poor and black people. It concentrated on an astronomical spending program for the Pentagon—all military and space programs. This hardly seems in the interest of peace, poor people, prosperity, or progress.

Here in Mississippi the Civil Rights Movement gave us our first political base in this century with the Freedom Democratic Party. The gains of that movement must not be lost now. The strength of the black vote has only been estimated by its potential in the United States. Whether it is used as a balance of power can only be determined by the test of the black bloc vote. This has never been measured because black people are inclined to be like all potential voters and groups in the United States regardless of their ethnic heritage. We vote Republican and Democratic and independent. Despite black involvement in the Democratic Party for more than fifty years since Roosevelt's coalition including labor, blacks, and other minorities, we have never reaped the political harvest. We have never voted our strength as black and poor people. And that is how we ought to vote for just one time! Vote our concerns, vote our interests, vote our needs, and prove our power. Vote not only for the man who promises us the most but vote for the party or ticket we can influence and make do most for our people. The rich man is not about to fight the rich. Labor is not going to vote against unions and the working man. The Jewish voter is not going to vote for anti-Semites nor against Israel. Why should black people vote against the interests of black voters? How can we hope to determine who is best for us? Let us try one of our own. Try building the strength of that Black Caucus. Remember in *unity*, there is strength. One of us may not be much, but all of us working together means POWER!

One hundred years have passed since a black man from Mississippi sat in the United States Congress. In 1881, John R. Lynch was elected to the Forty-seventh Congress. We have not elected a black man since that time. Hiram Revels, Blanche Bruce, and John R. Lynch all represented Mississippi in Reconstruction years, but since that time we have not heard a black voice from Mississippi speaking in Washington. We need a *voice*. We need a black voice speaking, fighting, and working for the interests of black Mississippians. Such a voice will best represent the common people in Mississippi for he who champions the poor, black, and downtrodden speaks for the best interests of all the people.

We black voters in Mississippi need to send a message to our lily-white brothers and sisters in the Democratic and Republican parties and tell them our time has come. We want our share, and we are no longer willing to sit idly by and let them use us only for themselves. We need to go to the polls on November 4 and send a message to the district, to the state, to the nation and to the world. Vote for a qualified black man from Mississippi. Tell everybody we are tired of the scraps and the leavings from the white man's table. Tell them we are a half-million voters strong; we can elect our own man; we can go to the polls rain or shine, hot or cold; we will be there. Tell them we are tired of shoddy, obscene, immoral white men taking our votes and fighting us, oppressing us, and using us. Our black history in Mississippi is a proud and glorious one. After the end of Black Reconstruction, the great black protest movement began and despite lynching, poll tax, white demagoguery of the Bilbos and Vardamans, despite Senator Eastland, we have won our rights and we have learned our political lessons. A state that can send seventeen black men to the state house and elect black mayors, black constables, black officials on every level, that state can elect a black congressman. If Tennessee and Georgia can do it, Mississippi surely can. The Voting Rights Acts of 1964 and 1965 were laws of liberation. They made us free to vote without reprisal of a grandfather clause, the poll tax, and the threat of the lynch rope. Remember the deaths of our martyred leaders in Mississippi: Medgar Evers and Ditney Smith, Reverend Lee and Fannie Lou Hamer, and those thousands lynched like Emmett Till and Mack Charles Parker and Willie Magee. Remember how they died and what they died for and exercise your right to vote. This is why we have had voter registration drives. Go to the polls and vote. Vote the right way, vote for a black man.

This may be our last chance to make and participate in a democratic society that has never fulfilled our democratic dream nor its full potential for freedom, peace, and human dignity. This may be our last opportunity to turn the clock around and give us a chance.

What about welfare that threatens the life of our people? What about jobs for black Mississippians? What about health care for poor black people in Mississippi? What about the condition of our schools and universities? What about the rape of our land? Our farms and institutions? Send a message, black Mississippians, in this next congressional district election!

We need a *black voice* in Washington for the people of Mississippi. Elect a black man and insure black people a voice. Send the world a message.

A century is long enough to wait. We can't wait any longer. Look at this sorry mess you white congressmen have made of our rights and our lives. White Mississippians, what have your representatives done lately for you?

BLACK MISSISSIPPIANS, send them a message!

(1989)

On the Civil Rights Movement in Mississippi

IN 1949, when I came to live in Jackson, Mississippi, segregation had a stranglehold on the nation, the state and the city. I have seen eleven governors in forty years. Five of them demagogues, racists, segregationists, all Democrats or Dixiecrats, or boll weevils, and six of them moderates, intelligent and recognizing the need for change in the racial climate in Mississippi.

From 1948 to 1972, the following Mississippians have been governor: Fielding Wright, Hugh White, J. P. Coleman, Ross Barnett, Paul Johnson, John Bell Williams. William Waller was the first moderate because for the first time, Charles Evers was included in the governor's race. In the mid-1970s, black political power began to raise its head and set the stage for a more liberal climate. Consequently, Cliff Finch was elected in 1976, and William Winter, Bill Alain and Ray Mabus soon followed.

Although the Supreme Court decision of May 17, 1954, had outlawed segregation in the public schools of the United States, there was massive resistance to any form of integration, especially in the southern states. Since the masses of black people in this country still lived in the South, the Supreme Court decision was of no use if it did not benefit the black masses. Yet, blacks rode in the back of the bus. Water was colored and white. No restaurant, hotel or gas station provided comfort for black people. Department stores did not allow blacks to try on clothes. Interstate travel was strictly segregated. All education was strictly dual and substandard. Newspapers, radio and, subsequently, television promoted racism with a flourish. Ugly epithets were hurled and printed repeatedly. No black person's name held a title. Human dignity was not considered.

A continuing struggle of protest against segregation had existed from the beginning of the century. But until 1954, the law of the land was still *Plessy vs. Ferguson* of 1896, when a black person had no rights that a white person was bound to respect. Almost every southern state found itself the scene of a pitched battle between black and white.

When did this end? And to whom are we indebted for this ending? The first of these painful encounters occurred in Montgomery, Alabama, with the bus boycott involving Rosa Parks and E. D. Nixon of the National Association for the Advancement of Colored People (NAACP) and forcing to the forefront the leadership of Martin Luther King, Jr. The NAACP was the first of the civil rights organizations to take note of the disturbances and seek redress in the courts. In Mississippi, three persons are martyred to the cause: Medgar Evers, Fannie Lou Hamer, and Vernon Dahmer.

Medgar Evers led the first fights against segregation in the late 1950s. He became field secretary of the NAACP in 1954, and moved to Guynes Street in June of 1956. He was one of the first to apply for admission to the University of Mississippi and worked closely with James Meredith toward that end. Beaten on the bus in Meridian for refusing to sit in the back of the bus, he made his own little children the first guinea pigs for school desegregation. Evers organized voter registration drives and counseled Tougaloo students in the first sit-ins to desegregate the public library. Yet, it was his organization of economic boycotts against the white power structure in downtown Jackson on Capitol Street that was most effective. His last words were the commanding ones, "Let's march!"

Fannie Lou Hamer said she did not know she had a right to register and vote. When she made this discovery, she was a timekeeper on James O. Eastland's plantation in Ruleville, Mississippi. Hamer decided to go to the county seat to exercise her rights, for which she lost her job and was thrown off the plantation.

Nevertheless, she continued to organize her neighbors to register and vote. In fact, Hamer was one of the first people to organize the Freedom Democratic Party. What she lacked in education, she made up for in courage, stamina and determination. For she had the nerve to go to Atlantic City, New Jersey, and say to Vice-President Hubert Humphrey when a compromise was suggested, "We didn't come up here for no two seats."

Hamer, together with Aaron Henry, Reverends Lawrence Guyot and Herbert Lee, Ditney Smith, Ella Baker, Andy Devine, Victoria Gray, Unita Blackwell, David Jordon, Dr. Gilbert Mason, Jasper Neely, Bennie Thompson, Hollis Watkins, and other community leaders who followed in the footsteps of these brave and martyred people who organized the state of Mississippi into congressional districts; held precinct, county, and state meetings; elected their own delegates, and challenged the Mississippi state Democratic and the National Democratic parties.

For her efforts, Hamer was beaten in Winona, Mississippi, where she was jailed. Two black prison guards were ordered to beat her with night sticks. One guard beat her unmercifully until he was exhausted. Afterwards, she was unable to move. Many believe that her death from breast cancer resulted from those beatings. Fannie Lou Hamer stirred America's soul with her rendition of "This Little Light of Mine, I'm Gonna Let It Shine."

The Mississippi mud and clay are red with the blood of black men and women. Nobody paid for the death of Emmett Till, a four-teen-year-old black boy who was killed and weighted down in the river. Nobody paid for the murder of Mack Charles Parker who was taken from jail and lynched. His body was also later found in the Tallahatchie River. Both of these black males died right after the Supreme Court decision. Certainly nobody paid for the deaths of Medgar Evers, Fannie Lou Hamer, Vernon Dahmer, Reverend Herbert Lee, and Ditney Smith.

Mississippians looked on as Daisy Bates and nine high school students fought and integrated the Little Rock High School. Martin Luther King, Jr., was jailed in Albany, Georgia. White mothers of schoolchildren in New Orleans contorted their faces with hate, screaming, "Two, four, six, eight, we will never integrate!"

The entire decade of the sixties was marked by these pitched battles and eruptions of violence and riots. In a Louisiana jail, James Farmer confronted the Ku Klux Klan while Gloria Richardson led the cause in the Tidewater country of Virginia and Maryland. Clinton, Tennessee, had its troubles as well.

Although every year within the sixth decade of the twentieth century was violent, the most heinous of them all was 1963. It was the year of Medgar Evers's assassination. Evers was shot in his back while in his own front yard on June 12. Four little girls died while attending Sunday school in the bombing of the Sixteenth Street Baptist Church in Birmingham, Alabama, in September. Finally, President John Fitzgerald Kennedy was also assassinated in Dallas, Texas.

The battle of Birmingham raged, and in 1964, Freedom Summer in Mississippi was marked with the Ku Klux Klan murders of three civil rights workers: Michael Schwerner, Andrew Goodman, and James Chaney in Philadelphia, Mississippi. Nevertheless, the Voting Rights Act of 1965 was the first positive result to combat racial violence and bigotry of ten years. This is the Voting Rights Act that began to work in connection with voter registration drives for the election of black public officials.

Years later, Mississippians now have many elected black public officials, including mayors of cities, state legislators (senators and representatives), a congressman, and a black national committee man in the Democratic Party. Indeed, the Jesse Jackson campaigns for president in 1984 and 1988 are direct results of the civil rights movement in the 1950s and 1960s and the Voting Rights Act of 1965. In 1983, Jackson led a southern crusade of voter registration which resulted in forty thousand new black voters in Mississippi alone. This is also the year when Harold Washington was elected the first black mayor of Chicago, Illinois, as a direct result of a Jesse Jackson–led voter registration drive.

Jackson first came to Mississippi with Martin Luther King, Jr., as a member of the board of the Southern Christian Leadership Conference which met in Laurel, Mississippi. He was in Selma, Alabama with King in February 1965, and in Memphis when King was assassinated in April 1968. Although Jackson was only twenty-six years old then, King's death sealed his mission and destiny. Later that year, Senator Robert Kennedy was also slain by an assassin's bullet in California after winning that state's primary.

And still, this was not enough to squelch the black political fervor that swept through black people's hearts long ago. Jackson challenged Mayor Richard Daley and the Singer delegation in the 1972 convention in Miami, Florida and forced the powerful Illinois delegation from the floor because there were no blacks represented. This was also the year that Richard Hatcher (mayor of Gary, Indiana), Amiri Baraka (LeRoi Jones), and Jackson organized an independent black political party which ended four years later in Kansas City. Although Congresswoman Shirley Chisholm made a bid for the presidency in 1980, it was 1984 when Jesse Jackson made a spectacular bid and carried four hundred delegates to San Francisco.

Jackson's Rainbow Coalition seeks social justice in America, peace in the world, a drug-free society, and education for excellence, which is only reminiscent of Franklin Delano Roosevelt's coalition in the 1930s. This political plan of that radical era also envisioned Blacks, Jews, and Gentiles together, labor and management sitting at the table of fellowship. Roosevelt's coalition turned a society that was demoralized by its Republican president, Herbert Hoover, and helped us turn the corner to prosperity.

Not surprisingly, the coalition of the New Deal and this civil rights movement became targets of Nixon/Reagan/Bush Republicanism. The Reagan revolution toward neofascism and fascistic terror began in 1964 with the defeated campaign of Barry Goldwater. The arch-conservative wing of the Sunbelt and the West revolted against the leadership of the liberal northeastern Republicanism of Nelson Rockefeller, Senators Javitz and Brooke, and Eisenhower, who were Republicans who had dominated that party's political scene for fifty years.

The arch-purpose of Reagan and Bush administrations has been to destroy all forms of liberalism in the Republican Party, the New Deal of Roosevelt and Truman, the Warren Supreme Court, and the civil rights successes of Kennedy, Johnson, and Carter.

Jackson is the last best hope of Black America. For some, he is the anointed messiah. For others, in the words of George Bush, "that hustler from Chicago." Somewhere in between is the man Jesse Jackson.

(1980)

Mississippi and the Nation

MISSISSIPPI STANDS on the threshold of a decade of destiny. Her potential is great and her future is, indeed, brighter than usual. As we compare our state here in the Sunbelt with other states in and beyond this region, we have reason to take courage today and hope for a bigger and better Mississippi. Of course, when we look at the past and the future, we must take into consideration the outlook for the nation and a global look at the world in general in order to see Mississippi in perspective.

This state has never been the typical sample of the United States because we have here a unique and peculiar position. History declares that we have been among the last of the states formed along the Mississippi River when that body of water was the western frontier of colonial North America. When she was admitted to the Union in 1817, Mississippi was still largely wilderness with hundreds of acres of virgin forest and soil. A rural state with an agricultural economy, Mississippi remained almost virtually untouched by

This essay was originally delivered as a speech at Mississippi Governor William Winter's Inaugural Symposium, 1980.

the Industrial Revolution for a hundred years, from the middle of the nineteenth century until the middle of the twentieth century.

Then, suddenly, like an explosion of time, this state felt the weight of both the Industrial Revolution and the Einsteinian or electronic revolution almost simultaneously. The result of that explosion has been nearly a quarter of a century of phenomenal growth, an attempt to balance diversified and light industry with agriculture and the establishing of three major economic assets: the Space Center NASA, expansion of Ingalls Shipyard at Pascagoula, and the great Tombigbee Waterway. Mushrooming manufacturing centers, with major plants and industries from the Northeast establishing branches in the Sunbelt here in Mississippi, cause a healthy economy to assume a brave new look, and all this in the face of mounting unemployment and inflation all over the nation.

Mississippi may not be typical of the national economy; however, we are typical in that we are a part of the great pluralistic fabric of this nation. Historically, Mississippi has been home to four races in the family of mankind: Native Americans were here first—the Chickasaw and Choctaw, the Creeks and the Natchez. The white men from Europe imported Black Africans to build their cotton plantations, and the Delta has for more than a century been home to a group of Asian Americans. They came when the railroads were crossing this land. Mississippi is, therefore, multiracial as well as multicultural. William Faulkner has written this history in prize-winning fiction, and Richard Wright, a "Native Son," began his search for a common ground of humanity here in his native Mississippi. It is along these multiracial and multicultural lines that I wish to examine the challenges that face Mississippi and our American nation.

The economic, political, and social factors are only the necessary background for more specific indicators of a good life in Mississippi and what we can hope and expect in the future. As an African American woman, I am concerned about what type of opportunities will be available for people of color during this decade as far as education, family, community life, health, recreation, and the cultural life of Mississippi as well as the country. If the world is at war, then we are at war. If inflation persists and unemployment rises while the problems of energy and world hunger remain unsolved, Mississippians cannot help but be affected in every area of our lives.

Perhaps an even greater challenge lies in what may seem intangibles and abstractions, but which are of utmost importance if we as a state and a nation are to develop the indomitable will and the stamina we need to meet the challenges of a new decade and a world already in social upheaval. These intangibles and abstractions are no less than the spiritual, ethical, and religious values which form the bedrock of our American culture that we have from its inception considered fundamental. Today, the superpowers of the world are locked in a deadly ideological conflict. We now can look back on several decades of war and revolution. Europe, Asia, Africa, the Caribbean islands, and the South Pacific have been drenched in a blood bath of combat and upheaval. Although the United States has escaped war on its own soil during the twentieth century, that is not to say we have not been involved.

Mississippi has given her sons in every war of the century, for her finest youth have bled and died in foreign wars. Foreign policy involves us and is as relevant as any national or global issue. Whether that foreign policy is one of isolationism or globalism, the necessity for intervention in foreign affairs must continue to place us on the horns of a dilemma. Yet, foreign combat is only one of the specters and phenomena of the century. In the short space of our lifetime, the world has witnessed the horrible specter of famine and hunger in at least five countries: China, India, Bangladesh, Biafra, and now Cambodia. These are non-European countries, but this segment of suffering humanity must not and cannot be ignored. World famine and the problem of raising enough food to feed the world is a preeminent challenge to a state that is largely rural and agricultural as well as a test to the nation as a whole. This demand must be met now. Obviously, the problems of energy must be seen as inextricably bound to the problems of unemployment and inflation as well as oil and our foreign policy.

When the twentieth century began, the price of a loaf of bread in the world marketplace was determined by the cost of grain, whether wheat, corn, oats, millet, rice, or barley. Now it is determined by the price of a barrel of oil. We have recently witnessed a shift in the economic order of the world. We must now meet the challenge that the shift demands.

The challenge to state gubernatorial administrations is to meet the crisis in leadership that we are witnessing all over the world. Our governors promise positive and competent leadership. Nothing short of this will suffice. Certainly, this is a Herculean task and I am sure they recognize that leadership for tomorrow must come from our youth of today. Therefore, we must re-examine our educational system in Mississippi and America in order to develop the creative thinking of our young people and prepare them for imaginative leadership if they are to meet the challenge of destiny. All over America we are still basing our educational system on Newtonian physics together with a fundamentalist religious faith and a narrow and bigoted belief about people who look and think differently from us. In the past, the Einsteinian revolution gave us a new concept of the universe, and although our post–World War II world has seen an electronic revolution in space, atomic energy, cybernation, and automation, we have still not witnessed an intellectual change in basic ideas about education, religion, race, and culture.

We need to stretch our minds and faith in order to accommodate our thinking to the problems of our systemic crises so that we can meet the current demands. We need to understand the Einsteinian principles of unity in diversity—racial and cultural diversity as well as an illimitable universe with a space-time continuum. Then we can better understand our pluralistic world. We need to develop international understanding and peace on the basis of such unity in cultural and racial diversity. We need to develop religious tolerance so that we respect all religious faiths and know that God is truly the Father/Mother of all humanity. Every man is our brother. Every woman is our sister. Every child has the light of God. All human personality is holy and divine.

My family has been involved in education for African Americans in Mississippi for over one hundred years. In 1878, my great-uncle, James A. Ware (the Jim of *Jubilee*), and my grandfather, the Reverend Edward Lane Dozier, a Baptist minister (who married Minna in my novel), came to the Mississippi Delta and established a school for black children in the oldest black Baptist Church in Greenville. Uncle Jim died there in 1932. During the school year 1920–21, my mother and father taught school at the Haven Institute in Meridian and there I went to school for the first time.

In the 1940s, my sister came to Prentiss Institute for her first teaching experience, and I have been in Mississippi since 1949 at Jackson State University, where I retired in 1979. When I came, it was with the full intention of staying and making Jackson my home, as well as a home for my family, husband, and then three children (a fourth was born several years later) and now my grandchildren. Why have I remained in Mississippi so long and, now that I am retired, why don't I leave?

I believe that despite the terrible racist image Mississippi has had in the past, despite her historic reputation for political demagoguery, despite racial violence and especially lynching, despite all the statistics about being on the bottom, Mississippi, and especially urban Mississippi, offers a better life for most black people than any other state in which I have lived or visited. I have lived in the Middle West, the Northeast, the border South, and the Deep South. I have traveled through thirty-five of these United States, particularly the eastern half and this side of the Rocky Mountains. I observed on first coming to Mississippi in the 1940s that most black people in Mississippi are thrifty, proud, and generally intelligent, notwithstanding substandard and dual systems of education. In Jackson, the average African American family struggles to own a home, pridefully maintain it, send their children to college, and participate in their community as law-abiding and voting citizens. Mississippi has an impressive number of African American public officials.

Our martyred dead, Medgar Evers and Fannie Lou Hamer, as well as Martin Luther King, have not died in vain. Not only is Mississippi noted for beautiful women (past Miss Americas and Miss Black Americas have been from Mississippi) and great athletes, but it is also a proven climate for genius for William Faulkner, Tennessee Williams, Richard Wright, Eudora Welty. The folk culture of Mississippi is part of my heritage; therefore, it is home.

Superficially, Mississippi has an ideal climate, a mild winter and a long growing season. She also has a growing economy, better housing for all her people, and widening recreational opportunities. The problems with welfare and public programs are the nation's dilemmas. Yet health costs, hospitals, doctors, and pharmaceuticals are less in the South than in the Midwest and the Northeast. Even high taxes are comparatively lower. If school integration has worked well anywhere in the nation, which is doubtful, it has worked better in Mississippi than in most other places. There is documented proof of this. Life is not idyllic in Mississippi for black or white. The same hard realistic facts of American life prevail here as elsewhere;

however, the radical climate is certainly no worse. The civil rights movement liberated both black and white. A more liberal racial climate has helped business and politics; therefore, the society is more open and generally better. Today, there is hope for a change and an improved tomorrow. Mississippi has been the determining factor in past presidential elections. She may well be again in the future.

All of us must be prepared for the drastic changes coming, if for no other reason than that we are already living in another age, and the next century is already upon us. Mississippi, like all the rest of this nation, must be prepared to meet the challenges and cope in every respect with the changes of a new decade. A decade of destiny.

We must be prepared to deal with world revolution and sinister war threats, to cope with ideological conflict and culture shock, to deal with a shifting economic order and, not least of all, with multiracial, multicultural diversity. We must test our spiritual endurance and our religious faith if we are to survive, not only as a state and a nation, but as a people, as humanity on the planet earth.

(1988)

Jesse Jackson, the Man and His Message

JESSE JACKSON is first a black man and secondly a Baptist preacher. Born in South Carolina in 1941, educated at North Carolina Agricultural and Technical College and Chicago Theological Seminary, he is in the tradition of the black Baptist preacher who has led black people from the antebellum days of Nat Turner to Adam Clayton Powell, to Martin Luther King, Jr., his mentor. Jackson is a direct disciple of Dr. King, working from his youth with the Southern Christian Leadership Conference.

Highly articulate, dynamic and charismatic, he has proven himself a national leader with the stature of an international figure. As a minister of the gospel—good news—of the Christian faith, he is one of the prophetic minority with a sense of mission and of destiny. Calling himself a country preacher, and having a gift of wit and humor together with an athletic training and background, he relates to all young people, and as a civil rights activist, he brings a special dynamism to the black struggle for political power and social freedom. With a marriage of more than twenty years and father

---

This essay was originally prepared for a volume in progress under the title "Jesse Jackson's Role in Mississippi Black Politics."

of three sons and two daughters, he presents a stable family life as an example to the nation and the world of positive African American life.

He understands the metaphysical connection between contemplation and action which all his predecessors as religious leaders understood from Turner to Powell to King—how to touch what I call the "feelingtone" of black people. This feelingtone exists in black music and religion, and draws its spiritual and intellectual power from one's innate divinity. With this equipment which is more than theological, metaphysical, and intellectual, but unquestionably all three, Jesse Jackson brings to the American political arena an excitement generated in the Democratic Party by Franklin Delano Roosevelt, John Fitzgerald Kennedy and Lyndon Baines Johnson and in the unfulfilled hopes of Harry Truman and Jimmy Carter. In 1988, news commentators called Jesse Jackson the greatest political orator since William Jennings Bryan. He promises to do what only one of them (FDR) was able to accomplish, which is to turn this nation around from a depressed, demoralized society and a hell-bent, death-dealing course toward war and nuclear destruction—to a look forward toward peace, health, prosperity, domestic tranquillity, and world security.

Jackson alone on the political scene has both the knowledge, charisma, and the spiritual power needed at this tragic moment of destiny in American history. He is not a "me-too-man" like all the other pygmies around a giant's feet. He neither resembles the neoconservative fascism of the present administration nor the colorless do-nothing policies of those Democrats afraid to speak out of fear they may lose their blind and helpless constituents.

On the economic front, Jackson used both Operation Breadbasket and PUSH (People United to Save/Serve Humanity) to bring economic gains to the black community. He confronted big business with economic boycotts and literally forced some of the money made in the black community by such corporations as Coca-Cola, Pepsi Cola, Kentucky Fried Chicken, Budweiser beer, and Seagram whiskey back into Black America by means of franchises, employment, and other forms of affirmative action. Nearly a decade ago, he began with PUSH to move a program for excellence in education through the black community. This caught on nationally and is now a number-one priority in the nation for our educational needs.

Voter registration is undoubtedly Jackson's greatest political contribution, first to the city of Chicago, second to the South, and third to the nation at large. There is no doubt that voter registration in Chicago was a large factor in the election of Chicago's first black mayor, Harold Washington. This is a direct carryover from the civil rights movement in the 1960s. The challenge now to the National Democratic Party is buttressed by the large potential of a registered black electorate. "One man–one vote" and the ending of racial quotas is a part of Jackson's campaign for the presidency. With this large voter registration he hopes not merely to challenge the status quo of politics as usual but also to achieve parity through the election of many black candidates on the local, state, regional and national level. This parity is one of the goals of his campaign. Regardless of the final outcome, this is a worthy goal. This is not just a means to an end, it is both the means and the end.

Watching Reverend Jackson on television, one has to admire his style, aplomb, wit, and common sense. His judgment has been unerring. Cries from critics of his flamboyance were also used against the equally handsome, self-assured Adam Clayton Powell. The Reverend Powell was also articulate, magnetic, and zealous for the redemption of black people who he served in the halls of Congress. Yet, we broke Adam Clayton Powell's heart with our ingratitude. The enemy killed Martin Luther King, Jr., and the racist writers demeaned Nat Turner. We should remember and learn well the lessons of history.

Jackson threatens to break this nation out of the box of "do nothing" stagnation at home and abroad while the neoconservative right-wing politicians continue to restructure our nation and world into a fascist nightmare of nuclear war and terror. Be wary of this enemy, for he is both powerful and formidable. Hunger, disease, ignorance, the children of poverty, and widespread unemployment are sapping the life out of our American people today while a few multibillionaires determine the course of our world toward Armageddon.

Jesse Jackson's achievement in bringing Navy Pilot Robert Goodman out of Syria is the *piece de resistance,* for it says to the world three things: (1) An ecumenical approach of conciliation and reconciliation is the only method that will work in the Third World toward peace and economic stability. (2) Only a black person in the present world order can deal effectively and successfully with that larger Third World of billions of people who are not white; for, Jackson did not speak down to this Third World nation in ugly racist condescension, but looked them right in the eye. (3) It says that prayer, religious faith and other weapons of spiritual power effect more by talking than guns, threats and money can ever do.

What is Jesse Jackson to these United States of America? He wants to be president of the U.S.A.? If that were all, it would be a little more than an empty fantasy. There are several others making that vapid statement. His candidacy is enough, however, to raise the sights and consciousness of every poor, black, and nonwhite child in America, those millions in a rainbow coalition who have been told, "No Negroes, Jews, Catholics, or women need apply."

Yet, what can he do against the twelve oil companies who brought Ronald Reagan to power after twelve years of preparation? What can Jesse Jackson do against the twenty-five corporate structures determined to prevail with money and the military, those powerful tools of fascism used against the people? Alone he can do nothing; however, leading a nation with unity and vision, he can powerfully help to effect real social change. He can turn this nation around and look with health, intelligence and fortitude toward a better world. If White America, and particularly the establishment in the Democratic Party, turns thumbs down on his sensitivity and insight, ignores and obstructs his push toward political empowerment and social freedom for black people, gives the usual order to kill or assassinate him, and once more frustrates one-third of a nation by denying this last chance for civilization and humanity to prevail, what can America say about the doom of impending Armageddon? More than that, what will poor America do?

Equally devastating and annihilating as assassination is the combined efforts of neoconservative Republicans and Democrats to nullify Jackson. Don't kill him and make another martyred black leader. Neutralize and nullify him, but do not crucify him!

There are all kinds of strategies and propaganda used against Jackson. Money from the Arabs and Third World foreign countries? What about it? How many White Americans have taken and continue to receive Arab money? Or more specifically, how much Arab money is invested in real estate and other markets in this country? Is it better that good Americans have financed Israel to the tune of a million dollars a day to buy peace in a land where there is none? All of Jackson's campaign money could not be coming from Arabs. Some of us know it is also coming from the grassroots of the people. We know that he could not have qualified for matching funds without those grassroots.

What does Jesse Jackson mean to black people in Mississippi? What can he do to address the problems of African Americans here as well as other places in the country? How has he been involved already in Mississippi politics? What do African American people in Mississippi owe Jackson? How does he compare with other presidential candidates on the issues that affect black people in Mississippi? Who does Jackson represent?

Jesse Jackson is not as old as African Americans' involvement with the Democratic Party in the U.S.A. In the 1930s, Franklin Delano Roosevelt formed a coalition with black people, labor, northeastern Jewish liberals and intellectuals, as well as poor whites from the grassroots of Appalachia, and he won election to the office of the president four successive times! A rainbow coalition of women, Hispanics, and black people has potentially the same thrust.

Mississippi's black Democrats, however, reach back only to the Freedom Democratic Party of the 1960s. It was that party that challenged the old conservative wing and Dixiecrats of the National Democratic Party and won seats in the national convention. That party was an outgrowth of the civil rights movement in Mississippi with the martyred leadership of Fannie Lou Hamer, the intrepid Medgar Evers, and Martin Luther King, Jr. Yet the most effective tools of that movement are Jackson's voter registration drives which play a crucial role in ending dual registration in the county and city hall as well as the double primaries which are deliberately designed to defeat all black candidates on the basis of race.

What are the issues facing this country now, issues critical to Jackson's 1988 presidential campaign, and to any candidate for national election? The first issue is jobs. Bread and jobs are the most crying needs in the black community. While the Bush era declares 6.8 percent unemployment nationally, black unemployment is 12.1 percent and for black teenagers, 34.3 percent.

The end of an industrial phase of our economic system and the beginnings of a new world of high technology and electronic revolution have left black people without the skills needed to enter fields of high technology. This is equally true for poor whites and Hispanics. Women are doubly discriminated against by men in the marketplace. At the same time, the United States government has bolstered the economics in countries of Western Europe (particularly in a defeated Germany) and the Asian countries of Taiwan in China, Japan, and Korea so that their technology equals ours and threatens to surpass us. Their cheaper labor enables them to produce and sell us more goods than our troubled economy can produce and provide. Welfare recipients in Mississippi, both black and white, belong to the vast army of the unemployed, while our clothes, toys, appliances, automobiles, china, and even our foods are imported goods. Our biggest export market is in guns and ammunition or war materials, and we make few of those in Mississippi.

A second major issue, if not alternating as number one, is the issue of war and peace. Foreign policy does not concern us? When black boys from Mississippi have shed their blood and died on foreign fields in every war in this century? So many blue boxes from Vietnam came home with black bodies. Some of them were the last surviving males in their families. Of course, African Americans protested to our senators and the war department with scarcely no effect. Decimating the black population has been a desired goal on the part of white Mississippi politicians from the days of slavery through the career of ex-governor J. P. Coleman, who said, "The trouble with Mississippi is we have too many black people."[1]

Lynching, starvation, northern migration, and foreign war have all served to decimate the black population in Mississippi. From a vast majority we have become a barely equal number, yet we don't have an equal representation in political action on the local, state and national levels. This is one point on which Jackson offers relief to black people in Mississippi. A fight for parity in elected officials through immediate and radical social change from an oppressive system to a more just and representative society and using the political process to effect change on all levels. It begins with voter registration and proceeds with lawsuits to enforce the voting rights laws and concerted efforts to end dual registration and double primary elections. Two cannot be a primary. Only one election is a primary. In Mississippi, we are living with constitutions and governments so outmoded as to be seventy to one hundred years old. They date back to a time before the industrial revolution came to Mississippi, much less the electronic revolution of the mid-century.

Jackson has repeatedly come to Mississippi to address the problems of black people here and to help with voter registration, elections and key political issues affecting everybody. Justice in the courts, jobs and action in the marketplace—ending the arms race and the development of nuclear missiles around the world—these were great issues in the presidential race of 1984. Where did other candidates stand on these issues and the multiple problems of black people? Jesse Jackson was number one on all the issues that faced black people. Walter Mondale was perhaps second, despite his mistakes in Chicago during the Harold Washington mayoral campaign. Gary Hart was third, and Ronald Reagan was fourth, if anything.

"Who is Jesse Jackson?" was the question asked by the white press in 1984. "What does Jesse Jackson want?" was 1988's inquiry. The implication in these two queries tells the story. He is a threat to the political status quo. From the summer of 1984 in San Francisco to the summer of 1988 in Atlanta, an entire eternity of time seemed to pass. We went from night to broad daylight, and the meaning of the twentieth century in America bourgeois democracy was summed up in one word: "racism." Jesse Jackson is the most knowledgeable candidate, speaks to the issues, has the right ideas, but he cannot win because he is black.

In 1984, Jesse Jackson was knocking on the door of the Democratic Party asking the party to let us in—African Americans, Hispanics, Native Americans, Asian Americans—the whole Rainbow Coalition. Insofar as rule platform and delegates were concerned, the party of Walter Mondale offered no concessions to Jesse Jackson. They had already decided that his voting strength in delegates would be one-fourth or approximately four hundred delegates. They believed that a white woman must be considered for vice-president before a black man could be considered, and there would be no minority planks in the platform.

Jesse Jackson had his foot in the door, and he was allowed to make a conciliatory speech—apologetic and humiliating to his followers, but nevertheless a great speech. For it was a sermon and it brought tears to the eyes of black and white regardless of their chosen candidates. However, I was not crying. I was too mad to cry. I looked around in amazement to see delegates dissolved in tears. And as my more militant fellow delegates declared, "We had nothing, not a thing to take back home from that convention. After all, any good black Baptist preacher can preach—my grandfather knew how to preach a hundred years ago." What kept ringing in my ears was the gospel song in that speech, "God is not through with me yet."

I was a delegate-at-large in 1984, and I found it impossible to be aware or conscious of everything that was happening. It was my first convention, and I lived too far away from the center of things. I was living all the way up at Fisherman's Wharf, and the convention was down in the cavernous depths of Moscone. Nevertheless, in 1988, I was a delegate from the fourth district, and I went to the meetings diligently. I lived with the Mississippi delegation and that made the difference. I knew people on the rules and platform committees both times, but I was really stunned to see how hard work and careful plans went awry in 1984.

Most of the delegates from Mississippi were my friends, and they were divided into two camps—Mondale and Jackson. When Jesse Jackson delegates booed Andrew Young and Coretta Scott King cried, a young woman reporter from the *Wall Street Journal* came over and accosted me. She could see my lips were closed and my face in a frown. I was truly upset. "Why are these people booing? Aren't these people your civil rights leaders?" I told her, "Yes, they are, and they have always been respected as such, but that is not the issue here." "What was the issue here?" she asked. I replied, "The issue is the vote on the majority plank versus the minority plank. Jesse Jackson delegates are for the minority plank, and Mr. Young has just spoken for the majority plank. And I presume Mrs. King is upset and embarrassed because they are booing him."

Needless to say, the minority plank lost. All the planks proposed by Jesse Jackson lost, even though Gary Hart delegates joined hoping to get their plank in the platform. They lost as well. The black vote was split—actually fragmented among Mondale, Jackson, and Hart. Mondale supporters, including Andrew Young, were part of the Carter administration; therefore, their loyalties were divided. Young's distinguished career in Washington was within the Carter-Mondale administration.

Jackson won the Mississippi primary in 1984, and went on to win Super Tuesday in 1988, which gave him seven southern states. This was a base to build labor votes in the North until he was stopped after a successful campaign in Michigan. Wisconsin was a clear indication that Democrats had broken the rules by allowing Republicans (who had already elected Bush) to cross over and vote against Jackson in the Democratic primary.

My first pleasant surprise came at the Jesse Jackson meeting in the Marriott Marquis in 1988. The place would not hold the people. The press was all but asked to leave—they were pushed back against the wall and delegates were sitting on the floor and standing around the place. I was not impressed with any of the speeches by the stars and dignitaries. They were not saying anything of consequence, but I was impressed with the diversity of race and class in the delegates for Jackson. My mouth fell open when I saw signs reading "Jews for Jesse Jackson" after all that publicity over the "Hymietown" incident, Mayor Koch's remarks that "any Jew voting for Jesse Jackson had to be crazy," and even the Willie Horton manipulation which came later. After all of that, here were groups of people with signs that read, "Jews for Jesse Jackson."

The full-blown flowering for Jackson came the next day when one got the impression that this was Jesse Jackson's convention—the crowd and program, coupled with the rules and platform, and the National Democratic Committee with twelve hundred delegates—were only exceeded by Michael Dukakis. Remember the Democratic presidential nominee field began with eight men, among them Paul Simon, Richard Gephardt, Joseph Biden, Gary Hart, Albert Gore, Michael Dukakis, and Jackson. Jesse had everything to gain and almost nothing to lose (except the nomination and that was not really the greatest prize). I kept hearing the echo of that song, "God is not through with me yet." This time the black vote was not fragmented.

Yet, once we were inside the party, they suddenly changed the rules. The Wisconsin vote and all others after Michigan participated in the "Stop Jesse" movement which had begun. Sadly enough, its participants were black and white influential delegates within the Democratic Party. They were from the South, Midwest and Northeast parts of the country. Then we learned that even the far West, where hard work in voter registration should have paid off, would collapse under the weight of money. The campaign chests in the Democratic Party were just too unequal; Jackson, like the Baptist preacher he is, built most of his campaign on volunteers and donations from poor people.

I realized when I went to Atlanta that it was all over, except the shouting. And what a shouting show they gave us! That Tuesday night the Jesse Jackson red signs appeared to equal if not outnumber the black signs for Dukakis, but that was not the reality. Tuesday was a great day, yet it was an illusion. When I was asked by news reporters if I would work during the campaign in the fall for Dukakis, I told them I didn't think I would be physically able— too old and sick—and I was sitting in a wheel chair then. Then they inquired, "If it were Jesse Jackson, would you work?" I laughed and said, "Of course, even on crutches."

For the first time in fifty years, I seriously considered not going to the polls, but I knew I would, if for no more than making a personal statement for myself. I'm still a Democrat and the only way to change the Democratic Party is inside.

When people in the press asked what African Americans would do in November, 1988, they got the same answers all over the country: (1) vote Democratic as usual, (2) vote Republican in protest, (3) not vote at all, (4) throw away their vote on a third party, or write in a candidate. All the talk about a third black political party seems nonsensical. We have been down that road in the 1970s, two or three times already. We should have learned that lesson of Robert La Follette in Wisconsin. Voting for Lenora Fulani or Lyndon Larouche can only help the Republicans. One man said to me that he could not believe at first that Americans would elect the former head of the CIA to be president, but after Nixon and the Reagan revolution, he knew anything was possible.

And what of the future? Will Jesse Jackson run again? Why not? Is it possible to put any black person in the presidency during this century, such as David Dinkins, Andrew Young, Sharon Pratt Kelly, or Douglas Wilder? The Democrats may control Congress, but do the Republicans have a stranglehold on the presidency? And if the Democratic Party refuses to change any and all of its racist politics, will black politicians accept this racism? Or, will the American people consider the possibility of changing an inflexible system? If change cannot come from the inside, perhaps change will come from the outside, yet change is inevitable. The process of change has already begun.

Note
1. J. P. Coleman (1914–91) was governor of Mississippi from 1956 to 1960.

(1992)

Whose "Boy" Is This?

THE ANITA HILL–CLARENCE THOMAS
episode on national television gives us a cosmic picture of race, gender, and class in twentieth-century United States of America. Politics, education, and religion are reflected in the mirror of ever-changing sexual and monetary morality. Family, church, and school kit-and-caboodle seem nastily exposed in the whole spectrum to our appalled viewing. Recovering from the shock of this subtle, and not-so-subtle pornography, we struggle to analyze its meaning, its purpose, and its attendant phenomena now and in future use.

If we begin with the premise that we have a fascist, sexist, and racist society, understanding this whole sorry spectacle should not be difficult.

Fascist means forced government by the strong, powerful, big money, and big guns. Sexist means a disregard for the rights of women, using women's labor and sex for male purposes, placing women on a lower salary scale than men for the same work, and, most of all, male chauvinists exploiting or using sex to dominate the lives of women.

Racism is the Anglo-Saxon or white man's fight for power and

control over all nonwhite people in the world. Anglo-Saxon strong-
holds are European, American, South African, and Israeli. Let us ask
ourselves a half-dozen questions in order to analyze, assess, and
summarize this conundrum.

Who are these people?
From whence have they come?
Why are they doing this?
How did our country get to this point?
What can we do about it?
What is the lesson we are learning here today?

According to their testimony, Anita Hill and Clarence Thomas
have known each other a considerable length of time. He was her
boss on at least two jobs. Even though she brings the charge of
sexual harassment against him, she continued to have contact with
him, to be recommended by him, and to telephone and congratu-
late him on his promotions and his sudden rise to very powerful
positions until his interracial marriage. This would seem paradoxical if it were not for our basic premise of fascism, sexism, and racism.

Who are these people? They are admittedly buppies—black, up-
wardly mobile, conservative Republicans. They are conservative in
spite of themselves in *race, religion, and politics.* Although he was
educated—first in Roman Catholic schools before prestigious Yale
University, and she was connected to a fundamentalist Protestant
school—they both fit the bill for conservative Republicans—obviously against abortion, or against women's reproductive rights to
control their own bodies, affirmative action, and the basic premises
of the New Deal and the civil rights movement—freedom for justice and human dignity.

Do not misconstrue their protestations. Their ambivalence
merely reflects their confusion. They are both buppies. All their
combined successes in our ultra-corrupt society makes this a positive fact.

How corrupted is our society? From whence did all these people
come? We live in a drug empire. This entire hemisphere is affected
by an economy based on drugs and drug-related crime in a politically fascist police state. We are suffering from a world plague of

sexually transmitted AIDS. We have lived through a century of war and revolution, over land, money, property and race. Although neither Anita Hill nor Clarence Thomas may claim to be paragons of virtue (which they very well may be), they certainly are victims or examples of this corrupted society. They are not outside the pale of this culture. They may believe they are. We know they cannot be.

Sexual and monetary morality question all our behavior. In our biblical morality, lies are as big a sin as adultery—if not as big as blasphemy—against the Holy Spirit. Who is as pure as the driven snow in this case? Do they know what they are saying about each other and about themselves? Psychologically, is he really a sadist and she a masochist? Is he mad with the world because he is black and both white and black men have abused him because of his color? Does she look around her and see herself mirrored in all the dozens of black women whom black men have used and then married white women? What's going on here? Whether they are telling the truth or lying, they have allowed themselves to be trashed on television before the nation, and the mark of Cain is on their heads. Americans still give lip service to standards of biblical morality in the face of ever-changing fascist, sexist, and racist standards where the old ways do not matter anymore. Family structure, religion and school (education) are no longer guided by ancient meaning. The world is not the same place.

One decibel of credit goes to Judge Thomas for realizing this public manipulation of life in a fascist, sexist, and racist society masked under a confirmation hearing is not worthy of the position and is shameful. But the shoe was on his foot. He still got the job. What is the future for Anita Hill? She is the woman, the accepted victim in this sexist mess! Although she never intended it, she was the one trashed before our eyes. She may not have intended to dig a ditch but she certainly did dig two. You can't hurt your brother without hurting yourself. But that is "old" morality.

And that brings us to the racist remark made by Thomas's white wife that Anita Hill was in love with her husband and wanted to marry him. I have heard that infamous remark before this incident. Why would a woman like Anita Hill—good looking, well educated, holding a substantial position—having accused a man of sexual harassment, want to marry that man? Is that snide remark her punishment for having come forward? If she is telling the truth she would have to be out of her cotton-picking (or wool-gathering)

mind to marry any such creature, snail, worm, caterpillar, or croco-
dile! (Silly rabbit.) Then perhaps you say it is all sexual and racial
jealousy of a scorned woman. *Maybe* Clarence Thomas was interested in Anita Hill and if he made those pornographic remarks, he
was trying to titillate her into his bed. How does that sound for
starters? This further elucidates the sexual ingredient in racism.

Contrary to the remark by Clarence Thomas that he was the
victim of racism—that was a red herring of false and mammoth proportions. He placed himself on the side of the racists, sexists, and
fascists—in the bosom of powerful Republicans. True enough, these
are the enemies of all black people regardless of gender, class and
color. I could not believe my ears to hear his mixed metaphors, il-
lusions, and innuendoes in the name of race. Going back to pre-
desegregation days, this man qualified as a white man's "boy"—
bought, paid for, and guaranteed to deliver to "the man." Most
black people view him this way.

I could understand his awkward and painful position as a candidate in the confirmation hearing, but I fail to see him singled out as a
victim of racism. Anita Hill holds that unenviable position. She was
and is the victim of racism, sexism, and fascism. But how sorry can
we feel for her because she has willingly joined a system which she
knows is fascist, sexist, and racist? I know she does not want my pity,
and I have none for her. She is not ignorant, unconscious, nor naive.
She knows about playing with fire and getting burned. I save my con-
tempt and pitiful scorn for Clarence Thomas. He has paid a fearful
price. God help the poor soul who comes before him to be judged! He
is the victim of the kind of abuse and misuse black people cruelly
show their own—within our own ranks—the kind of treatment uppity
blacks or buppies show other blacks because of color, class, and location. Here was a *"nobody"* who came from the misnamed *"lower
class"* black with no money, no position and no prestige. Only whites
befriended him, the nuns first of all. He owes his allegiance to whites,
not to blacks, certainly not black middle-class uppity buppies. He is
exactly where he belongs with a *white conservative Republican* court.
Even in the choice of a mate, he reveals an insecurity in his blackness—perhaps, also in his maleness. Rumor has his first wife, who is
black, saying he was a wife-beater. But he has only three strikes against
him—he has been chosen by friends who are fascist, sexist, and racist.

How did we get to this place in America? Truly television seems
the fourth arm of government, and if we examine the headlines for the

past twenty-eight years, the television story and the printed news should answer all our questions. It is basically a Republican story—a Republican plan, revolution and success story. We could begin with personalities before movements but these will eventually coalesce into our present fascist predicament. We could begin in 1946 with Richard Nixon's election to Congress and his defeat of Helen Gahagan Douglas, but it really does not mean much until Barry Goldwater in 1964 when the southwestern Sunbelt rebelled against such Republican northeastern liberals as Nelson Rockefeller and Senator Javits and their so-called authoritarian control of the Republican Party. The country has since elected three presidents from that conservative Republican Sunbelt—two from California (Nixon and Reagan) and one from Texas (Bush). Kennebunkport, Maine, is Bush's summer home. He votes in Texas. As early as 1968, the fringe of extremist hate groups such as the John Birch Society, the Ku Klux Klan, the neo-Nazis, the Americans for the Preservation of the White Race, and the military–paramilitary America First, and the Skin Heads began to rear their ugly racist and fascist heads in the Republican Party. In these minds, black, liberal, and leftist Democrats are dirty words. The Democratic revolt in the South began with Roosevelt and Truman when the solid white South and white Democratic Primary, which had scorned the black and tan Republicans, began to form the lily-white Republicans. Nixon had the "*plan,*" Reagan had the revolution, and George Bush brought his operation as head of the CIA to form the bases of his foreign policy. All the scandals of Watergate, the Iran-contra affair, the sale of American land and industry to Japan, the breaking of the back of American unionized labor with the aid of the Mafia and the stockpile building of armaments while downgrading education, health, welfare, and the domestic infrastructure. This is how we got to this place. This is why the country can put on a circus on television with complete impunity such as the Anita Hill–Clarence Thomas controversy. This is what the society has been breeding for twenty-eight years. And the worst is yet to come. We have sown the wind. How can we escape reaping the whirlwind?

Does it matter whether the presidential election gives us a Democrat or Republican? Will it end a fascist, sexist, and racist society? Will all the global problems of our planet continue to escape the U.S.A.? Will a new political administration turn around the economy? In our present police state—is there such a thing as the difference between bourgeois democracy and a people's democracy? What is the lesson we are learning here today, and what can we do about it? One, if you play with a puppy, he will lick your mouth. Two, based on the past, the future will take care of itself. We can do nothing to keep it from happening.

In the black 1970s, black nationalists made a crude, raw, and vulgar prediction: "There's a shit storm coming!"

Part IV

What Is to Become of Us?

Notes on Education and Revolution

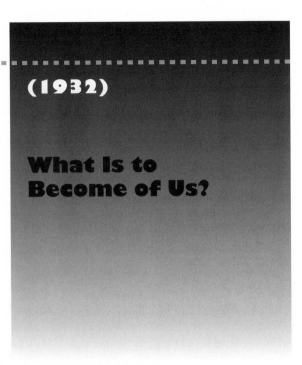

(1932)

What Is to Become of Us?

FROM THE RANKS of hundreds . . . who stand yet within . . . college I venture to ask—What . . . of us? . . . of fellow students who have graduated and been thrown into life by their alma maters. Already they are thrown into a maelstrom of strugglers and seekers who like themselves beat against the doors of employment with frenzied and desperate clamors for entrance with little response.

Many of them are looking back with regret on the courses they took in college in that they were denied vocational guidance. With just two or three months out of school, they send back the message of specialization and vocational emphasis.

Realizing the importance of an education, our race is gradually crowding itself with well-trained high school and college graduates. But in a rush for the necessary education, an important and invaluable item has been overlooked, a worthwhile lesson left unlearned.

This essay originally appeared in 1932 in *Our Youth*, a magazine published by the Colored Juvenile Delinquent Rescue Association in New Orleans. Ellipsis dots indicate text missing from the only copy of the essay available for publication.

Photographed by C. B. Claiborne.

But you brought me to this country.—Gentle-
men, I'm here to stay.

Princes shall come out of Egypt and shall
dwell upon this sod;
Ethiopia is stretching forth her dusky hands
to God;
Righteousness shall stand forever and shall
triumph over sin;
There shall be a peace abiding here within
the hearts of men;
All the low and false conceptions will at
last be done away;
You have brought me to this country,—Gen-
tlemen, I'm here to stay.
                                   E. D. Tyler,
                           Shreveport, Louisiana

DON'T QUIT!

When things go wrong, as they sometimes
will,
When the road you're trudging seems all up
hill;
When you want to smile, but you have to
sigh,
When the funds are low and the debts are
high,
When care is pressing you down a bit,
Rest, if you must, but do not quit.

Life is queer, with its twists and turns,
As every one of us sometime learns,
And many a failure turns about
When he might have won had he stuck it
out,
Don't give up though the pace seems slow—
You may succeed with another blow.

Often the goal is nearer than
It seems to faint and faltering man;
Often the struggle he's given up
When he'd almost grasped the victor's cup,
And he'd learned too late, when the light
came down,
How close he was to the golden crown.

Success is failure turned inside out—
The silver tint of the clouds of doubt,
And you can never tell how close you are;
It may be near when it seems so far;
So stick to the fight when you're the hardest
hit—
It's when things seem worse that you must
not quit.
               —Victorian Railways Magazine
          Selected by Mr. George H. Carpenter

VACATION TIME

Hurrah! for good old Vacation Time,
With cool breezes, clouds, showers and sun-
.... of roses,

Filling [?] children's hands with posies;
Then comes forth beaming hot July
With some days wet and others dry
The children run to the swimming pool,
Forgetting all their books at school;
What care they for the silent books,
When they can swim in the murmuring
brooks.
In a nice cool, quiet place
With mosquito hawks galore to chase?
Now comes August with its lucious fruit—
Every longing appetite to suit;
Oh! for the sweet days of childhood;
Wandering in field, vale and wood;
All hail to Dame Nature
For her blessings rare
Given to childhood days
That know no care.
Could we but use a magic wand, we fain
Would call back those happy days again.
                               Martha A. Sears.

IN THE VORTEX

The author was prompted to write this
article by the conditions of the time. In
this period of great economic depression,
the individual, as well as the nation, is in
the mazes of the vortex of ever changing
existence. Much vision is needed, or he
will be lost in its labyrinths.

It must be borne clearly in mind, however,
that individual, as well as national adjustment, is not a matter of mere chance. Every
act or every series of acts is purposive in
the process of development.

Now, the business world passes through
four regularly recurring cycles, more or
less marked, before it attains its maximum
development. The stage of panic, the
third stage in such a condition of affairs, is
usually termed its vortex. This stage,
nevertheless, is not purposeless, although
apparently chaotic. There is order, for
every subtle event of this cycle is endowed
with a relatively rapid, rotary motion around
the very core of the nation's economic existence. If one were to look below the sur-
face of the ever-varying scenes of this national phenomenon, one would see, or rather
discover, the laws or the general tendencies
which make one condition of events glide
almost unhesitatingly into another. In the
end, the nation finds itself on a firmer foot-
ing than before.

The world has never found itself in such
a vortex as it finds itself to-day. The vortex,
however, has shifted from a national viewpoint to an individual one. The adjustment
must be individual, indeed, versus national;
and in addition to a sane vision, previously
mentioned, as a requisite of national success, another element must be added; namely, a pragmatic but at the same time idealistic philosophy of life.

The formation of such a philosophy is
indeed difficult, but the philosophy as such
is comparatively simple,—simple in diction,
simple in application. "Life—take it as
it comes and make the most of it." Such a
philosophy is within the reach of all. It is
optimistic and not at all fatalistic as it
would appear before a careful scrutiny is
made of same. It is large and catholic; it
is in essence a motive force, truly, however,
incapable of precise scientific analysis; it
is an unquenchable spiritual impulse and is
an adventure to be realized only in words,
for there always will be
Into "something richer and more strange";
"................................ a vortex of change"
it is an interpretation of the dream of Life,
and with its instinct humanity is inalienably
endowed. One cannot escape from such a
philosophy, for one must think one's self
out of the intricacies of the elements of the
present social vortex.

Such a philosophy is the very reflection of
Life in its external truth. It places every
individual above the other to experience
with fortitude "the adversities and the
slings of an outrageous Fortune" and enables him to fight nobly in the vortex; and
it enables him, if necessary, to suffer all,
ently for the mere joy of living.

Again, such a philosophy, "Life—take it
as it comes and make the most of it," sounds
a clarion cry of hope in the presence of
tumultuous ruin and inevitable change. It
develops a message of hope for all humanity, individually and collectively,—a message that is made on the lyre of each individual's personal emotions,—on the pain
or the ecstacy of each human heart; and,
although in the vortex, or in the maelstrom of human existence, the victim may
pass out of the personal into the universal,
at which moment life, in its fullest sense,
is begun, and he may see beyond the vortex,
beyond the whirl of ever changing or even
shifting events, beyond its storms, a new
awakened world, the outgrowth of th[e] vortex, the beginning of a better life for humanity as well as for himself.

With such a sane philosophy one
may greet his every day exi[stence]
feeling:

O winds of Adversity
If the vortex is here
the best of Life
Be far behind."
                                   Geo. H[.]

WHAT IS TO BECOME O[F]

From the ranks of hundreds [of stu-]
dents who stand yet within [the]
college I venture to ask—Wha[t]
of us?

Only a few weeks ago we [...]

passing of fellow students who have graduated and been thrown into life by their Alma Maters. Already they are thrown into a maelstrom of strugglers and seekers who like themselves beat against the doors of employment with frenzied and desperate clamors for entrance with little response.

Many of them are looking back with regret on the courses they took in College in that they were denied vocational guidance. With just two or three months out of school they send back the message of specialization and vocational emphasis.

Realizing the importance of an education, our Race is gradually crowding itself with well trained High School and College graduates. But in a rush for the necessary education an important and invaluable item has been overlooked, a worthwhile lesson left unlearned. As a result the graduate just out of school has found that his education has not been properly guided, he has not been educated to do the thing he is best fitted for, his book learning has not enhanced his native equipment.

We make a mistake when we think any one of us may be either a doctor, lawyer, preacher, teacher, or social worker. All of us are not made to fit into some one of these. But if after careful observation and searching we are able to definitely ascertain whether we have an intellectual or industrial trend of mind, a college education can then make a better cook or gardener or farmer or nurse. In short a college education is not meant purely for those who are specially equipped for the professions alone but if applied the proper way in any field of endeavor coupled with inborn talent it will prove a quicker solution to many of our problems in more ways than we have ever imagined.

As a result of shortsightedness on the part of many of our people heretofore certain industrial phases of life have not been [...] fed by members of our group and [...] too weak to support the professions [...] business concerns that look to [...] open maintenance and growth.

[...] us will invest our college [...]table occupations, with the [...] edge that is necessary to [...] and pay, we shall soon find [...]ell as other Races on a fair [...]erity and economic independ [...]do not, we will remain in the [...] distress, facing the same di- [...]day. With the race compara- [...] stricken, while we continue [...] pittance of our earnings in [...] necessities of life; with the [...] number of openings in prom- [...] employment for the Youth [...] enter, while we are denied

positions in the lucrative but less concerns of others even though conversely our businesses are often through much trickery wrenched from our hands; and with sheer ignorance in many instances blinding us to the importance of cooperation for the benefit of all, despite the fact that we are noticeably progressing, with these cold truths confronting us, what is to become of us if we do not carefully thread our way out of the acute situation we are now in?

The sooner we realize the importance of the common task in the upkeep of the more complex one, of the industrial in conjunction with the intellectual and cease regarding such with an air of condescension and a secret fear of soiling our hands, the sooner we sense the inestimable value of the little job, just so soon will we be able to operate bigger businesses on larger and more successful scales.

The best and quickest way for individual and collective progress is through organized vocational guidance in our Secondary Schools and Colleges. Through it those of us who were meant to be successful, first class carpenters, mechanics or bricklayers would cease striving to be what we often end up as: unsuccessful, second class teachers, preachers, and doctors.

Moreover a good and sure way to succeed in our various occupations is to apply our knowledge wisely in our own environment with a view to bettering conditions there. Thus we follow the principle and words of our great teacher, Booker T. Washington, "Let down your buckets where you are." A further inference from these words may be summed up in this manner: The Negro has a bucket, the tool is in his hand, he has used it and given it to others all over the world, his manual labor has brought enormous profits and stupendous results to nations who have used him as the tool to realize their dreams and ambitions, to materialize their ideas and plans, NOW he must use what is his own for himself, he is putting his brain to school daily, it should and it must supply him with the IDEA, the SCHEME and the PLAN. And now the two together,—his BRAIN and his BRAWN, must work out his own salvation.

Most of the solution to our problems and much of the discoveries on the road to our goal will and does depend upon us. True we have a hard road before us with many heavy odds against us but we are encouraged when we think of the splendid progress made so far and know that in proportion to the difficulties our fathers faced and the hindrances we face today we are indeed fortunate.

Let us bear in mind that if we continue in the way many of our schoolmates have un-

wittingly gone we shall be part of the cause for the coming generations asking and facing the same question as we do, "What is to become of us?" but if we decide to cast our lot in the places where our native talent and equipment can be used to greatest advantage and all in the conquering faith of our fathers we may feel sure not only of a high plane of intellectual and spiritual growth but we will know the answer of "What is to become of us?" politically, financially, and economically.

MARGARET WALKER.

CHILDREN'S PAGE

Continued from page 6
THE BUDS OF HOPE CLUB

The Buds Of Hope Club is for children of all ages, both boys and girls. It does not cost you anything to join. These are the requirements of a member of the Club: You are asked to send in your name, age and address. You are also asked to send in poems, jokes, letters and short articles to the Magazine for publication. Aside from this, you are asked to compile a scrap book containing pictures of great men and women of our Race, poems, jokes and other beautiful pictures and scenery. The Editor of the Children's Page would be glad at anytime to have letters from boys and girls regarding the Children's Page.

NEW MEMBERS OF BUDS OF HOPE CLUB

William Marcus Jackson, 2 yrs., 2228 Dryades St.; Joyce Elaine Butler, 2 yrs., 2127 Loyola Avenue; Carol Elaine Carter, 2009 Loyola Avenue; Audry Davis, 10 yrs., McDonogh School 37, 1508 Iberville St.; Harriet Bourgeois, 12 yrs., St. John Of Arc. 466 Brooklyn Ave.; Doris Mae Gibbs, 8 yrs., Holy Ghost, 2105 Louisiana Ave.; Marguerite Hausmann 12 yrs., Thomy Lafon School; Vallery Hausmann, 9 yrs., McDonogh School 36; Helen Williams, 13 yrs., Danneel School; Quentin Williams, 12 yrs., Danneel School; Catherine Sanders, 13 yrs., A. P. Williams School; Anthom Mitchell, 12 yrs., Valena C. Jones School; Mildred Dennis, 9 yrs., 2517 Derbigny St.; Delorous Bardel, 10 yrs., 2411 Soniat St.; Aline Fowler, 17 yrs., 2013 Iberville St.; Bernadine Alpough 11 yrs., Palmetto, La.; Moses P. Thompson, 12 yrs., 3425 Saratoga St.; W. E. Roberson 5½ months, 2418 S. Liberty Street.

All of the above named members of the Buds Of Hope Club, with the exc[...] ous, reside in N[...]

As a result, the graduate just out of school has found that his education has not been properly guided, he has not been educated to do the thing he is best fitted for, his book learning has not enhanced his native equipment.

We make a mistake when we think any one of us may be either a doctor, lawyer, preacher, teacher, or social worker. All of us are not made to fit into some one of these. But if after careful observations and searchings we are able to definitely ascertain whether we have an intellectual or industrial trend of mind, a college education can then make a better cook or gardener or farmer or nurse. In short, a college education is not meant purely for those who are specially equipped for the professions alone but if applied the proper way in any field of endeavor coupled with inborn talent, it will prove a quicker solution to many of our problems in more ways than we have ever imagined.

As a result of shortsightedness on the part of many of our people heretofore certain industrial phases of life have not been . . . by members of our group and . . . too weak to support the professions . . . business concerns that look to . . . maintenance and growth.

. . . us will invest our college . . . occupations, with the . . . that is necessary to . . . and pay, we shall soon find . . . as other races on a fair . . . and economic independence . . . do not, we will remain in the . . . distress, facing the same di . . . . With the race compara . . . stricken, while we continue . . . pittance of our earnings in . . . necessities of life; with the . . . number of openings in prom . . . employment for the youth positions in the lucrative business concerns of others even though conversely our businesses are often through much trickery wrenched from our hands; and with sheer ignorance in many instances blinding us to the importance of cooperation for the benefit of all, despite the fact that we are noticeably progressing, with these cold truths confronting us, what is to become of us if we do not carefully thread our way out of the acute situation we are now in?

The sooner we realize the importance of the common task in the upkeep of the more complex one, of the industrial in conjunction with the intellectual, and cease regarding such with an air of condescension and a secret fear of soiling our hands, the sooner we sense the inestimable value of the little job, just so soon will we be able to operate bigger businesses on larger and more successful scales.

The best and quickest way for individual and collective progress is through organized vocational guidance in our secondary schools and colleges. Through it those of us who were meant to be successful—first-class carpenters, mechanics, or bricklayers—would cease striving to be what we often end up as: unsuccessful, second-class teachers, preachers, and doctors.

Moreover, a good and sure way to succeed in our various occupations is to apply our knowledge wisely in our own environment with a view to bettering conditions there. Thus, we follow the principle and words of our great teacher, Booker T. Washington, "Let down your buckets where you are." A further inference from these words may be summed up in this manner: The Negro has a bucket, the tool is in his hand, he has used it and given it to others all over the world; his manual labor has brought enormous profits and stupendous results to nations who have used him as the tool to realize their dreams and ambitions, to materialize their ideas and plans. Now he must use what is his own for himself, he is putting his brain to school daily, it should and it must supply him with the idea, the scheme, and the plan. And now the two together—his brain and his brawn—must work out his own salvation.

Most of the solutions to our problems and much of the discoveries on the road to our goal will and does depend upon us. True, we have a hard road before us with many heavy odds against us but we are encouraged when we think of the splendid progress made so far and know that in proportion to the difficulties our fathers faced and the hindrances we face today, we are indeed fortunate.

Let us bear in mind that if we . . . wittingly gone we shall be part of the cause for the coming generations asking and facing the same question as we do, "What is to become of us?" But if we decide to cast our lot in the places where our native talent and equipment can be used in greatest advantage and all in the conquering faith of our fathers, we may feel sure not only of a high plane of intellectual and spiritual growth, but we will know the answer of "What is to become of us?" politically, financially, and economically.

(1972)

Reflections on May 1970

The Jackson State University Massacre

THE EVENTS OF May 1970 which we remember today were happenings of far greater significance and of wider scope than many of us supposed at that time. When we remember the two young men, Phillip Gibbs and James Earl Green, who lost their lives here, and consider the serious injuries of others at that time, nothing seems more fitting than the words Lincoln uttered at Gettysburg, and nothing seems more tragic than the cold reality of our specific situation. Even now, two years later, we recall our deep physical malaise and our even greater mental anguish as we suffered the trauma of those immediate and terrible days.

Although it may be small comfort now either to the bereaved families or to their friends and comrades of all concerned, we must recall those painful hours and re-examine what happened here and know why we must never forget those martyred men nor misunderstand the significance of the trouble then if we would understand our lives today and what is happening to us now.

This essay was originally delivered as a commemorative lecture on the second anniversary of the Jackson State University massacre.

The future of our world, our country, and community, and yes, even of our college, depends on a clear understanding of what was hanging in the balance then and what continues to hang in the balance now. And by balance, I mean the scales of justice where all our hopes of freedom, pride, and dignity are weighed. It is not enough to say that the events of May 1970 at Jackson State College were only a precious fragment of the whole rage of dissent and discontent that spread itself across the nation if not the entire world at that moment. For if we fail to understand the national and international implications of our local predicament, we fail to understand what is most challenging to all our people everywhere in this crucial decade of the 1970s.

We know now that the eruption of violence on campuses all over the nation was not a spontaneous thing. It was planned and organized and powerfully manipulated by forces outside our control. We also know that, although the Committee on Campus Unrest reported the deaths of two students here as "The Killings at Jackson State," none of the murderers was apprehended, indicted, or even reprimanded. In the words of a high official of the state, "The responsibility rests with the protesters." This is what the forces of repression would have us believe. And so, in this sense, justice remains blind, and their deaths go unavenged.

On the other hand, we may not know to what extent the depth charge or bombshell set loose at that time succeeded in retarding and repressing three national movements. As black people, we witnessed systematic attack by local white police on black communities throughout the length and breadth of the land for the next six months. Sometimes these attacks were disguised under the ambiguous term of "shoot-outs," and their victims were specified as Black Panthers or rioters, or merely restless and violent blacks. Specific cities can be recalled but what is more significant is that ninety percent of the United States was affected. Whether we realize or recognize the fact, the racist forces of white control considered a growing wave and movement of black people as a real and present danger to the security of this country. Consequently, the black people were systematically repressed. And no one knows how many of our blacks were killed.

The youth culture or organized student movement was, moreover, berated and vilified as being constituted of "bums," "hippies," "junkies," and young hoodlums. This radical and revolutionary student group was openly attacked and summarily put down as a part of total repression.

And finally, but probably most significantly, the rapidly growing and overwhelming tide of a peace movement was regarded as a definite menace to government foreign policy and the conduct of the Vietnam or Indo-China War. The monthly moratorium marches and demonstrations that began in October 1969 reached a climax in May 1970, and although many white youths risked serious head-breaking in Washington, D.C., in the first week of May of 1971, the multiple and mass arrests with costly fines and/or jail sentences served eventually to restrain this very volatile and voluble mass of war-weary demonstrators.

Obviously no amount of force could contain it for, even now, we observe the same effort to quell the peace demonstrations. Nothing confused and deceived us then of the far-reaching implications of death at Jackson State in May 1970 and nothing confuses or deceives us now.

This was more than a local or isolated incident. The social and political meaning in the local trouble had national and international significance.

On August 13, 1970, it was my painful duty to testify before the President's Commission on Campus Unrest as to what I thought were the reasons behind the awful outburst of violence on this campus where I have worked for more than twenty years. I refer you to that report for details of testimony, but I mention it here in passing because of the kind of repercussion it received. As I have already indicated, I expressed the personal belief that this act of violence perpetuated against our people and our institution was an overt act of repression indicative of national repression and the direct results of racism and the widening of the war in Asia.

As a consequence of my testimonial, I received a number of pieces of hate mail which were quite revealing. These letters and marked clippings revealed a sad state of sick minds, definitely psychotic and full of paranoid fear. All of them revealed the same obsessions, misunderstandings, and racist aberrations. These, in the order they were listed, were: (1) fear of the Black Panthers; (2) complaints about their tax burdens as though no black people pay taxes; (3) resentment of welfare recipients; and (4) attacks or charges of wanton illegitimacy leveled against all black people. This is the usual racist gimmick of taking half-truths and making whole cloth from them. Each of these prejudicial expressions placed in its proper frame of reference and with explanations of statistics in true percentile ratios would reveal startlingly opposite conclusions from those drawn so hastily here.

I was amazed at the tremendous amount of fear and hostility in the white community against the Black Panthers. Perhaps their fears are well founded but when they tell *me*, a black person, to get rid of the Black Panthers, I don't know what they mean, nor what they think I can do. I do recognize why the white police have wantonly murdered Black Panthers even in their beds, but in spite of the national efforts to exterminate the panthers, I do not believe they have yet succeeded.

As for illegitimacy, black people have no monopoly on illegitimacy any more than what some consider adultery. There are reasons why the statistics reveal so many cases in the black community, and we should understand first that our system of welfare forces the black man out of the home so that his wife or woman can get the check. If he and she work, no matter how little they make, the check is affected. Moreover, the masses of black women are less educated concerning contraceptives or birth control and less willing to perform abortions once they are pregnant. But don't tell me the white girls *never* get pregnant unless they are married! They do have more homes for white unwed mothers, and they are not exposed as often as black women to the public records of county hospitals but, again, this is a racial gimmick used against all black people. And, as for as the tax burden of whites, that is a national joke. Not only are the statistics clearly showing that rich corporations pay no taxes, the rich whites who live in the suburbs pay no city tax. It seems to me that the black people could also have something to say about the tax burden. We are the residents of the inner cities, and don't tell me we don't pay taxes. Enough about answering my hate mail.

What we must understand above all, at the base of these attacks, is a fundamental racism with the false assumptions of white supremacy and racial superiority, "'Cause the white man's got a God complex."

These letters imply a deep hatred and resentment of all black people and all of them attempted to justify the violent deaths here at Jackson State in May 1970. Most of all, they confirm our belief that racism is a moral and mental sickness that pervades and permeates all American life.

Granted that we are aware of all these facts—and granted that polarization of races in this country continues, that a perpetual foreign war which began at the beginning of this century continues in Asia after twelve years of neither winning a political or military victory, the deaths of hundreds of thousands and the destruction of other nations' land and property, not to count the materials cost running into billions of dollars. Who do you suppose profits from a war? The factories who make the uniforms? The munitions factories? The bombs and guns? Nuclear weapons and germ warfare? Granted that these facts are obvious in the face of obdurate hatred and violence, war, and racism: How best can we memorialize these two young men who were victims of disaster on the morning of May 15, 1970? How can our lives best serve their memory? What dedication can we bring to this occasion of horror so easily accepted by the white community and flimsily excused by white racists? Are we dulled in defeat or are we awakened to a new awareness of man's continual struggle to be free? Must we forget so soon or do we dare to remember? What is the mandate these martyred men have handed us?

Do we accept our fate as colonized people less than slaves, or is there such a destined dream as freedom, peace, and human dignity to bless us with their truth?

A nation cries out to be delivered from the death and despair and destruction that pervade our world. Two black youths have spilled their blood on these hallowed grounds where we daily tread. Do we dare forget? The least we can do is remember.

What is your role as students in this black struggle for freedom? Our first step is an understanding of the forces that seek to enslave and re-enslave us. Recognizing the forces of repression as an enemy to all black people is our first step. As Mari Evans says, to identify the enemy is to free the mind. And when the mind is free, the people *will* be free to build a new and better world. The second step is understanding the potentials and the uses for your education. Is it relevant and viable? Can your class establish, lead, and maintain an entire dynamic community? You may be called upon to do just that. Your service is needed in your communities. And that is the third step—your dedication to the struggle for the complete liberation.

I challenge you to remember what happened on this campus two years ago. Remember and think again. Ask yourself, and remember. On pain of your own death—do not dare to forget.

(1969)

The Challenge of the 1970s to the Black Scholar

A FEW MONTHS ago when someone approached me about joining a group of black scholars in a scholarly endeavor, I asked them and myself, why me? What constitutes a scholar, what is his work, and to what special world does he belong? What does it mean to be a scholar? When does an ordinary student become a scholar? Is it a question of grades? Does it mean that he must hold a Phi Beta Kappa key from some great university, that he belongs to an honor society, and that he excels in his chosen profession? Or does it mean that he is a hack writer laboriously pulling himself up the academic ladder by some publication no matter how worthy or how unworthy? What goes into the making of a scholar? And why is it important to a college student, involved in an honor's program? Who should aspire to scholarship, and why?

I believe it is an absolute necessity that we develop a whole generation of scholars and that they understand their obligation to

---

This essay was one of several speeches written and delivered during the 1969–70 academic year.

black people as we seek to change our world and our society from what it is to what it ought to be.

Let me begin by quoting from a scholarly journal a definition of the black scholar. The black scholar "is a man of both thought and action who thinks for his people and acts with them, a man who honors the whole community of black experience, a man who sees the Ph.D., the janitor, the businessman, the maid, the clerk, the militant, as all sharing the same experience of blackness, with all its complexities and its rewards."

In these times, black people of necessity are rearranging priorities. One of the first places to begin is with school and education. We must redefine our lives and our means of obtaining the goals we seek for our people. The black intellectual community is responsible for the leadership of our people. The scholars provide the ideas, and the colleges must develop these scholars. Indeed it is here in the college years that we should first learn the tools of research, the importance of creative thinking, and the ways toward a meaningful definition and understanding of black existence.

In rearranging our priorities, our first task is a redefinition of the uses of education. It is not so essential that we train people to operate machines and thus depersonalize human beings into robots, as it is necessary that we inspire our young people to become creative and independent thinkers. It has always seemed to me that the one duty of the teacher is to inspire his students to think and to think for themselves. He guides him into methods, but he must first inspire him to think so that he learns to do independently the intellectual tasks set before him. When I was busily engaged in teaching freshman composition, we generally began with the business of thinking. We read Robinson's excellent article on "Various Kinds of Thinking." We emphasized creative thinking, which is the highest kind and leads to knowledge and invention. We also emphasized the technical process of thinking, from concepts to thoughts to ideas, figurations and configurations of ideas, and pointed these up with the analogy of words and sentences, paragraphs and themes, but above all we illustrated it with a little story about the differences in ordinary people, intelligent people, and intellectuals, who of course you know are distinguished by the kinds of conversation in which they indulge: ordinary people discuss people, intelligent people discuss events, and intellectuals discuss ideas.

In my parents' day, there was a great deal of attention made to what was called culture of the head, the heart, and the hand. Schools for black people emphasized the training of the hand so that black people could get jobs and become employed. This pointed up the deep controversy between W. E. B. Du Bois and Booker T. Washington who took the philosophy of Hampton College to Tuskegee and opposed Dr. Du Bois's theory of the talented tenth. Somewhere in the confusion of education for the elite versus education for the masses, we lost perspective and purpose. Today there is a real need for a reassessment of the value of education in the struggle of our black masses for freedom, human dignity, and peace. The student enters the scholar's world, first when he becomes an independent thinker, when he ceases to accept everything he hears without question, when he develops an inquiring mind, when he seeks to know, and when he discovers a love of learning, a thirst for knowledge, a desire to understand or fully comprehend. Second, he begins to be a scholar when he discovers the unity of knowledge, the relationships of all subject-matter fields to each other, and thirdly, but not the least, when he realizes the unity of mankind, and of all people in terms of biological, moral, spiritual, and ethical law. When he stands off the ground of working humanity and perceives the universe as a working wholeness, with cause and effect, supply and demand, unity and diversity, and the man-made concepts of time and space as one continuum, he is on the threshold of intellectual adventure.

The university is therefore and supposedly a community of scholars. The university is a generator of ideas, a place where knowledge is acquired and where learning is not merely dispensed in capsules or by prescription but where the student learns to organize the raw and chaotic elements of his personal and social experience into meaningful expression in the scientific and artistic world. We are not here merely to train the hands and cultivate the heart, we are here to sharpen the mind and hone it to a razor's edge. Therefore, method is not the first thing we learn without substance. The subject-matter field must first be surveyed, and then completely analyzed and synthesized so that the scholar is not only grounded in the tools, he is clearly master of the content. He does not merely memorize and learn in a rote fashion but he seeks to apply his thinking skillfully and effectively. He is ready to leave these "hallowed" halls when he has more than ingested and digested the whole animal of his choosing, and is now ready to apply the principles of his academic experience to the larger experience that awaits his intellectual maturity. It is therefore a mistake to suppose he is preparing for life, for he is already living here. He may be undergoing a preparatory phase of scholarship, but it is a bit redundant to say this preparation is for life. All of his life he is learning, sometimes consciously, sometimes unconsciously. It is what he does with his learning. If he is a true scholar, his education will last a lifetime for he continues to grow beyond the degree level and will not suppose that once he has completed the graduate-postgraduate syndrome that he may now seek the level of water from whence he recently lifted himself salary-wise and is no longer expected to read books, to enterprise, or to venture with the unknown. Rather, he continues searching for that new knowledge and invention which will advance mankind.

In recent years, the college campus has been the scene of much social upheaval; perhaps more student unrest has expressed itself on college campuses in the past dozen years than ever before in the history of the American people. Is it a conservative and apolitical question to ask if learning and scholarship can survive in an atmosphere of social unrest and constant protest? Most of us have heard the rich alumni of large American universities cry out that students who want to learn and study and think are not allowed this privilege because of their protesting and radical schoolmates. They contend that these students do not want an education and will not let others get an education. It seems to me we can quickly ask the question, what kind of education goes along in the same old-fashioned way, dead and insensitive to the needs of the people, irrelevant to the social issues of poverty and rapid change taking place in our world today? The true scholar is not an isolationist. He does not bury his head in the sand nor hide in an ivory tower. All life is his arena, and he follows the great example of Francis Bacon, who said, "I have taken all knowledge to be my province." I believe that the black community should be more than a laboratory for the university. It seems to me in these years of crisis, the black scholar must relate all his endeavor to that community. Whether he is a sociologist and follows the examples of Du Bois, Charles S. Johnson,

E. Franklin Frazier, Horace Cayton, St. Clair Drake, or Andrew Billingsley and Joyce Ladner, he is both teacher and scholar, he deals in the very life of the people, he learns from them, and he pours back into them his knowledge or his learning. Even more than the historian who keeps our records does the writer and author belong inseparably with the community. Frequently he is not the teacher for the writer must be free and the academic atmosphere tends to stifle his creativity. But we are badly in need of scholars today who will deal with the great body of literature by black writers, music of the black man, and the history of art by black people. The natural scientist like the social scientist has a wide field of endeavor beckoning him. Such endeavor demands a dedicated life and that life must be lived in the midst of the people. All our problems are in the streets. The black cities of America are crying out to black people and asking that the politics and the economics of these same city streets operate on behalf of the black people and not against them. The problems of education for black people are irrevocably tied to our political and economic problems. We cannot be politically and socially unconscious. We cannot afford to talk against change nor do nothing about it. We must actively engage in changing our society and we must accept our roles as intellectuals, as scholars, as teachers.

I do not think it is an accident that Stokely Carmichael and Angela Davis were philosophy majors in college. We cannot afford to go along in a dull, plodding, middle-class, middle-aged fashion fearful of change and fighting the very word "revolution." We have no choice but to seek to liberate our people for all our fortunes are bound up with whether black liberation forces succeed or fail. . . . We have reached an impasse, a point of no return. Our situation is desperate. We must have relief from oppression and repression, and all our relief through social change begins first with this idea.

The challenge of the seventies to the black scholar is to change our society. That is a big order for intellectuals who are not inclined to be activists. The role of a scholar is an intellectual role first and foremost. He is the theoretician of the black struggle. He must create the new paradigm for a new existence. He must find the way out of the impasse, the dilemma between integration and black nationalist separation; he must design the new world while the old world falls around our heads.

We are not a violent people, but violence has been thrust upon us. The prisons are full of our black people, and they are not all criminals. The streets are not safe because the white police are our enemies, tools of an oppressive and repressive racist society that constantly deal in our death. Our young men who have gone to the war come home maimed and crippled in body and soul because of the racist treatment in the war—a war designed to kill gooks and niggers! The rich men have turned loose the torrents of narcotics upon us purely for the sake of the dollar while the masses of our people suffer further under this demoralizing typhoon. Our southern black colleges are threatened daily, and all the old forces of racism and despotism continue. We have no choice but to fight with all the weapons we possess. Our greatest weapon is the word. The black scholar is a man of thought and action who thinks for his people and acts with them.

There are some who believe that the decade of the seventies will not see violent confrontation of the races nor overthrow of our political and economic system; rather they hope it will be like the cold war of the fifties, a decade of repression, a decade of regression, a decade of counter-revolution in which we sink deeper into a morass of fear, of poverty and crime, of war and pestilence, doped into submission, enslaved by greed and lust and possessed only with one incentive: another day, another dollar.

God help us if this is true. God help us if we regress now from the deaths of Medgar Evers, Martin Luther King, and Malcolm X. Surely our martyrs have not died in vain. Surely they have killed all the dreamers; have they also killed the dream?

(1992)

Education in the Global Village

THE GLOBAL VILLAGE is here—now. No longer is it scheduled for the future. The technological age, the high-tech jobs, the human touch—the global village, you name it. We are already there. Our twentieth century of blood and guns of war and Marxist revolutions, that century is over. We have begun a new age, the Age of Aquarius; the twenty-first century is already upon us. But, we are unprepared to deal with it. Our educational systems are two hundred years behind. We are still dealing with an educational system based on Newtonian physics. The Einsteinian revolution began this century, but we are yet failing to implement both the technological and the humanistic meaning of the Einsteinian electronic revolution. Oh, yes, we have watched our planet shrink to a smaller world—to that global village—with telecommunications, space travel, and computerized business institutions. We are struggling with the new math and science while the liberal arts lag behind. And, we know

This essay was originally delivered as a speech at two Award Day ceremonies in 1992: one for the Mississippi University for Women and one at Tougaloo College.

we have a need to understand our multicultural, multilingual universe to become tolerant of world religions and more humane toward all races, creeds, genders, and classes; but we still insist on all the methods of a fascist, racist, and sexist society. These, we know, are the enemies of a democratic society. We know our pluralistic global village is too small to endure such contradictions, and we know the tragic consequences if we continue to deny our human condition, our human potential, our truly spiritual destiny.

Education in the global village must deal with disintegrating social institutions—the family, the church, the school, and the neighborhood that encompasses these three. We can no longer abide a truncated and split society with rifts of cliques and factions of race and creed and gender. We must all work together or we will die and be destroyed together.

Education in the global village must be for the people—all the people—for the masses and not only for the elite, but for rich and poor, for black and white, for women and men; it cannot discriminate by declaring the welfare recipient defective in mental capacity, by refusing the poor a chance to work and grow and live an abundant life. Less than two hundred years ago, higher education for women was denied and declared ludicrous, ridiculous; a woman's place was in the kitchen and the bedroom. In the global village a woman's place is anywhere she chooses to be.

Less than two hundred years ago, it was against the law to educate an African American. In the global village, this formerly oppressed people occupy high political positions—women and men in Congress, in the state houses, even in a governor's mansion.

Mississippi has too long been considered at the bottom of the national social ladder. In a nation where the rate of literacy is the highest of any industrialized country, Mississippi is among the four states on the bottom. The poverty level in Mississippi is among the lowest in the nation.

Yet, Mississippi is considering closing its University for Women, its professional schools of dentistry and veterinary medicine, and of course, its two predominantly historic and black schools. All this under the pretense of desegregation and in the name of poverty.

The problem of education in Mississippi is the same as it has been for one hundred and fifty years. The solution in the Ayers's case[1] is really not race, but equitable spending of money. Racism, sexism, and fascism are the true elements in the global village.

The word "education" comes from the Latin word meaning to lead out. Higher education is designed to make the individual an independent, creative, and organized thinker, so that she becomes a leader whenever the individual finds herself.

I firmly believe that the main purpose in life is to glorify God by serving humanity; and coupled with that, I believe intelligence has more intrinsic value than money. That the only aristocracy is the aristocracy of the mind. Every person is a human being; no one can be more or less. Every human being is born with a brain. Each person is obligated to use that brain to fulfill the highest human potential. The global village demands a society of educable, intelligent people with vision and courage and the human knowledge of our spiritual destiny.

Note

1. The Ayers case refers to the desegregation of higher education in Mississippi. The case originated in the courts of Mississippi and was eventually heard before the U.S. Supreme Court. For more recent developments, see *Black Issues in Higher Education*, March 23, 1995.

(1975)

Tribute to Black Teachers

THERE WAS ONCE a time when the teacher was venerated. From ancient times the teacher was regarded as a semi-god, a community leader, a moral example, a foundation of knowledge, the symbol of wisdom, the walking truth of life, and an encyclopedia of culture. This revered personality was expected to live without blame or censure, but everything in our society is undergoing change. Social change is so rapid and radical that we are left breathless. Change is the name of the game. The twentieth century is an age of revolution, a transition from one age to another. These revolutions and wars have piled upon one another with such velocity and accumulated in such incremental rhythm that they are like a ball of tumbleweed in a windstorm or a snowball in a blizzard.

We have come through revolutions; we are in revolution; to-

This essay was originally presented as "The Image of the Teacher" at the opening orientation session of the Holmes County Public Schools in Lexington, Mississippi. It was later published in *The Lexington Banner* in 1975.

morrow we will make more revolutions. The concept of the instructor has suffered in this atmosphere and like everything else is caught in a revolution and state of change. Like all role-playing—roles are out of style—the role-playing or popular perception of the teacher has changed and not for the better. They stand for authority, law and order, servile respect for our elders, and blind obedience. Revolution and rebellion has not only threatened this image but changed the image of the teacher into a false god. The teacher has toppled from the pedestal of veneration, an ordinary human being, not a semi-god. However, the image of the teacher should be a positive, strong, influential image as our humanity demands and deserves.

We have a great history of the teacher, a great tradition from Iknaton in Egypt; Moses, the lawgiver; the eighth-century Hebrew prophets; Confucius; Jesus; Krishna; Mohammed; Buddha; Socrates; Plato; Aristotle; Erasmus of Rotterdam; and finally the great Einstein, Edison, Mary McCleod Bethune, George Washington Carver, and our beloved leader W. E. B. Du Bois. These were all great teachers of civilization. They imbued our lives with great ideas, ideas of spirit, love, freedom, peace, human dignity, truth, and justice. Steeped in this tradition are also the ideals of the bicentennial from such patriots as Thomas Paine, Benjamin Franklin; and finally Absalom Jones and Richard Allen, African American religious leaders.

Consider the ideals of God and the fellowship of humanity. Consider also the ability of individuals to think and, therefore, govern themselves. America is based on the belief that all people are created equal before the sight of God, that they are entitled to life, liberty, and the pursuit of happiness, domestic tranquillity and the five freedoms: freedom of speech, freedom of assembly, religious freedom, freedom from want, and freedom from fear. These are the universal ideas of human value and satisfying people's needs. These are the teachings of the greatest teachers.

This is what the teacher must understand is part of the new image we must give to a suffering world; crying for food, fuel and energy, money, land, and most of all for leadership. I am the example of a family of three generations of teachers. My great-uncle, Jim Ware, and my maternal grandfather, the Reverend Edward Lane Dozier, taught school one hundred years ago in

Greenville, Mississippi. My mother and father taught more than fifty years ago in Meridian, Mississippi. My sister, Mercedes, gave Dr. Joyce Johnson Bolden, head of the music department at Alcorn College, her first music lessons in Prentiss, Mississippi; and I came as a teacher of English to Jackson State University over thirty years ago. My family has been involved with education in Mississippi for at least one hundred years. Another sister, Gwendolyn, taught in the public schools of New Orleans and a brother, S. C. Walker, Jr., taught in that same system. Mercedes, who went on to become a concert artist and fulfilled the requirements for a doctorate in music, is now retired from teaching in New York. We are all teachers and each one, from my grandfather, who spoke the King's English, has made a reputation as a great, creative, and natural-born teacher.

After more than thirty years of teaching, I have found it a most rewarding profession. You will never make a lot of money teaching, for no one becomes financially rich teaching. In terms of the service rendered, the teacher is often the poorest paid member of society. Until recently, the black teacher, and particularly the black woman teacher, worked for a pittance, hardly making enough to buy bread and keep body and soul together—regardless of how expensively she appeared to be dressed. She was in debt for those clothes that she bought mostly on credit. Not only have I had the opportunity to mold minds and character, but I receive letters almost every two or three weeks from former students who have achieved and gone on to greater tasks. They thank me for the lessons and the days they sat in my classroom. This is the greatest reward of teaching.

The black teacher, particularly the southern black woman teacher, has been the first positive image some poor African American children have known. Instilling a good self-concept of worth in the black child is the most important task their teacher can accomplish. The black college, like the private black high school and the church-related grade school, gave African American children an education long before the state school existed.

I have always had wonderful teachers. They believed in me, inspiring me to achieve and believe in myself. My teachers were first my parents; then a Meridian native named Mrs. Harris and beautiful black women in Birmingham and New Orleans. When I went to

Northwestern University, I was seventeen and a junior in college. My test scores on entrance examinations were in the upper third of that junior class. I am a product of southern black teachers, mostly women, and as a result of those good teachers, my image of the teacher is reflected in what I am today.

Despite the electronic revolution in teaching, mostly reflected in the machines for visual and audio aids, we are still facing an intellectual revolution in education and ideas. This is necessary in order to update our educational systems from the twentieth and nineteenth centuries to the ideology of the twentieth century and to implement the principles of the Einsteinian revolution. In our pluralistic or multicultural society, we need education that is also more relevant, modern enough for the twenty-first century, and more humanistic. The Einsteinian revolution that brought nuclear power from atomic energy has changed our lives and concert of the universe in which we live.

The teacher must be cognizant of these facts. The teacher should be aware of the cognitive and affective aspects of learning in young children as well as in adolescents. She must fight racism in all its subtle and blatant forms. Every teacher must help to develop a worth and positive self-concept in every child or pupil in order for them to grow to respect every human being without racial, class, or religious prejudice. Every teacher must not only guide and inspire, but teach each child to think, and how to think. Teachers must avoid selective teaching and learning. Not only must Johnny read better, write better, spell better, run races better, but Johnny must learn to think better or she cannot survive. No person should ever accept a job teaching unless she or he loves people. The child who is taught without love is not well taught, and that child will neither like school, nor learning. Each teacher should have an abiding love for humanity, believing that human personality is potentially divine and every living soul has a spark of God, and the breath of God within her or him.

Yet, the teacher should also love learning and seek knowledge for its own and reward. To be prepared is an obligation. Moreover, the teacher must have respect for herself before she can have respect for others. The smallest child and the oldest person must be respected first as a human being. I have always told my students that they must always remember everyone is a human being, no one is any less, or any more. When the teacher understands these facts, loves people and knowledge, and respects one's own person, only then can the teacher aid in enhancing the self-concept of each child.

The teacher must, therefore, be solidly grounded in the methods of her educational field. They must be thoroughly prepared in the principles, precepts, and concepts of their profession. Grades are not always indicative of ability, for general intelligence and consideration for human beings are beyond grades. Some years ago, a county superintendent of schools from the Mississippi Delta visited me while I was in the hospital and complimented Jackson State University on its fine teacher education program. He said, "We get very fine teachers from Jackson State."

Although the state of Mississippi has supported Jackson State University's teaching program for a mere thirty-five years, the program has grown and developed to such an extent that it has won national awards for excellence. Moreover, we can point with pride not merely to our many successful graduates who are teaching all over the state, nation and the world, but most importantly, to the vast improvement in the quality of students produced in the public and county schools of Mississippi over the last twenty-five years. Accreditation of high schools, equalization of teachers' salaries as well as pay raises, better buildings, educational equipment, facilities, more and better libraries across the state; all these are evidence of growth in educational opportunities and achievement in Mississippi during the last twenty-five years.

The image of the teacher must live up to its history. Teachers must all make that image greater today than it was yesterday, and in the future hope to bring to pass the fulfillment of humanity's destiny which is spiritual. We are asked, more than we are challenged, by a changing world order to present each child with a new, positive, and strong healthy image of the teacher in order that they may grow into the intellectual giants we must have as our leaders of tomorrow.

When I was beginning my teaching career and was leaving for my first teaching position, feeling woefully inadequate and unprepared, my mother said to me, "Remember, make it with your students. Be prepared with your subject matter every day and make sure they respect you for your ability, character, and personality.

Attend strictly to your own business and keep your nose out of everybody else's personal business. Behave yourself, and you can stay on any job you have as long as you like." I have never forgotten her words, and I have never been fired from any job.

During my first commencement at Jackson State University, and every ceremony thereafter as long as Jacob Reddix was president, he gave a charge to the graduating class and asked them to repeat after him a paraphrase of the oath of Hippocrates. It was called the Hippocratic Oath of Teachers. I quote this oath, verbatim:

> I now take upon myself the sacred responsibility of the ministry of teaching. Into whatever community I shall go, and if any man shall entrust his children to me for the teaching of letters, I shall not refuse to receive and teach such children. Moreover, I shall teach them from pure affection, even as my own brethren, remembering that it is written, "The wise shall shine as the splendor of the firmament," and "They that instruct many in righteousness shall shine as the stars in the heavens forever and forever."

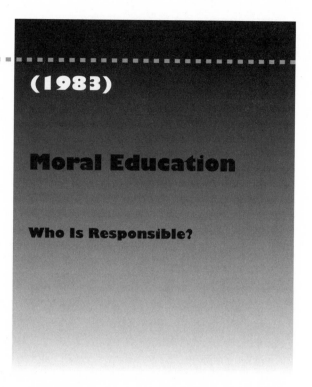

(1983)

Moral Education

Who Is Responsible?

WE ARE LIVING in desperately disturbing times. A societal crisis is worldwide. Our economic system has collapsed, and Western world capitalism is now in chaos. Mounting unemployment, inflation, devaluating currency, a fluctuating stock market, and a banking dilemma of bankruptcy are the obvious signs of economic distress and problems that have reached the point of no return.

The entire modern world is caught in the meshes of this worldwide catastrophe. We can no more escape our world crisis than we seem to be able to extricate ourselves from this death-defying destruction.

Reaganomics served notice of restructuring society into neofascist terms with strong emphasis on the military or force and the complete elimination of what the administration regards as the welfare

This essay was originally delivered as a speech at the Fourth Annual Reading Conference, sponsored by the Mississippi Committee for the Humanities and the Department of Reading at Jackson State University in 1983.

state and socialism or social programs for the poor and disadvantaged.

We have witnessed a century of war and revolution. These wars have been expensive, costing mankind untold numbers of human lives, costing too, in money, property, bartering power, and influence. A complete revolution in power and energy resulting in high technology now dominates our age. This century-old revolution began with five great thinkers of our age. Their ideas have influenced every aspect of life in the twentieth century. They have dominated our human undertakings—all inventions, knowledge and power—and they are the keys to our morality, our moral judgments, our value systems, and our moral education.

These five men are: first, Albert Einstein and his pioneer leadership in our electronic revolution resulting in atomic energy or nuclear power and proliferating from theoretical physics and mathematical equations to a new concept of our universe. This revolution has taken us through rapidly developing high technological systems of cybernetics and automation to a wonder world of space, computer chips, video games, and instant telecommunication systems.

At the same time, a second man, Sigmund Freud, has led us into a world of self-analysis and inner consciousness or psychological experimentation. His pioneering efforts in psychoanalysis or psychiatry resulted in a better understanding of human personality and sexuality, the self and society. This new world of human behavior reveals our dream world and the symbiology of brute fact and reality of our existence. But yet another man, Søren Kierkegaard, has sought to link our finite world with an infinite world of metaphysical proportions and mystical power and thus better understand our earthly and spiritual existence through a philosophy of existentialism.

A fourth man, Karl Marx, has further determined our economic and political lives through the empirical tools of historical and social analysis resulting in worldwide social revolutions throughout this century, socialist, Communist, and fascist systems of totalitarianism, thereby perpetually changing governments and social institutions.

The fifth man, W. E. B. Du Bois, a sociologist, has looked at all these changes—socioeconomic, political, and philosophical—through the modern phenomenon of race and nationalism or urban, rural, national, and international experiences based on the modern myopia of race and culture.

Now we are in a time of crisis. Our century of social, political, economic, and geographic change not only faces chaos and crisis; we are in the birth throes of another century. Therefore our crisis is as much, if not more so, a moral crisis.

Our problems of war and revolution, of nuclear energy, of world hunger, of monetary crisis, of human relations and leadership, all of these problems are moral problems, and clearly the solutions are people-oriented and dependent upon our moral stamina, moral education and responsibility, and our ability to make right decisions for right action and right conduct and social behavior.

Moral decadence and moral corruption are eating through the heart of our very existence. There is no phase of our lives in which we cannot see this moral corruption and decadence. We could liken our American empire in the world today to the last stages of the Roman Empire. When that empire fell, it was the Christian church under the leadership of Saint Augustine who set about building an eternal city of God on the ruins of Rome.

Our modern materialistic empire of money, rampant crime and violence, sexism, racism, and militarism is collapsing around us. We are caught in this chaos of decadence and corruption. Who will rebuild the city, and who will lead us to the citadel? Where is the paradigm for the twenty-first century? Who is morally responsible—who is responsible for our moral education? Who will implement the moral concepts and value systems of our new concept of the universe?

Who is able? Who is capable? Who will make the human response to the challenge of nature in this desperate age? Surely there will be a response. If it is not to our liking, whom should we blame?

What are our options—annihilation of the planet earth or tyranny from men who choose to be beasts rather than gods? Who is morally responsible for the moral education of our future generations?

Ask yourself if you are. If all our society is not morally responsible for the evil mess we are now experiencing, who is responsible for our new, creative, constructive and positive moral education?

MORAL EDUCATION—Who is responsible?

We should first recognize that the strength of the people is in our moral, spiritual and cultural values. It is not in money and material things. It is not in magic, superstition, mesmerism nor hypnotic powers. It is in our deeply spiritual and moral beliefs and values and our cultural expression. If we are people of spirit, we are also people of great creative imagination; we are people of moral and ethical values and standards, and the strength to sustain us for our survival as well as our contribution to the world around us lies in these values. Sometimes in our five centuries of acculturation in a Western world and American materialism, we have become confused and lost track of these values; we tend to assume the inimical standards of a world totally opposite from our own, and we find ourselves in conflict. It is especially important that our youth, the young people coming on to lead us into the twenty-first century, understand clearly what is our value system and help to construct the values of a new society, the moral imperatives for our world community.

These are four areas in which these moral imperatives must exist and out of which areas our moral imperatives not only must rise but also develop. They are, first, the individual personality; second, the home, marriage and the family; third, the church and religious expression; and fourth, the school and education.

What then are these moral imperatives? First, for the individual personality we must consider all the aspects of personal health— physical, mental, and spiritual—and personality development as well as good self-concepts and development for high achievement in career goals. Second, in the home, marriage and the family, one finds the basic value system of morals, ethics, and spiritual guidance. Third, church and religious life provide the cultural and ethnic ethos that can maintain religious tolerance and cultural pluralism. Fourth, for the school and education, we need a new educational system based on Einsteinian principles and the development of creative thinking and creative leadership for the future.

Our present-day system of education began in the nineteenth century when the scientific revolutions of the eighteenth and nineteenth centuries were charting a new universe with Newtonian physics. The Einsteinian revolution has outmoded such thinking. We no longer live in the nineteenth century. Even the twentieth century is largely behind us. Yet our religion is still that of the

Middle Ages and the Protestant Revolution. What should a creative and spiritually vital religion do for our society? Why is the Christian church in America today derelict in its duty and slow to move its feet toward full integration of all Americans into the mainstream of American life? All America knows that institutionalized religion has lost its basic meaning because it has too long been in the employ of racism that has viciously used the church and the Christian religion for selfish ends and vested interests. Segregationists like the Ku Klux Klan and the American for the Preservation of the White Race have so long declared themselves as the true representatives of Christianity, the true American patriots, and the standard bearers of such nonsense as racial purity and integrity that they have whipped the truth of Christianity—the truth of the brotherhood of man and the fatherhood of God, whipped it senseless beyond recognition. Their lynch ropes, high explosives, boxes of dynamite, long-range rifles, and burning crosses are all used in the name of Christ and the Christian religion. Our burned churches are quite symbolic of racial hatred and spiritual decay. Our people deserve something better than a begging ministry in the employ of a powerful and wealthy hierarchy. The pages of history that tell the true story of slavery and segregation are stained with the blood of black men who were crucified by white Christians. No hypocritical whitewashing of moribund congregations that are stinking with moral decay will deliver us today. Perhaps it is time for a new avatar. Violently shaken by class, caste, and racial disturbance, the church in America craves a new awakening in which spiritual meaning is reborn and revitalized. Religion in a society should be the underlying philosophy of the people which undergirds the basic institutions of that society and gives dynamic impetus to all the group action and subsequent phenomena of that society. When the religion of the people is dead, then they are without visions and without moral imperatives.

When we talk of moral education, moral re-education, and moral imperatives, we do not wish to be confused with the Moral Majority. This is something altogether different, a horse of another color, and more inclined toward what we regard as immoral rather than moral. But perhaps the Moral Majority can best illustrate what has happened under a decadent and materialistic society and how twisted our patriotic American and Christian ideals have become under the guise of values based on money and property.

The Moral Majority is racist, neofascist, fundamentalist, arch conservative, and completely materialistic. In 1958, Reverend Jerry Falwell, leader of the Moral Majority, denounced the Earl Warren Court and the 1954 Supreme Court decision by declaring that integrating public schools was a satanic plot against God's will. He also declared that liberals in this country were all left of center and in the lunatic fringe.

He is a strong advocate of prayer in the schools, but he wants it to be Christian prayer. He does not regard Roman Catholics as Christians and does not look highly on Jews, Moslems, and Buddhists. So he does not want universal prayer; and since all these people have children attending public schools, he obviously does not want them to pray. He wants prayer limited to Christians. Perhaps he does not understand how all religious people pray. We have a cultural pluralism in America not limited by caste, race, and creed. This pluralism demands total tolerance and respect. It demands new moral, ethical, and spiritual values.

The Moral Majority is strongly fighting abortion, but perhaps we should look a little more closely into their motives. They are not against abortion *per se* as long as the person having the abortion is a relative or friend with a private doctor and not a welfare mother using the taxpayer's money or a teenager with an unwanted pregnancy. These strong forces against abortion are not against nuclear war or war in any form. They do not object to killing soldiers and civilians in Vietnam nor men, women, and children in Asia and Africa. They are only against killing unborn babies at home. So their personal morality is really social immorality. They are against the poor, and they object to our government helping the poor. They are against Darwin's nineteenth-century scientific ideas of evolution and insist on special creation being taught in the schools. They insist on literal interpretations of the Bible, word for word, despite translation and centuries of multiple versions. They insist on censorship of all movies and television and a failure to recognize either women's rights or gay rights of fellow human beings. They are fundamentalists, and they batten themselves by feeding on the emotions of the gullible and semi-ignorant. This is not what we mean by moral education. This is immoral in the most immoral sense. They have even threatened to burn the books.

Yet they are staunch supporters of the ground swell for Ronald Reagan. They are in total accord with Reaganomics and the neofascist restructuring of American society. If anything, they feel Mr. Reagan does not go far enough and is not conservative nor fascist enough in the Nazi sense. Here is a blatant example of immorality in politics and social legislation.

No social institution has suffered more moral decay than the American family. Basically in America marriage is an economic institution relying heavily on money or income for its preservation. The more important elements of character, disposition, and intimate relationships of filial and conjugal love, sex, and friendship are subject to the bread-and-butter nuts and bolts of marriage. In times of economic stress and depression, many marriages collapse. Divorce and separation have the highest percent of statistics in the so-called civilized world here in America, and the number-one culprit or correspondent is money. Runaway children, kidnapping, teenage pregnancy, child abuse, alcohol and drug abuse are symptomatic of serious trouble in the American family. Both petty and major crimes committed and juvenile delinquency have grown out of these problems. A breakdown in interpersonal relationships and communication may be the first symptoms of serious trouble in the family but these are not all.

A family deeply grounded in spiritual, moral and ethical principles and buttressed by religious faith is more than likely to be a happy and healthy situation. This is far from being easily achieved in our present world of crime, chaos, confusion, and corruption, but is not impossible. It is especially difficult for the single-parent head of a household, but again such a household is not doomed to social destruction given the undergirding of moral and ethical values, religious faith and principles, and the overriding spiritual atmosphere. The problem is basically moral. What kind of morale can you develop and sustain in your family?

What is the role of television in family life and society? Does your child read books or look at TV and play video games? How much do you believe of what you read in the newspaper or see on the boob-tube and the idiot box? This mass communication medium manipulates the minds of the people and daily programs us for panic and paranoia. How can this medium be used constructively and positively in the rebuilding of our society, as an educational tool, to mold public policy, public opinion, delight, and instruct us in morality at the same time?

Our moral problems in education are manifold. From the common school through the postgraduate programs in higher education, we have fundamental and systematic crises and challenges.

The Einsteinian revolution discards the two-century-old educational system based on Newtonian physics. Such a worn-out system is obsolete. Our new concept of a new illimitable universe beyond space and time demands a new system of education. In the face of high technology, of unbelievable changes through satellites, computer chips, and other devices of automation and cybernation, our classrooms no longer have boundaries of walls and our curricula must constantly be changed.

Twelve million people unemployed may never go back to their old jobs. Are they doomed to violent crime, drink, drugs, and insanity, or can they really be retrained into new jobs and skills? Will there never be enough work not displaced by machines and robots? Unemployment insurance, leisure time, or re-education? In which direction are we going? Our problems are basically moral.

We have another specific instance or example to illustrate our dilemma. This problem grows out of institutionalized racism in our American colleges and universities. In the days of segregation, our black athletes were unwanted, unrecognized, and unpaid. They did not play in the big leagues, on the professional teams. Many sports were all white, and competition was purely limited by race, class, and sometimes creed. Bravely, these black athletes have fought and broken down the barriers of racial discrimination and proven themselves not only competent but in many cases superior in every sport. Now in so-called integration, they are winners, the heroes, the champions, and they are also pawns in a brutal and most immoral arena. Black colleges can no longer compete in recruiting black athletes, and since the name of the game is money, the black sports programs on black college campuses are slowly doomed to death. The white university sends its recruiter to the black high school athlete and promises the world—a house for his poor struggling mother, a Cadillac for his deprived family, and a girlfriend of another race for himself. How immoral can you get? There is no law against this immorality. It is just a part of our system, our corruption. And didn't you black athletes want to play on an integrated team? You don't need an education; all you need is money. Thus they corrupt the flower of our youth.

Reinhold Niebuhr in his book *Moral Man and Immoral Society* (1932)[1] cautions the moralist against his idealism and altruism, and I quote:

> Yet the moralist may be as dangerous a guide as the political realist. He usually fails to recognize the elements of injustice and coercion which are present in any contemporary social peace. The coercive elements are covert, because dominant groups are able to avail themselves of the use of economic power, propaganda, the traditional processes of government, and other types of non-violent power. By failing to recognize the real character of these forms of coercion, the moralist places an unjustified moral onus upon advancing groups which use violent methods to disturb a peace maintained by the desire to break the peace, because he does not fully recognize the injustices which it hides. They are not easily recognized, because they consist in inequities, which history sanctifies and tradition justifies. Even the most rational moralist underestimates them, if he does not actually suffer from them. A too uncritical glorification of cooperation and mutuality therefore results in the acceptance of traditional injustices and the preference of the subtler types of coercion to the more overt types.
>
> An adequate political morality must do justice to the insights of both moralist and political realists. It will recognize that human society will probably never escape social conflict, even though it extends the areas of social cooperation. It will try to save society from being involved in endless cycles of futile conflict, not by an effort to abolish coercion in the life of collective man, but by reducing it to a minimum, by counselling the use of such types of coercion as are most compatible with the moral and rational factors in human society and by discriminating between the purposes for which coercion is used.

Our music, art, and literature born out of our folkways and folk-beliefs are also part and parcel of our cultural gifts and heritage.

Like religion, the poetry of a people, their art, songs, and literature come from the deep recesses of the unconscious, the irrational, and the collective body of our ancestral memories. They are indeed the truth of our living, the meaning, and the beauty of our lives, and the knowledge of our heritage is not only fundamental to complete understanding of us as a people, it is a fundamental ingredient in the development of our world consciousness.

Our cultural arts are therefore vital in moral education. The purpose of poetry, according to Horace, is to delight and instruct. Therefore, all cultural activity is twofold in purpose, to entertain and at the same time to teach. Morality is taught both by precept and example. Determining first what kind of morality the individual wants and the society will accept is perhaps not always easy, but this is our first step toward healing the nation, toward a world that is morally whole and a world community of moral rectitude.

Note

1. See Reinhold Niebuhr, *Moral Man and Immoral Society: A Study in Ethics and Politics* (1932; New York: Charles Scribner's Sons, 1960), 233–34.

(1968)

Religion, Poetry, and History

Foundations for a New Educational System

THE THEME "Religion, Poetry, and History: Foundations for a New Educational System" immediately poses questions and demands definition of terms. Why do we need a new educational system? How are the values of a society formed? What is the role of religion in a society? What is the meaning of poetry? And what is the essential worth of a people's heritage in developing their social consciousness? The answers to these questions should then automatically lead to a set of basic assumptions: one, that the philosophy and aesthetic values of a society are fundamental to the development of certain basic institutions and the social phenomena of that society; two, when these social phenomena and institutions erupt in chaos, the basic philosophy must be re-examined and ultimately changed; and, three, when the society thereby undergoes such violent change, the people are morally responsible to create a new set of values on which they can build better institutions for a better society.

This essay was originally published in *Vital Speeches of the Day* 34, no. 24 (October 1, 1968).

Why do we need a new educational system? We stand today in the throes of cataclysmic social change. We are caught in a world-wide societal revolution that breeds ideological and military conflict between nations. We are impaled on a cross of constant economic problems which automation and cybernation have brought us with the electronic revolution. We are deeply distressed by the conditions of our inner cities. We are equally concerned with the confusing drama on our college campuses which reflects the search of our young people for values different from our own.

Our young people seem to be seething in a boiling caldron of discontent. Like the youth of every generation, they want to know, and they demand to be heard. Like youth in every age, they are the vanguard of our revolutionary age. They are the natural leaders of revolution, whether that revolution be of race, class, or caste; whether it is sexual or academic; whether it is political or intellectual. Today, the revolution we are witnessing encompasses all of these, for the violence of revolution not only threatens but definitely promises to sweep out every corner of our outmoded existence. Violence today is more than a tool of tyranny, as it has always been; it is also the tool of revolution.

We are not only shedding the old ways of the past. We are overwhelmed by the problems of a new universe. We stand under the watershed of the twentieth century totally unprepared for the innovations of the twenty-first century already rushing headlong upon us. The historical process, of which we are a part, does not necessarily mark off the cycles of our progress with the man-made dates or hours we have set for change. The life of the twenty-first century has already begun while the debris of the structures in a dying twentieth century crashes all around us.

Our basic institutions of the home, the school, and the church are threatened by the same violent destruction undermining our socioeconomic and political system, for they are part and parcel of the whole. Three hundred and fifty years ago, when the American colonies were not yet a nation, a set of built-in values were superimposed upon the American continent and people by European powers. These values were composed of three basic philosophies: (1) a religious body of belief containing the Protestant work ethic with duty and work as a moral imperative, with the puritanical and Calvinistic aversion to pleasure of secular play, song, and dance, coupled with (2) the economic theories of a commonwealth only groping for the rising industrialism and capitalism that did not fully emerge until a century later, but which were hidden under (3) the American political dream of democracy. This democracy was based on the idealism of Christianity which declared all men are brothers and the children of God. Except for the facts of chattel slavery and inhuman segregation, the ideal dream might have become a reality. Slavery and segregation as institutions contradicted the ideal dream, and America developed instead a defensive philosophy or rationale for racism, the fruits of which we are reaping today.

The Black people in America have so long borne the stigma of slavery and segregation that every community, black and white, has been warped by this wanton subjugation. For a very long time after slavery, almost a century in time, the federal government gave tacit consent to Jim Crow, and segregation was supported boldly by law which of course became custom. Now it has been outlawed, but the mark of Cain is still on the land. White America has educated black and white children with a set of monstrous lies—half-truths and twisted facts—about race. Both black and white children, as a result, have been stunted in their mental growth and poisoned in their world outlook. The American white child in the North and South is just as distorted in his thinking as the black child although the expressed manifestations are not the same. The white child has been taught to value race more than humanity. He has been taught to overestimate his intelligence and human worth because of race, and at the same time, to underestimate the human worth and intelligence of anyone who is not of his race. The white American is therefore basically ignorant of the cultures of other people, and has no appreciation for any other language, art, religion, history, or ethical system, save his own. He is in no way prepared to live in a multiracial society without hostility, bigotry, and intolerance. He believes that he must convert all people to his way of thinking because he cannot possibly conceive that his way of thinking may not always be right for everyone else. Everyone must dress, think, pray, and amuse himself as he does. Every socioeconomic and political system must emphasize or epitomize the values of his mechanistic and materialistic society. He falsely assumes that his values are idealistic and altruistic, that he is democratic and Christian while all others are totalitarian and pagan, yet in all his actions, he contradicts his preaching. His every waking hour is spent getting and spending for himself, while denying his brothers any and all of the same rights he claims for himself. Self-righteous and self-centered, he thanks God daily that he is not as other men (meaning other races) are.

On the other hand, our black children have been taught to hate themselves, to imitate people whom they have been taught to believe are superior. Every day they read in the schoolbooks, the newspapers, the movies, and the television the monstrous lies that deny their existence and denigrate their world. They have been led to believe that we have no black history, no black culture, no black beauty, nor anything black that has value or worth or meaning that is good. They have been told that our world is white and Western with a cultural heritage that is Graeco-Roman, Christian in religion, Protestant in ethic, and democratic in politics; that all these things are right and of necessity good and civilized while all the opposites of these are wrong and of necessity evil and savage. The non-Western world which is colored is therefore primitive in culture, heathen in religion, pagan in ethics, communistic in economics, and totalitarian in politics. This of necessity is evil, anti-Christian, and anti-white, and therefore anti-American. Ancient civilizations and empires of Egypt, Babylonia, and Persia, ancient cultures and empires of Ethiopia, Karnak, China, Mali, and Songhai, to say nothing of that famous city of Carthage which the Roman orator Cato constantly declared must be destroyed; these ancient names are not recited in our history books, nor is the fact that both Asians and Africans and all the Arab world enjoyed their great Renaissance eras before the Europeans and the Christians. Thus our world has been divided into East and West, into black and white, and given the separate connotations of good and evil. For the most part our people have been gullible and believed the half-lies and the half-truths denying our blackness and wishfully affirming their whiteness by seeking to become carbon copies of white people. But the fact remains that we are living in a multiracial world in which there are varying cultures, religious beliefs, and socioeconomic or political systems, and whether we like or dislike it, our children must be educated to live in such a world. They must learn to live in a world that is four-fifths colored, nine-tenths poor, and, in most cases, neither Christian in religion nor democratic in ideals.

The struggle of black people in America in this decade of societal revolution must therefore re-emphasize the battle for intellectual emancipation. A new self-concept must be instilled in the black child, and a new perspective must be developed in the white child. Moreover, it becomes the awesome task of every well-meaning, clear-thinking American, black and white alike, to rectify the wrongs caused by racism, to change the basic attitudes and twisted facts still erroneously held by segregationist America, by racists who are white and black. All America must move toward a new humanism with a preoccupation toward providing a full measure of human dignity for everyone. We must create a new ethic that is neither Protestant, Catholic, Jewish, Moslem, Buddhist nor any other ethic narrowed by creed but liberated into respect for the human rights of all men. Our ethic will then become a universal blessing of mutual respect and concern for every living spirit. We need a new educational philosophy in order to achieve this. A knowledge of world religions, world cultures, and all the racial and nationalistic strains that make up the human family will make such an ethic possible. The appreciation of other people and their cultures is predicated upon an understanding of them and understanding is predicated purely upon genuine knowledge. We need a new educational system. The recent revolution in teaching has been largely electronic; an intellectual revolution is of necessity a revolution in basic ideas.

Anything false that is used in the name of religion is then the opiate or drug by which men lull themselves into a false consciousness, into deadly apathy, and supine complacency. A vital and dynamic religion is necessary to the cultural advancement of all people. Religious faith is personal, but religious institutions are of necessity social. As such they must serve all the people or they have no value.

Black people, before they came to America, had a religion and ethic that was tribal or communal and that was based on their group participation in rites and ceremonies that gave impetus to their living and moral order to their community. White Puritan Americans at home and abroad as missionaries frowned on this a superstitious nonsense. In America black people lost their ties with Mother Africa, but they have neither lost religious faith nor mystical charisma. We are still a people of spirit and soul. We are still fighting in the midst of white American racism for the overwhelming truth of the primacy of human personality and the spiritual destiny of all mankind. We fight for freedom and peace because we know these are spiritual entities and have nothing to do with guns and money and houses and land. Contrary to the prevailing belief of racist society, all black men do not necessarily believe that a guaranteed employment of all the people is the highest essence and accomplishment of a society. Artists and the religious of all nations know this is not so. Wise men are not all bankers and soldiers. Some are philosophers and poets and they too make their religious contribution to society. Some men therefore serve their society with the creative gifts of themselves, neither for money nor fame but for the cause of righteousness and with human integrity for the advancement of all mankind. Whether we remain the test of democracy, the soul of the nation, the conscience of America, the redemptive suffering people of the world, or the tragic black heroes of a dying society, we know that the essence of life is in spirit, not in cars, whiskey, houses, money and all the trappings of an affluent society. Call it soul if you wish, but it is our gift and a part of our black heritage. We declare it worthy to offer on the altars of the world toward the enduring philosophy of a new and necessary humanism.

Black people today in America are more than ever before socially conscious, aware of the damage that racism has done to our psyche, the traumatic injury to our children's morale and mental growth. We know the effects of the brutalizing, stigmatizing, dehumanizing systems of slavery and segregation under which we have existed in America for three hundred and fifty years.

A new awareness of this black history has taken hold of us in the wake of the riot commission's report that white racism is the creeping sickness destroying America. How, then, shall we diagnose this racism and prescribe for its cure? Will more jobs, better housing, more ballots, and fewer guns cure racism? Hardly. This is a battle for the minds of men. In the words of one of our greatest thinkers who predicted that the problem of the color line would be the problem of the twentieth century, in the words of that classic, *The Souls of Black Folk*, let us remember that we have three great gifts: a gift of song, a gift of labor or brawn with which we have helped to build a nation, and a gift of spirit or soul. Let us stir up the gift of God that is within us and let us create a new world for all Americans. Let us use our heritage of religion, poetry, and history as foundations for a new educational system. Let us teach our children that we are a great people, that they have a great heritage, and that their destiny is even greater.

It must come as a shock to many of our people living in the inner cities of America when they read about the deplorable conditions in the ghettos, to discover that all this abuse directed against criminals, against dope addicts, against looters and conspirators, all this abuse and condemnation directed against those of us who live in subhuman conditions of black colonies of the white power structure, all of this is a blanket condemnation of us as a race and as a people. What, then, is a ghetto and how did it come into existence? Must we be blamed for this, too, on top of all the other racist hatred and injustice vented upon us? Who owns all this property and where do the owners live? Do they value their property more than they value our lives? Is this why they send the police to protect their property while only God protects our lives? Is it not true that the ghetto is a black colony of the white power structure in which we are exploited with no representation in the political and economic system? Do the people in the ghettos control their economic and political lives? Is the money spent in the ghetto returned to the ghetto? Do the people living in the inner cities run the governments of those municipalities? Somewhere we must truly place the blame where it belongs. Poor black people can no longer be the scapegoats who bear the blame for everything in our society. We not only must build economic and political power in the ghettos; we must change the thinking in the ghettos as we must change the thinking of all America. We must create a new mental climate.

Fortunately for many of our people, all of us have not been blighted by ignorance of our heritage. Some of us have come from homes where all our lives this positive healing process has existed. While we were simultaneously reading the lies in the history books at school, we were learning our true history at home from our parents. We have neither the segregationists' views of the South nor the racist views of the North about slavery, the Civil War, and Reconstruction. Some of us grew up reading *Opportunity* and *Crisis* magazines, reading the *Louisiana Weekly*, the *Chicago Defender*, and the *Pittsburgh Courier*, or whatever our local newspaper was. We heard the poetry of Du Bois and James Weldon Johnson and

Langston Hughes, and the music of Roland Hayes, Paul Robeson, and Marian Anderson. We learned the names of our leaders such as Harriet Tubman, Sojourner Truth, and Mary McCleod Bethune. We knew our great blues singers and Broadway stars and prizefighters and Olympic winners. I was delighted to hear Dr. Sam Proctor say at commencement that he did not need Stokely to tell him he was beautiful, his mother told him that. That is what mothers are supposed to do. But all our children do not know how beautiful they are, for all of them have not been so fortunate. All of them do not know that physical beauty is relative according to man-made standards and that what we believe in our minds and hearts is what we are, that we need not become what our enemies wish us to become. We can be what we want to be and most of all we want to be ourselves, and not an imitation of other people.

Contrary to what some of our black brothers believe, this new educational system must not be one of racial exclusion, or this will become another face for racism. This learning must be all-inclusive. Any notions that a wide cleavage in the American people is based on race, class, caste, sex, or age—any such notion is unrealistic, naive, negative, and detrimental. Whether black and white Americans are divided by yellow men, red men, or the little green men of Mars, the result can mean nothing but chaos. Shall we divide and conquer? Who will conquer, and who stands to benefit from such cleavage? If any foreign nation can divide us by indoctrination, it can also completely destroy us. Some of our black brothers seem confused by the conflict, and the tactics of the struggle seem to cloud the issues. When we were subjected to segregation by law, we sought to become assimilated into the mainstream of American life. We regarded this as a worthy and positive goal. Now some of us seem to have some extreme thinking in the opposite direction. These seem to be appalled with the apparent failure of integration, and disappointed with the slow business of desegregation. Shocked and stung by the ugly face of white racism, they now declare that the sickness of America makes segregation and apartheid more to be desired than either desegregation or integration. This is not a clear incentive toward building power in the ghettos nor rebuilding the moral fiber of America. Whatever we have learned from our struggles in the past, at least a few facts should be clear: We fight with faith in the goodness of the future. No matter how troubled we have been, we have not lost our perspective. Our sense of history tells us that our human personality is potentially divine, hence our destiny must be spiritual. These may not seem much but they are enough, if in terms of these truths we teach our children the worth of their human personality, a pride in their heritage, a love for all people in the recognition of our common humanity, and a sense of dignity and purpose in living. They help us realize that freedom, like peace, is spiritual. It is with such tools that we must build our houses for tomorrow.

Just as we minister to the physical needs that are human, we must minister to our mental needs that are also human. We must recognize the worth of every living person. All America is crying for this new humanism, for a new educational system, for a new and creative ministry from a new and spiritually vital religion, meaningful and with a genuine moral imperative. A new Space Age of the twenty-first century craves a vital and new religion to usher in the millennium. A new century promises to erase the color line. A new humanism must prevail. We must find the strength and the courage to build this new and better world for our children. Many of us will die trying in these last years of a dying century, but in the twenty-first century, our progeny will raise their eyes to more than a vision of a brave new world. They will occupy the citadel. Their truth will be honored and freedom understood and enjoyed by everyone. Racial justice and understanding will be a prelude to international peace and good will. But we must begin now to destroy the lies, to attack the half-truths, to give our children something in which they can believe, to build faith in themselves, love for mankind, and hope for the future. Most of all, we must teach them that righteousness is more to be desired than money—for the great possession of money without guiding principles, without judgment, without pride and integrity, such possession is nothing—and that cars and houses and whiskey and clothes and all the trappings of an affluent society do not dress up empty minds, and ugly hearts, and loveless lives; that meaningless living is without immortality in that it does not give us heroes to honor. Our martyred dead are great because they died for freedom. Our list of heroes is three centuries long, but they are deathless and forever with us. Wisdom and understanding cannot be bought in the Vanity Fairs of the world. Justice and freedom are prizes to be sought and our martyred men of goodwill have already proved they are well worth dying to obtain.

Teach them, our children, that their heritage is great and their destiny is greater. That we are a great people with a great faith who have always fought and died for freedom. Teach them that life and love are for sharing and, above all, they are never to forget that we are all a part of the mainland, involved with humanity. We are not alone in our beauty and our strength. We are part of all mankind, who throughout all recorded time have bravely fought and nobly died in order to be free.

Our religion, poetry, and history—they are our folk heritage; they are our challenge today to social commitment; they are the foundation of a new education, a new moral imperative, a new humanism on which we base our cultural hope for a free world tomorrow morning in the twenty-first. These things shall be:

> A nobler race than e'er the world hath known shall rise
> With flame of freedom in their souls
> And light of knowledge in their eyes.
> They shall be gentle, brave, and strong
> To spill no drop of blood, but dare
> All that may plant man's lordship firm
> On earth and fire and sea and air.
> Nation with nation, land with land
> Unarmed shall live as comrades free
> In every heart and brain shall throb
> The pulse of one fraternity
> New arts shall bloom of loftier mold
> And mightier music thrill the skies
> And every life shall be a song
> When all the earth is paradise.

(1969)

Revolution and the University

REVOLUTION TODAY IS sweeping away the past, ushering in a new century, and changing our lives so rapidly that what we experienced six months ago is already outmoded. Worldwide societal revolution seems to have overtaken the United States of America. Revolution that was sweeping the streets in the early sixties began sweeping our campuses in the late 1960s. There is a new order in education. The entire educational world is in the throes of cataclysmic change, in a chaotic state of revolution, and what the end may be is anyone's guess, for the end is clearly not yet in sight.

Many people are therefore so confused about the issues that each crisis finds them unprepared and defiant or resentful. They thrash around for answers, and they offer threats toward the so-called militant or rebellious youth. They argue that the administrations of various colleges and universities should handle these youth, should stop the nonsense, and put down any notions of revolution or violent actions. These people are totally unaware of the

---

This essay was originally written at Northwestern University in 1969.

tremendous forces for change that are at work today in our world society. They cannot understand why this worldwide societal revolution is not only necessary but also completely irrepressible.

The role of black students who demand black studies on predominantly white campuses is further misunderstood, and what has happened at Cornell, Columbia, City College of New York, San Francisco State, Berkeley, and countless others seems further complicated by the support of young white militants for the demands of these students.

I was literally born on a college campus, and there I have spent most of my life in one capacity or another. My father and mother taught school in three southern states—Alabama, Mississippi, and Louisiana—and I grew up on those college campuses where they worked. My mother taught music, and my father, a Methodist minister, taught religion and philosophy. At seventeen I entered the junior college at Northwestern University. After spending my eighteenth year as a dropout because it was the middle of the Depression and we had no money, I returned to Northwestern a year later. Exactly one month and ten days after my twentieth birthday, I graduated from Northwestern with the B.A. degree and with a major in English. Four years later, I entered the University of Iowa in September, and the following August I took the M.A. degree in English with a creative thesis, "For My People, A Volume of Verse." Immediately after graduation, I went home to the South hoping to teach English in September, but eighteen months passed before I found my first job. I was employed at Livingstone College in Salisbury, North Carolina, for one semester and a summer. I left Livingstone to teach for a year at West Virginia State College Institute.

Meanwhile my thesis was published by Yale University in the Yale Younger Poets series edited at that time by the late Stephen Vincent Benet, and I was prevailed upon to undertake a lecture tour reading my poetry. In six months I visited approximately fifty colleges in twenty states. These included black colleges in Alabama, Georgia, North Carolina, Tennessee, Missouri, Texas, Arkansas, Mississippi, Florida, and Oklahoma. Also included were white schools, colleges, and universities in New York, New Jersey, Massachusetts, Minnesota, Pennsylvania, Ohio, Illinois, Wisconsin, Maine, and Connecticut. Over a period of five years, these engagements totaled more than one hundred and fifty lecture–recitals, and sometimes they were return engagements. After that first year I thought I was retiring to the private life of marriage and a family only to find myself returning to Livingstone College—again for part of a year. I left on maternity leave and never went back. Three years later I began teaching at Jackson State College in Jackson, Mississippi, where I was employed until my retirement.

After rearing four children almost to adolescence I returned in mid-life to the University of Iowa. In three years while teaching and writing I fulfilled requirements for the doctorate in English. With the publication of a second book—also a thesis, but this time a novel—I found myself again in demand as a speaker on college campuses. Recent tours have taken me to such campuses as Columbia, Wisconsin (Milwaukee campus), Fisk, Howard, North Carolina at Durham (now North Carolina Central), Stillman in Tuscaloosa (where the University of Alabama is located), LeMoyne, Grambling, and the predominantly white campuses of Milsaps, Ole Miss, Mississippi State, and Mississippi Southern, to speak before teachers in two Ohio communities, and before such national bodies as the Conference on College Composition and Communication of the National Council of Teachers of English, the National Conference of the Urban League, and the National Human Relations Council of the National Education Association. I have talked in various places with teachers, students, administrators, alumni and parents.

After more than thirty years since my graduation from Northwestern, I returned to my alma mater as a visiting professor in creative writing. Sudden circumstances that seem very strange took me there. In the spring of 1968, Northwestern felt its first revolutionary thrust from the demands made by the black students on the Evanston campus. At that time black students on predominantly white campuses all over this country began to demand an education more relevant and sensitive to the needs of black people, more knowledge of African American history, and more understanding of black culture on the part of White America. They demanded more concern with the issues confronting America because of race and racism. In agreeing or assenting to these demands, the university promised to hire more black teachers and to try to recruit more black students.

Like many other college campuses in America, Northwestern faced a painful state of revolution. Young black students, brilliant and militant, were joined by equally militant and brilliant white students. Faculty members were concerned, administrators were harassed, alumni horrified, but the fact remains that the university faced change. Education throughout America seems destined to change in every aspect of curriculum, administrative policy, and racial complexion of faculty and student body, because revolution promises ultimately to change all our world society.

This is the revolution that took me back to Northwestern. I found the university in the middle of a student crisis. One after another is likely to arise without warning from any conceivable direction. The university must expect one crisis after another, whether it is white resistance to black rebellion or vice-versa. It cannot presume that any one crisis settles a revolution, for this is clearly a revolution.

I am sure it is a great honor to be asked to return to one's alma mater in any teaching capacity, and I am aware of this honor even though I returned at a difficult time. I am also aware that a teacher's first business is to teach, to inspire and stimulate students to think, but it is also difficult to teach when one's students are involved in a crisis; marching and picketing and occupying buildings and going on hunger strikes and in turn being suspended, arrested, or placed on disciplinary probation. Never in my wildest dreams did I ever imagine myself in such a situation.

I cannot avoid making comparisons with the Northwestern I knew in the 1930s and the Northwestern I found in 1969. My memories of my adolescent days at Northwestern have always been too painful to bear recollection. Young, poor, and black, my life at Northwestern was restricted to a very narrow sphere. I could not live on campus in any dormitory nor eat in any place in Evanston except the dime store. It was nothing unusual to hear a ranking professor tell "darky" jokes in the classroom. Very seldom did any fellow student who was not black speak to me. I made very few friends among teachers or students, but those rare friendships I made have lasted a lifetime and influenced all my endeavors. I was not prepared for race prejudice in a great university above the Mason–Dixon line, in an institution founded by the very denomination of the Christian church to which I belonged. Then, too, I had never before seen such opulence, grandeur, and obvious display of wealth. Naturally I was bewildered, and it was only after graduation while

I was working in Chicago with black and white people that I began to understand. Nevertheless, the university was very influential in molding my life. Despite obvious prejudice I was allowed to stay even when my parents could not pay my bills, and I graduated owing the university.

June 1969 I found myself in a more friendly atmosphere. Students and teachers greeted me pleasantly. I lived in a comfortable apartment in university housing, and I found free interchange and communication among many of the people I encountered. Yes, the university was changing. Suddenly, it has changed. You ask me how it has changed, and I answer I know that if it had not changed, I would not have been there. If Northwestern were not changing, nothing else would matter but my black skin. Do not misunderstand me to say that change at the university has been complete or even sufficient. Nor is it a fact that blackness could reaffirm such an untruth. But there is a revolution taking place in the university, and hopefully a better society will be the result.

Why the university? Why student unrest? Why a revolution? Every day we discover through the mass media that "solid, good, well-meaning citizens" are muttering against this nonsense and demanding to know why the university officials do not put an end to this or let the police and law and order prevail. None of this grumbling is likely to stop permanently a worldwide societal revolution from grinding out necessary, even imperative, change. Neither political power nor great wealth will be enough. Legislation may impede but not long prevent progressive change in its inexorable march forward. Why must the university change? Because the philosophy under which it has operated for more than a century is already outmoded. It belongs to the early nineteenth century and the age of Newtonian physics rather than to an Einsteinian world of relativity, unity in diversity, and the space–time continuum, or to an ever-accelerating technological universe. Today in a technological universe, education must keep step with technology.

One hundred years ago the Industrial Revolution and rising capitalism changed most of American society, and today this long technological revolution is necessary to prepare us for the twenty-first century. No person and no institution need hope to escape. Whether one wishes progress is not the point. Progress will insist and proceed on its destined course.

What is the function of the university if it is not expected to lead to this avant-garde of progress? Surely the university has a moral and spiritual obligation to all society as well as an intellectual purpose to fulfill. The university is a social institution with a social function, and in this community of scholars, social theory is of no value without practice application. To preach one text and practice another is neither expedient nor wise. The university must accept the challenge of contemporary society and respond as best it can to every segment of that society.

It seems to be very difficult for White America to understand why these calamities have come upon the university and why they seem unable to escape the problems of racism and the effects of that racism on black people wherever they turn or seek to escape. Many university students and faculty members join with some politicians and decry student unrest because they say it is disrupting education for those students who have come to get an education. *What kind of education?* Classes as usual and the status quo? Education that is as dead as a doornail and can have no meaning in a multiracial society?

A great university like Northwestern is situated in a predominately white suburban community on the North Shore only a few miles from the inner black city of Chicago. It is just because of this, among other facts, that the university cannot escape its obligations and must deal with that black city and all its teeming millions. The politics and economics of the black ghetto offer Northwestern University a laboratory at its own back doorstep! The facts of black culture whether in literature, art, music, politics or economics, sociology of urban and rural living, whether in the psychological diagnosis of racism as a mental illness or in the genetics of race and the physical or cultural facts of anthropology, these are the facts of America, and they are first and foremost in the province of any educational institution. Americans, black and white, must learn to live and work and deal with each other if America is to survive. This is the immediate problem and the reason black people are determined to take care of their own business first. The university in America is not relevant to the needs of Black America, and revolution is changing that fact. Hence, the black studies programs.

It would also appear that White America remains complacent with the belief that this is a white man's country and the black man is only a small minority. This is a fallacious assumption. This country belongs to all of the people who live in it and have created it. Black America is not only a force in America to be considered but also a force in the nonwhite world. There are many forces at work in the society which threaten this fallacious assumption. The problem of the cities is only one. White Americans who sit comfortably on the knowledge that black people constitute only 10 percent of the population must also be awakened to the serious threat of a divided society destroying itself because of its basic inequities. Black people are not the only victims of the society, and we do not stand to suffer more in the final analysis if and when revolutionary or violent change undermines and topples the society. It should also be quite clear that a minority can change the majority.

It behooves the university and all true friends of the university to realize that this revolution cannot be deterred, that it is long overdue, and the only solution is to meet each crisis head-on and deal with its realities in a truly humanistic and practical fashion, positively and not negatively.

We should all remember the teachings of our great philosophers who have discussed the modern university and its role in contemporary society, such notable figures as Cardinal Newman, John Dewey, and Alfred Whitehead. All of them recognized the university as a social institution. Dewey has a special word for our times when he reminds us that sometimes the university becomes absorbed in its immediate interior concerns (such as how many languages should be required for the Ph.D.) and it ceases to be relevant; that one of its chief obstacles to the carrying out of social ideals is a certain "conservatism that isolates former ideals irrespective of the change going on in life at large. . . ." W. E. B. Du Bois in his *The Souls of Black Folks* further stipulates:

> The function of the University is not simply to teach breadwinning, or to furnish teachers for the public schools or to be a center of polite society; it is, above all, to be the organ of the fine adjustment between real life and the growing knowledge of life, an adjustment which forms the secret of civilization.[1]

The university is the generator of ideas for all mankind, and here should be formulated all the basic value assumptions and value judgments that undergird a growing society no matter how rapidly that society is changing. The university is called upon to move beyond the times and lead the world by example in learning what is just, what is true, what is real, and what leads to freedom and peace. If the university cannot do this, then the university does not deserve to exist. The university must therefore continue to work toward education for peace and progress; education for a multiracial society; education for a new age in the twenty-first century; education that is innovative and relevant and that touches the razor-sharp blade of life and hones that blade to its ultimate cutting edge. Northwestern's Black Studies Program proposes exactly this.

Revolution is often painful and violent, and those who destroy rarely trouble themselves to build again the institutions they have destroyed, but revolution on the university campus has only begun to make the necessary changes in our society. The university must therefore recognize the revolutionary forces at work in our society, forces which are irrepressible and must be reckoned with here and now. And, we must realize this necessity if we vaguely visualize why we live on this planet earth. Surely man is not made to grovel in the mire of ignorance and poverty nor struggle in the clutches of greed and lust, nor for the filthy wallowing of swine in mud and muck. Rather he has a mind with which to think and an immortal spirit to rise above the simple limitations of clay. He is expected to soar like a bird above the mundane prison of our world of phenomena and enter that nominal world of freedom, to reach the impossible heights, and to stride through the clouds into outer space.

The role of the university in a time of revolution is clearly not an easy one, but the job of reeducation is a big one that must be done. Indeed, it begins with the coed who is mother of the child yet unborn, with her infant in arms, with each preschool child. It is predicted upon a philosophy with one inherent truth, that all men are human creatures, none is any less and none can be any more. Mankind is challenged, and the university, in the name of mankind, is called upon to respond.

Note

1. See W. E. B. Du Bois, *The Souls of Black Folk* (New York: Fawcett Publications, 1961), 71.

(1976)

World Pluralism

The Human Encounter

AMERICA HAS BEEN called the melting pot of all races for truly all segments of the human race are gathered here on her soil, but this melting pot is not quite true. Anthropologists now tell us that prehistoric humans may have lived in this land, and others tell us that Orientals migrated across a land bridge from Asia to North America. But in any case, five hundred years ago, the white European found an indigenous people living here. Four hundred years ago black men were brought in chains from Africa. We were freed from these chains only a little over a century ago, and frankly we have never been a part of the melting pot. Neither the Native American nor the African American is an integrated part of the mainstream of American life. To be sure all nationalities of Europeans are represented here, and for the most part, they are part of the melting pot. The brown Caucasian race from India fears the stigma of Black America so much that he quickly dis-

---

This essay was presented before the American Association of University Women in Jackson, Mississippi, in 1976.

avows any racial connection with the black man. So what do we mean when we talk about the word "pluralism"?

Color and race are facts of the modern world; racism may be a special phenomenon, and race is too a social phenomenon of the modern world. The ancient and medieval worlds were not nearly so harried by race nor obsessed with the integrity of race as a biological fact as is the modern world. But even in modern times, the nature of our society is changing so rapidly that we must do more than recognize the pluralistic nature or characteristic of our world. Despite the great power struggle for economic and political ascendance in the modern world of the Western white and capitalistic world over against a nonwhite Eastern and noncapitalistic world, the facts are quite clear. Our world is made up of various segments or races of humankind all belonging to the human race or a common family of mankind. Sometimes when we see hate and malice generated into violent acts of terrorism and criminal acts of aggression against whole segments of mankind, we become distressed and confused and unable to understand the ulterior motives for money and power and ascendancy over the lives of others, which by the very nature of our political and economic system have given us a century of war and revolution in the world. We are in the bicentennial year of our nation, and if we look back over those two hundred years, we will discover that we have been at war almost continuously. First as colonists we fought a war of revolution for independence from the yoke of English tyranny. As soon as the American Revolution was ended, we found ourselves embroiled in the War of 1812. No sooner was that war ended when we fought the Mexican War of the late 1840s, and thirteen years later we were engaged in a fratricide over slavery that threatened to divide the union of states developed from those original thirteen colonies. Scarcely a generation after the Civil War we were in the Spanish-American War and fighting outside the borders of the United States, despite the Monroe Doctrine. This war occurred at the turn of the century, and in less than twenty years into the new century we were fighting a war to preserve a democracy, a war that reached world proportions. A generation later, we were involved in a second world war and from that we moved to Korea and then to Vietnam. We have had nine major wars in two hundred years. And yet we think of ourselves as a peace-loving nation and people.

If the history of our country has been one of war, certainly all other parts of our planet have been engaged in war and revolution. Kings have toppled from their thrones if not lost their heads, and the monarchy even in Europe is largely a form of government belonging to the past. No less than a half-dozen political revolutions in a century have swept through Europe—not counting those in Latin America, in Asia, and now the turbulence in Africa. As we talk here tonight war and revolution rage throughout the modern world. In three focal spots, there is great danger of war spreading to other nations on our globe. Ireland is in the throes of a bitter religious war. Religion is deeply involved in the Middle East in Lebanon and Israel or Palestine, and in Africa race and religion have entered into the wars in Biafra, Ethiopia, and now in Angola. It seems that the nature of our world is one of a competitive struggle for power and political control, aggression and terrorism. Racism and religious intolerance are only blind agents. If we continue in this death-dealing destructive way, what is to hinder our destroying our planet? Much talk has gone on concerning our environment and pollution in the face of ever more disturbing problems of energy, money, food, war, and leadership.

In the midst of this terrorism, war, revolution, chaotic destruction, competitive rivalries and dangerous games of intrigue, can we hope to have even peace, much less a recognition and enjoyment of the individual rights and liberties of all people in a pluralistic society?

Our churches are challenged with the ideal of brotherhood to avoid hypocrisy, cant, and misunderstanding. The home and family are threatened by the injustice of a society that will not recognize women's rights. A new ideal of family life is developing. Will the family remain merely fractured or become obsolete? I listened a few weeks ago to a young woman professor from Princeton who talked of a future when procreation would not be the result of human sexuality, and I was horrified with the kind of future in which less and less humanity will be evident, when dehumanization will be a part of regular regimentation. This is the nature of our world, and worse will occur if we let it happen.

While we have maintained the same form of government for

nearly two hundred years, the rest of our modern world has been undergoing violent political revolutions. Socialism and communism are feared so much by our democratic-loving-but-not-practicing people that we have nearly allowed the equally hated systems of Nazism and fascism to come into our land. Is there any way humanism can prevail? What do we mean by the human encounter? Do we mean physical touching of our loved ones who belong in the bosom of our single family unit? Do we have a sense of community beyond the limitations of me and my wife, my son John and his wife, we four and no more? I listened on Sunday as my pastor spoke about crime and lawlessness in our land, and he said part of our problem is that we have lost the sense of community. Add to our economic problems of simultaneous inflation and recession, of econo-spasms and the terrible economy of crime and drugs, the ring of rape, murder, and robbery aggravated by these facts and the fact that unacceptable crimes of violence are increasing, and ask yourself what we mean by the human encounter; is it not a fact that we are losing our sense of community? We hide in terror behind locked doors, we hear of bombs exploding, and hostages held at gunpoint with rifles, do we doubt that our society is changing or has been changed? Shall we add that the twentieth century is on the verge of collapse? If we do not change and continue on our polarized way toward more polarization, if the gap of polarization widens, can we save our society, redeem our culture and our people? Can we hope for world peace?

The history of the modern city goes back four or five centuries. What is the pattern of urban life today? Do you see a healthy future for our cities? Recently in an issue of *Southern Living,* I saw new and encouraging signs for the southern city, urban renewal, and a new pattern of living developing in our inner cities of the South. We have already lived through future shock as Toffler described it.[1] The econo-spasm is really no longer new or contemporary since such spasms were evident years ago. We are almost into the eye of the storm of the crisis of an old order. The modern stress which affects our physical selves and our psyche we must have release from. The chocolate cities ringed with vanilla suburbs are symptomatic of new patterns of living. The subcultures of the society are threatened but our ethnicity will not disappear. America was made by all races. Blacks proudly point to our cultural heritage and, having found the ground of our black awareness and identity, do not expect to lose this identity nor awareness in a cultural shuffle, certainly not in the melting pot. America comes to grips with her pluralistic nature and deals with all the cultural subgroups in her society. Aztec Indians in Mexico and in parts of South America have met a different fate in assimilation and cultural pluralism than the red man in the United States of America. Here he has almost been annihilated, become invisible. In Mexico and South America he is still not only visible but a part of a cultural rainbow that is culturally viable and healthy.

Can we change our society? We must if we hope to survive into the next century. We must preserve cultural autonomy and racial identity within our pluralistic society. Respect for the divinity in every living human being is the first step toward world humanism and religious peace and understanding. We must shape our world of tomorrow by shaping our society today. We must set goals and ask ourselves what kind of world we want for tomorrow. We must bring that world into existence now. Our destiny is a spiritual destiny. We must rise above the limitations of clay and circumstance to the rarefied air of gods. A technological universe which is demanding more and more nuclear power and sources of cheap energy must also be shaped into a world community developed out of cultural pluralism.

A new concept of education based in the realities of a new concept of the universe which the Einsteinian revolution has brought to the twentieth century must give us through re-education new uses for our education. Career goals of vocational, industrial, and liberal or technical education must also afford disciplines for life's meaning and sharing. We must be liberated into broader avenues of thinking for our fellow man if we hope for self-survival. We must learn to develop each individual in the society according to his abilities, "from each according to his ability, to each according to his needs." More understanding must be afforded for our gifted young, and both nutritional and scientific steps must be taken to develop the genius among us as well as remedy and cure the mentally ill among us; we must teach new uses of leisure in order to learn to relax and relieve ourselves of the pressures of modern technological living. Crafts and sports, reading, music, painting, the arts in our society, new meaningful uses of religion for meditation and renewal—all these belong in our re-education for a society that understands the true meaning of personal and social freedom and that hopes to live in peace with our neighbors in a world that has shrunk into a small community.

The spirit of man is truly invincible and immortal. Freedom of the spirit is what we hope to release in all human beings. In this bicentennial year we look back at the cultural heritage and major contributions of all ethnic groups that help make America a pluralistic society. Let us remember the events of our past, the freedoms that we constantly seek, the form of government we have learned to cherish, the contributions all races have made to America, to her founding, development and continuing sustenance. Let us celebrate a festival of the United States when we celebrate the traditions of all her peoples—multiracial, multiethnic, multicultural. Let us celebrate the diversity of our cultures as we celebrate together our nation's oneness, her indivisible sovereignty. Let us look ahead at the future as we view the horizons of today. Let us share today, let us set goals for tomorrow, let us secure the blessings of liberty to ourselves and our posterity. Let us involve every citizen, let us lift up our eyes and our heads and view the Utopia of tomorrow. Let us truly observe this bicentennial year by honoring our past and molding with honesty and great integrity the future of our society.

Note
1. See Alvin Toffler, *Future Shock* (New York: Random House, 1970).

(1992)

Epilogue

Race, Gender, and the Law

THE GREAT American poet Walt Whitman wrote:

> I feel I am of them—
> I belong to those convicts and prostitutes myself—
> And henceforth I will not deny them—
> For how can I deny myself?

In these United States of America, justice is tempered by money and power. Ever since the Constitution was framed more than two hundred years ago, the power structure of America has been composed largely of white Anglo-Saxon Protestant males—no Catholics, Jews, nor Negroes need apply. These excluded groups, along with all women, were considered the minorities. When the society is fascist, sexist, and racist, the judicial system can be neither better nor worse. But the law is of a dual nature. It is both an oppressor and a liberator. When segregation was the law of the land, established in 1896 by the Supreme Court in the *Plessy vs. Ferguson* case, the law was an oppressor.

Even before the Civil War under the Black Codes or penal system, black males were counted three-fifths of human beings and women were not counted as either citizens or human beings. After a brief period of twenty-five to thirty years when black males under radical reconstruction obtained the vote and held political office, *Plessy vs. Ferguson* revoked this privilege and disenfranchised most black males. In 1919, after a fifty-four-year struggle, white women received the franchise, but black women were still for the most part without the franchise until as late as 1965 when the Voting Rights Act made voting for all citizens a universal act—all races and genders included.

Racism, classism, and sexism are pernicious evils, and these three evils still persist in corrupting American society. Black people in this country have historically been the poorest of the poor masses. Money and power persist in excluding most African Americans. The Thirteenth Amendment, which was designed to eliminate slavery, added a clause which excluded criminals from emancipation. It reads, "except in the case of criminal actions." Thus, it is no wonder that the disproportionate numbers of black males or African Americans are in our overcrowded jails and, therefore, without voting rights.

The judicial system remains today both a liberating and oppressive force where *race* and *gender* are concerned. Whether in the realm of constitutional, civil, or criminal law, our American judicial system discriminates against most minorities, and women.

In antebellum days the records show that black women were beaten, branded, and murdered with no recourse to the law, which frequently included the overseer as sheriff and the master as judge and prosecuting lawyer. As late as the 1960s, a black woman, Fannie Lou Hamer, was beaten in a Winona, Mississippi, jail by two black trusties until she could not move. Sterling Brown used to tell a folktale about American justice where a goose was taken into custody by a fox and when she went to court the judge, jury, jailer, and prosecuting attorney were all foxes. African Americans are well aware that, when the goose is black, all the foxes may be white—judge, jury, and executioner. In 1952, Judge William Hastie spoke at Jackson State University at a seminar on American democracy, and a white man asked him if he thought the law could legislate men's minds and hearts and thus end segregation. Judge Hastie answered, "We are going to make segregation illegal in this country, and then we'll go from there."

During the past fifty years I have encountered the American judicial system on at least four different occasions. I hasten to add I have never been arrested nor spent the night in jail. I learned, however, during the 1960s that it is not always a disgrace to do so. A famous quote from "Civil Disobedience" by Henry David Thoreau says, "In an unjust state the only place for a just man is in jail."

In the early 1940s, in New York City, when my husband was flat on his back in an Army hospital in Wales, I was summoned to court on a charge of breaking and entering. I secured a good lawyer who later became a judge in New York City, and—taking my infant daughter—I went to court. I lost the case, and I was evicted from a coldwater flat in Greenwich Village where no Negroes had ever been allowed.

In the early 1970s, my son, who volunteered for service in the Marines, returned from a tour of duty in Vietnam. Two months after he returned, he was arrested in a black nationalist group of eleven persons including two women, one of whom was pregnant. They were accused and indicted for the murder of a white policeman. After seven weeks and a habeas corpus hearing, he was released on his own recognizance together with most of his friends. This was an example of false arrest. The incident succeeded in preventing my accepting a Fulbright Grant to teach in Trondheim, Norway.

In 1970, two days before two students were killed at Jackson State University by highway patrolmen, L. Patrick Gray came to visit me in my home. He was accompanied by a man from the FBI who refused to identify himself. When the killings occurred, Mr. Gray telephoned me to ask what I thought caused the incident. I told him violent white racism and the widening of the Indochina war in Cambodia were the causes of campus unrest and if they do not stop the war we will lose our country. Subsequently, when the President's Commission on Campus Unrest held a hearing in Jackson, I was called as a witness and asked to testify. I repeated what I told L. Patrick Gray.

During the same decade, nearly thirty years after my first experience with the judicial system in New York City, I had a mixed decision—I sued the apparent author of a blockbuster book for copyright infringement of my novel *Jubilee*. The judge ordered a hearing by a female magistrate. She rendered the decision in my favor, returning the case to the district judge. He ignored the female magistrate's opinion. Instead, he wrote a strong opinion against me and, within ten days, retired or resigned his judgeship.

Four years ago in 1988, my biography of Richard Wright was published by Warner Books. Six months later, his widow, Mrs. Ellen Wright, sued for copyright infringement. Eighteen months later, we won the decision. Then she appealed, and the Appellate Court upheld the District Court's decision.

My experiences certainly did not endear me to the system—particularly having to give a deposition. But after nearly a year since the last skirmish, which happily we won, I still believe what I said in the beginning: money and power temper justice in our judicial system.

People always ask, "What is it you people want? Haven't you made progress? What kind of change do you want?" We want a judicial system that treats all people alike, regardless of race, class, and gender—where the law is more the liberator than the oppressor—where women have more than voting rights, but also have reproductive rights—thus, having some control over our bodies and our destinies!

Recently, a reporter from *Mother Jones* magazine came to see me and asked how I could live in Mississippi with all the police brutality there. I wrote an answer to him in the form of a poem, and here it is—

On Police Brutality

I remember Memorial Day Massacre
Nineteen thirty-seven in Chicago.
And I was in the Capital of D.C.
May of nineteen seventy-one
When they beat all those white heads
And put two thousand souls in jail.
I wasn't in South Commons Boston
Neither when Crispus Attucks died
Nor South Boston when the rednecks rioted.
But I remember Boston
Where I couldn't buy a hot pastrami sandwich

In a greasy joint.
I remember living there in fear
Much as some would feel in Mississippi
I was neither in Watts, Los Angeles, California
In nineteen sixty-five
Nor Detroit in nineteen sixty-seven
And I remember all the fuss over LeRoi Jones
In Newark, New Jersey, too.
Now Santa Barbara, California, is remembered
As a separate incident, a separate thing
From Kent State in Ohio
And Jackson State in Mississippi
And Orangeburg, South Carolina
And Texas Southern
But to me, they were all of one piece
Of the same old racist rag.
And all of these things are part
Of what I call Police Brutality.

Bibliography

The Book of the Dead: The Hieroglyphics Transcript of the Papyrus of Ani. Trans. E. A. Wallis Budge. New York: Gramercy Books, 1995.

Du Bois, W. E. B. *The Souls of Black Folk.* New York: Fawcett Publications, 1961.

McKissick, Floyd. "The Way to a Black Ideology." *Black Scholar* 1 (Dec. 1969): 14–17.

Niebuhr, Reinhold. *Moral Man and Immoral Society: A Study in Ethics and Politics.* New York: Charles Scribner's Sons, 1932.

Toffler, Alvin. *Future Shock.* New York: Random House, 1970.

Walker, Margaret. *The Daemonic Genius of Richard Wright: A Portrait of the Man: A Critical Look at His Work.* New York: Warner, 1986.

———. *How I Wrote* Jubilee *and Other Essays on Life and Literature.* Edited by Maryemma Graham. New York: Feminist Press, 1990.

———. *Jubilee.* Boston: Houghton Mifflin, 1966.

———. *October Journey.* Detroit: Broadside Press, 1973.

———. *A Poetic Equation: Conversation Between Nikki Giovanni and Margaret Walker.* Washington, D.C.: Howard University Press, 1974.

———. *Prophets for a New Day.* Detroit: Broadside Press, 1970.

————. *This Is My Century: New and Collected Poems.* Athens: University of Georgia Press, 1988.

Wright, Richard. "Blueprint for Negro Writing." *New Challenge* 1 (1937): 53–65.

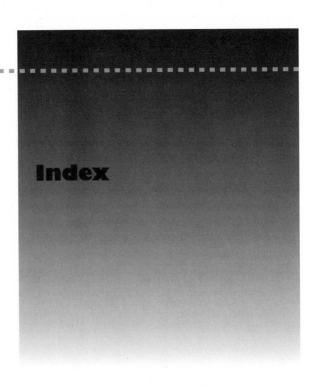

Index

Kline, Henry B., 112
Koch, Ed, 159
Krishna, 193
Ku Klux Klan, 31, 121

Lagerlof, Selma, 6
Lane, Pinkie Gordon, xvi
Lanier, Lyle, 112
Larouche, Lyndon, 160
Larsen, Nella, 44, 69
Lattimore, Jewel, 36
Lawrence, D. H., 51
Lawrence, Jacob, 69
Leadbelly, 70
Lee, Don L., 69
Lee, Herbert, 142
Lee, Jarena, 67
Lev, Barzillai, 67
Lewis, Edmonia, 69
Lewis, Ida, 36
Lincoln, Abraham, 109
literature: teaching of, 98–107. *See also*
    African American literature; south-
    ern literature
Locke, Alain, xvi
Lorde, Audre, 36, 39
Lovell, John, 21
Lunceford, Jimmie, 70
Lynch, John R., 138
Lytle, Andrew, 112

Mabus, Ray, 140
Madgett, Naomi Long, 36
Madhubuti, Haki, 69
Magee, Willie, 139
Malcolm X, 27, 77
March, Bessie, 33
Marshall, Paule, 46–47
Martineau, Harriet, xvi
Marx, Karl, 199
Mason, Gilbert, 142
Mason, Mrs. R. Osgood, 53n2
Matheus, John, 69
Maynor, Dorothy, 70
McCullers, Carson, 9, 49
McDowell, Deborah E., 44
McKay, Claude, 69
McKissick, Floyd, 94
Memphis, Tenn., 108, 109
Mencken, H. L., 121
Meriwether, Louise, 47, 59

Michelangelo, 19
Miller, Arthur, 27
Miller, May, 27
Millican, Arthenia Bates, xvi
Milner, Ron, 59
Missionary Baptist churches, 31
Mississippi: challenges facing, 146–50;
    civil rights movement in, 137–39;
    education in, 148, 190–91; history
    of, 145–46; industry in, 146;
    multiculturalism of, 146; segrega-
    tion in, 140–44
Mississippi River, 108–17
Mistral, Gabriela, 10
Mitchell, Loften, 59
Mitchell, Margaret, 46, 119
Mohammed, 193
Mondale, Walter, 157, 158
Monroe, Harriet, 20
Moore, Merrill, 112
moral education, 198–207
Moral Majority, 202–4
Morrison, Toni, xvi, 48–49, 69
Murfree, Mary Noailles, 111
music. *See* black music

Natchez Trace, 119
National Association for the Advance-
    ment of Colored People (NAACP),
    76, 113, 141
Neal, Larry, 59
Neely, Jasper, 142
"The Negro Speaks of Rivers"
    (Hughes), 109
Newman, Cardinal, 224
Niagara Movement, 76
Niebuhr, Reinhold, 206
Nixon, E. D., 141
Nixon, H. C., 112
Nixon, Richard, 166
Northwestern University, 219, 220–22;
    Black Studies Program, 225
"Note on Commercial Theatre"
    (Hughes), 95

Oblate Sisters, 34
O'Connor, Flannery, 49
Oden, Gloria C., 36
O'Neill, Eugene, 26
"On Police Brutality" (Walker), 235–36
Operation Breadbasket, 152